— THE SECOND —
BEDSIDE
— BOOK —

— THE SECOND —
BEDSIDE
BOOK

— AN ANTHOLOGY —

EDITED BY JULIAN SHUCKBURGH

WINDWARD

First published in Great Britain 1981
by Windward, an imprint owned by W. H. Smith & Son Ltd,
registered no. 237811 England,
trading as WHS Distributors,
Strand House, New Fetter Lane,
London EC4 1AD

ISBN 0 7112 0207 9

Typesetting by SX Composing Ltd, Rayleigh, Essex
Printed and bound in Great Britain by Morrison & Gibb Ltd,
Edinburgh and London

Conceived and designed by Shuckburgh Reynolds Ltd,
8 Northumberland Place,
London W2 5BS

Designers: Tim Foster and Roger Walton/Aardvark Design

Illustrations by David Davies, Tim Foster, Julie Hazlewood, Tony Kerrins,
David Sim and Helen Wilson

Contents

Introduction

One reviewer of the first *Bedside Book* criticised the effrontery of the definite article in the title, saying that the essence of a bedtime book was that a random sampling 'will unfailingly produce the old familiar faces and things. A sense of drowsy security ensues . . . and so to sleep.' This of course is a just criticism; but in compiling that book's successor I have not been able to confine myself to old favourites, and have not had the modesty to change the title. Once again the aim has been to make selections from recently published books by some of our best writers, while at the same time resurrecting a few older or classic poems and stories.

A few writers appear in both collections: for example Sir Isaiah Berlin, John Fowles, Iris Murdoch, Arthur Koestler and Philip Howard. There is rather less poetry and rather more fiction in the present book, including extracts from seven recent novels, and short stories by three other contemporary authors. Among the non-fiction pieces it will be seen that I have as before pursued a few themes by juxtaposing extracts which shed light on them. Western attitudes to Islam, and to the Eastern religious and spiritual outlook generally, is one of these themes; although I have not been able to find anything published in the last year on the extraordinary developments in Iran which seemed worth inclusion.

On one occasion (see pages 146–155) a review of a novel is reprinted here alongside an extract from the novel itself. I greatly admire the work of Clive James, a poet and gifted critic who is also greatly liked by the mass audience, and who has in the last year or so published not only an autobiography but a collection of his television criticism. I was anxious that he should be represented in these pages, but found it oddly difficult to select a self-contained extract from either of those books. His very funny review of *Fanny* has an underlying seriousness which is typical; but it is fair to add that other critics have taken quite different views of Erica Jong's book.

Until recently I had never read the poetry of Charlotte Mew, and her work does not seem to be at all widely known today; so I have included 'The Farmer's Wife' which was the title poem of her first published collection (1921). It gives some impression of the very individual tone of all her work; but I cannot resist also reproducing below the short poem 'Fin de Fête', referred to on page 186, which Thomas Hardy admired.

Sweetheart, for such a day
    One mustn't grudge the score;
Here, then, it's all to pay,
    It's Good-night at the door.

Good-night and good dreams to you, –
    Do you remember the picture-book thieves
Who left two children sleeping in a wood the long night through,
    And how the birds came down and covered them with
            leaves?

So you and I should have slept, – But now,
    Oh, what a lonely head!
With just the shadow of a waving bough
    In the moonlight over your bed.

Another enjoyable discovery was Mrs Leslie Stephen's *Notes from Sick Rooms*, which has just been republished, for Bloomsbury addicts, by a tiny American publishing firm in Orono, Maine, called the Puckerbrush Press ('puckerbrush', I understand, is a Maine country term for the secondary growth of trees). The piece on crumbs reproduced here seems to me to contain at least distant echoes of Virginia Woolf's style.

Finally I should like to thank all those who responded last time to my request for suggestions for inclusion in this anthology, and to extend the same invitation in the hope that it will become a regular event.

J.S.
June 1981

Kenneth Clark
Feminine Beauty

The discovery of feminine beauty, like so much that we value
in civilized life, was made in Egypt in the second millenium
BC. It was a sort of miracle; or perhaps we should say that
excavation has not produced a scrap of evidence to explain it.
The earliest women in Egyptian art, for example the two
goddesses who flank King Mycerinus in a famous group in
Cairo, although healthy, well-developed young creatures,
cannot be called beautiful. Then suddenly the Egyptian
sculptors invented a type of beauty that was not to be equalled
until sixth-century Greece. An example of how completely
the love of beauty filled the minds of Egyptian artists and,
presumably, of their patrons, is the tomb of Ramose. The
idea of filling a funeral vault with reliefs and paintings of
beautiful men and women is contrary to our notion of death,
but it expresses the Egyptian belief that the journey to
another world must be made as pleasant as possible. This
obsession with beauty reached its zenith in the entourage of
Amenhotep IV (Akhnaton), where a sculptor of genius, who
seems to have been called Imhotep, portrayed a group of
human beings so exquisitely beautiful that we could scarcely
have believed in them were it not that the same sculptor did

heads of other members of the court which are revelations of spiteful ugliness. Portraits of the Queen who, for convenience, we may call Nefertiti, reveal a delicate beauty which hardly appears again until fourteenth-century France, combined with a sweetness and humanity that we associate with the early Italian Renaissance. Although our present society can have little in common with that of eighteenth-dynasty Egypt, this is still beauty for today.

This moment of inspiration barely survived into the period of Tutankhamun, and thereafter Egyptian art relapsed into its thousand years of monotony. But occasionally a relief or a figure of no certain date has survived to show that the delight in feminine beauty had not vanished from Egyptian art. Where else could a measure of length be rendered as a beautiful woman with upraised arms? At some time during this period an unknown sculptor achieved a dazzling piece of feminine beauty; the *Lady with a Wig* in the Cairo Museum. If she was really done in the twelfth dynasty, as the museum catalogue says, she could be put forward as the first beautiful woman in art.

Meanwhile, the seafaring nations of the Eastern Mediterranean were producing styles as variable and irresponsible as seafront styles usually are. One of these – the art of the island of Crete – achieved, through isolation, a certain character, but precisely what this character was it is difficult to say. The reason for our uncertainty is that the discoverer of Cretan art

was the great archeologist Sir Arthur Evans, and the fragments he unearthed were so fascinating that he created in his
imagination a whole new style, different both from Egypt and
from the almost contemporary (*c.* 1400 BC) art of Mycenae.
Many of the original fragments were completed by a skilful
restorer. There seems to be little doubt that when Arthur
Evans returned to Oxford his restorer grew bolder and
executed whole figures, which Evans accepted with delight.
He was particularly pleased when people said how modern
they looked. It is with this reservation that I reproduce one of
these figurines. If they are old (which is by no means certain)
they support the belief that the beauty of women's faces is
dateless. This is confirmed by a unique example of the kind of
sculpture that must have been common in the Mediterranean
basin towards the end of the sixth century, the so-called *Lady
of Elche*, which survived because it had been exported to
Spain. A face of classic beauty is encased in a heavily-
ornamented head-dress, which was no doubt intended to
make her acceptable to a semi-barbarian people of the
Western Mediterranean.

In spite of two centuries of scholarship, the origins of Greek
art remain profoundly mysterious. What can we say, for
example, about that enchanting relief of the birth of Venus
known as the *Ludovisi Throne*? When and where was it made?
What was the original intention behind it? We can only say
that here, almost for the first time, we are aware of that gift
which Greece bequeathed to European art, an indestructible

love of physical beauty. We can study this in a series of standing figures of women, known as the *Kore*. They stood on the Acropolis of Athens, and must surely have had some ritual purpose. When ritual changed and the Acropolis was rebuilt they were thrown away, but have emerged (from the surrounding rubble) remarkably well preserved. The earliest (the so-called *Peplos Kore*) shows the simple column of the body surmounted by a head of adorable vivacity. She is succeeded by a series of almost equally seductive columnar figures, which at first look very much like one another, but when compared more closely (they are all in the same room of the Acropolis Museum) reveal remarkable differences both in design and in the character of the heads. Most of them show traces of a gentle smile, but a few are severe and relentless. One of the most famous is curiously self-conscious, as if posing for her portrait. She must have been a famous beauty.

The *Kore* contradict the popular notion that the Greeks were indifferent to feminine beauty, or at least rated it less highly than male. On the contrary, the ideal of feminine beauty that was to have such a long life in Western Europe goes back to Greek art of the fifth century BC, and has remained remarkably constant until the present day. The head below, which could date from any period of antiquity, is the

ideal beauty of the mid-nineteenth century, and would still be taken as an example of perfect beauty by anyone whose taste had not been influenced by the changing standards of the last fifty years. The nose and forehead run in a line which is indented by only a hair's breadth, the upper lip is very short, the ear is far back. All transitions are smooth. The same system is still apparent in what was once the most famous of all antique figures, the *Venus of Milo*, although the head, being subordinate to the whole figure, is more generalized. These heads show practically no trace of human emotion, but by the end of the century the eyes can look out into an imaginary distance with a certain pathos. A few surviving fragments show that Greek artists had always understood the meaning of pathos. The most familiar remains the most beautiful, the *Mourning Athena*. It is like an inexhaustible epigram that summarizes a whole complex of thought and feeling. Never again, perhaps, is the female body used with such restraint as the vehicle of deep emotion. One can also discover fragments that show the sentiment which we call romantic, which remind us how incomplete is our traditional notion of classical art.

The classical conception of beauty was diffused throughout the Mediterranean, partly from Greece itself and partly from the colonies of Sicily and southern Italy. The chief means of this dissemination was coinage. Greek and especially Syracusan coins were accepted as works of art, concentrating in their small diameter the finest talents in Hellenistic sculpture. One cannot call the Syracusan decadrachm a minor work of art; it is a small masterpiece of sculpture.

The Greek feeling for physical beauty was also spread by pottery. Just as coins were designed by the finest sculptors, so the leading painters decorated their elegant wine jars with figures which speak to us as directly as a drawing by Picasso. And then there issued from the workshops of sculptors in Athens and Tanagra figurines nearly all of which represent enchantingly beautiful women. What an aesthetically evolved society they imply! They tell no story, they assert no status; they were simply made to please the eye, and to remind the spectator of something agreeable.

Can we say that Roman art added anything to the concept of feminine beauty? Much of the antique sculpture found in

Rome was imported from Greece; we know that shiploads of marble sculptures left the port of Piraeus for Ostia. But it is fair to say that the Roman love of portraiture did produce a few heads of women that add to our concept of beauty, such as a small head of Poppea. They are more individualized than anything that has come down to us from Greece or Magna Graecia. And there are certain pieces of antique sculpture which seem to have a specifically Roman flavour. An example is the *Flora* of the British Museum, a work that, were it not for its impeccable provenance, we should consider an early nineteenth-century imitation of the antique. Anything less Greek, in our sense, than this effusive work it would be hard to imagine.

It is always a shock to read in literary sources that the Greeks rated their painting more highly than their sculpture, for not a scrap of it remains. But the eruption of Vesuvius in 79 AD has preserved for us a quantity of wall paintings which must, I believe, almost all go back to Hellenistic originals. They tell us that, as we should expect, feminine beauty was more often the subject of painting than of sculpture. To attempt a reconstruction of antique painting on such corrupt evidence would be a mistake. But one series of frescoes, those in the Villa Item, are of high quality, and show us an ideal of feminine beauty of which no precedent in Greek art has survived, although in fact they may well be copies of a lost phase of Hellenistic art. And in the fragments from Pompeii, Stabia and Herculaneum are some very pretty faces to tantalize us with a recognition of our loss. No wonder that the Hellenistic concept of feminine beauty remained embedded in European art long after all other elements of classicism had vanished. Yet this concept was to undergo what seems to us a dramatic change, for no one could apply the word 'pretty' to the ladies who surround the Empress Theodora at Ravenna. When did the change take place? A few surviving works of the late Roman Empire show that it was earlier than we would imagine; or at least that a new type of beauty, which seems to anticipate the style of Ravenna, overlapped with the tradition of classical urbanity. A beautiful example is an engraved crystal representing a mother and her two children, now in the Museum of Brescia. The oval faces, large eyes, and arched eyebrows are on the other side of that barrier of style which separates

Rome from Constantinople. The inscription tells us that it was made in the Greek-speaking East. It could be called the first great Byzantine work of art.

A critic of art in the last century would not have found that Byzantine art had much to contribute to my subject. But today we may feel that a Madonna in the style of Constantinople has a beauty of her own, and it was convincing enough to satisfy the faithful for at least four centuries. But it was more abstract or symbolic than the Greek type, which for some time ran parallel with it. If, today, a beauty in the Greek or Egyptian style were to enter a room, she would be accepted without question; but a Byzantine lady would be isolated, a source of wonder and surprise. As a matter of fact I have known two women (one Italian and one Greek) whose faces required only a slight simplification to become perfectly Byzantine; there is always abundant material in nature to justify any stylistic change.

From
Feminine Beauty

Joan Collins
Lifestyle

JOAN COLLINS'S *Lifestyle*

Sleep
Diet
Sex
Drugs

Relaxation
Smoking &
Drinking

The single most destructive factor in our emotional and mental lives today is stress. Our nerves and senses are constantly assailed by a barrage of tension-causing outside stimuli.

The noise level in today's society is reaching an almost intolerable level. Close your eyes now and unless you live deep in the heart of the country or are double glazed within an inch of your life, the amount of different sounds around you is quite amazing. Sitting in my bedroom right now in London I can hear the following: the radio in the kitchen, the phone ringing, a drill thumping away down the road, cars screeching their brakes and accelerating, and there goes the door bell again – it's an endless assault on the senses and on concentration.

Many of the diseases of today from which we suffer are caused by stress. Heart disease, insomnia, nervous breakdowns and disorders, skin diseases, stomach ailments – a long list of disorders brought on by modern living.

As an example of how stress can affect one's health and wellbeing, I will tell a personal story. A couple of years ago I was involved in a situation which was causing me intense grief. Because I am mentally quite strong, I did not crack up, nor did I have a nervous breakdown or commit suicide – all of which, at one time or the other, I felt I was coming close to. I went about my life and work as normally as possible. Only my family and very close friends knew that I was actually under enormous strain and suffering a great deal.

But the stress and pain evinced itself in my skin. Having had a good, healthy, more or less blemish-free complexion all my life, I suddenly developed spots! Not just one or two but dozens and dozens of the little monsters appeared on my face and neck almost overnight. This would be bad enough for anyone, but for an actress it was a catastrophe.

After trying all my own remedies to no avail, I finally saw a dermatologist. He examined my skin and questioned me thoroughly. He then informed me that I was suffering from a common skin condition called roseola nervosa, which I translated into 'nervous acne'.

There was nothing I could do, said the doctor. The condition of my skin would clear up when my personal situation was resolved. Since the latter did not seem likely in the foreseeable future, I resigned myself to months of disfigurement. Eventually, as predicted, when my problem sorted itself out so my skin started to clear up, and luckily today my complexion is much the same as it was before.

Good health is of course more than the absence of any apparent disease. Many people think that because they have no obvious symptoms or illness, they are healthy. They ignore the fact that they might be potentially ill through bad dietary habits, too much smoking, lack of exercise, and extreme stress and tension. Because our bodies are capable of adapting to these stresses and strains, at least for the first thirty or forty years of our lives, we are often not aware of impending disease until the symptoms manifest themselves outwardly. Illness begins in the body weeks, months, even years before you actually feel ill. And the seeds of this illness are usually planted by lack of care and attention to what we do with our bodies from the day we are born.

Many doctors still scoff at this. They would rather prescribe a pill or an antibiotic than trace the root of the problem. But prevention is better than cure, and that is why you should see your body as a finely tuned, complicated, sophisticated machine, which must be cherished and nourished with as much care as you would your newborn baby.

You may ask what you can do to eliminate potential problems and reduce or banish stress from your life. It is not easy, but examining and understanding the causes and then making a gradual change in your lifestyle can alleviate tension and may help a great deal.

Relaxation

Try to become aware of muscle tension in everyday activities and then to reduce it. As you go about your daily tasks learn to isolate the areas of tension you feel in particular parts of your body and concentrate on relaxing them. After a while you can do this automatically. For example if you have pain in the lower back, you are probably unconsciously tensing your lower back muscles when you are in a stressful situation – and by this I mean any of the petty day-to-day aggravations of modern life such as being shoved in the bus queue, jostled in the underground, fuming in traffic jams, and so on.

Once a day make time to sit in a chair or lie on a bed quietly and let yourself unwind. Take a deep breath. Close your eyes and try to identify the parts of your body that seem tense. Is it your back? Your neck? Your stomach? We all have different places in our bodies where tension builds up. When you have found the tension areas you must concentrate on relaxing them, and once you have done this you will feel the relaxation spreading and your whole body will begin to feel more at ease.

You may have to work hard to learn the art of relaxation, for it is indeed an art, but it will pay off in terms of mental and physical health.

Here are some complete relaxing techniques

Choose a quiet, calm environment with as few distractions as possible. This will contribute to the effectiveness of the relaxation by making it easier for you to concentrate.

Choose a comfortable position so that there is no undue

muscular tension. The easiest is a sitting position: if you are lying down there is a tendency to fall asleep. Although many people have reported that they use this relaxation exercise while lying in bed to help them go to sleep, if you fall asleep using the technique you are not experiencing genuine relaxation, which is quite different from sleep.

Close your eyes.

Begin to relax all your muscles, beginning at your feet and working up to your head; mentally hold the idea of each part of your body relaxing.

Breathe through your nose. Begin to become aware of your breathing and as you are breathing out say the word 'relax', silently to yourself. Breathe in . . . breathe out, 'relax'; breathe in . . . out, 'relax', and so on. While you are doing the exercise breathe easily and naturally. This device of repeating silently a word or phrase helps to break the train of distracting thoughts and allows the body and mind to relax.

Continue this process for 10–20 minutes. If your mind begins to wander, focus your attention back on the repetition of the word 'relax'. Try not to worry about how well you are performing the technique because this in itself will prevent true relaxation. Adopt a passive, 'let it happen' attitude.

I was taught this technique for relaxing by Dr Robert Giller of New York. I use it whenever I am in a particularly stressful period – which is quite often, I regret to say – and it definitely works for me.

Sleep

Just being asleep is often not as restful as it seems. How many times do you wake in the night? Does your partner disturb you by snoring or tossing and turning? Do the children come down for a drink of water? Does the baby wake up? You would be surprised if you counted up in actual hours how much deep sleep you have had, how much has really been beneficial. If you haven't had at least $6\frac{1}{2}$–$7\frac{1}{2}$ hours a night, try to get half an hour's nap or lie down during the day.

Sleep is nature's oldest and most trusted beauty treatment. Some of the legendary beauties of yesterday who still look good swear that they owe their looks and beauty to 12 or 14 hours' sleep a night! I myself think this is a waste of productive time which could be better spent doing many more interesting and valuable things.

You spend about one-third of your adult lifetime asleep, but what else other than rest do you get out of it? All your internal organs get a chance to rest and restore themselves. In the morning your stomach is flatter, because all food has been thoroughly digested. Any tension that may have accumulated during the previous day will usually have disappeared. Your batteries have been recharged and your cells revitalized, which is why after a good night's sleep your eyes have more sparkle and your skin more of a glow.

As we get older we need less sleep. If you couldn't exist on less than 9 hours a night aged twenty you may find that at thirty you feel fine with 7 or 8, and at forty you can get by with 6 hours. There are some lucky people who actually only need 1 or 2 hours' sleep a night and function perfectly on that. Think of all those extra hours of productivity or leisure one would have.

Sometimes you may need 8 hours a night and drop off as soon as your head hits the pillow, and sometimes you lie there unable to sleep, restless and frustrated until the early hours. This is really perfectly natural. Sometimes you need to eat a lot in one day and sometimes you don't feel hungry at all. Your body's metabolism is different at different times of the month or year. So don't fight it. Your body knows best. Read a book, have a hot scented bath or a glass of warm milk, and give up trying to force sleep on yourself. The more uptight and angry you become, the harder it will be to rest.

One night's lack of sleep or a small amount of sleep will not have a devastatingly dreadful effect on your body or looks. Try to catch up the next night. As far as amounts of sleep go, let your body judge how much you need.

Diet
Whatever sort of pressure you live under, tucking a healthy breakfast under your belt in the morning can do a lot to alleviate it. There is something to be said for the slogan 'Eat breakfast like a king, lunch like a lord and dinner like a pauper'. Going to work on a cup of coffee and a saccharin tablet, although it may be good for the waistline, is not in the

long run beneficial to the stress factor, which seems to be part of most people's lives today. Allow yourself plenty of time to have breakfast quietly; this will put you in a calm mood to face any problems that the day may bring. Being late or in a rush creates tension which may last all day.

Breakfast is important because there is likely to have been a gap of 8–14 hours since your previous meal. Your blood sugar needs raising, and your energy level must be revved up. Therefore some protein (e.g. eggs, cottage cheese), some carbohydrates (toast – wholewheat, please!) and some natural sugar (orange juice, grapefruit or honey) should be part of your normal breakfast.

If you do skip breakfast, you will suffer for it. It is much better to give lunch a miss occasionally and take a walk in the park than to leave out that all-important breakfast. Even when I have to get up at 5.30am to go to the studio I always have either a glass of orange juice or some tea with honey before I leave. (Those lucky actors whose call is before 7am get served a full breakfast in the make-up chair.)

I shall stress many times in this book the utter necessity of correct nutrition and diet. Let me emphasize one thing here, however.

What you *don't* eat is just as important as what you *do*. Try to eliminate or at least cut down the following:

Processed and over-refined foods
Foods full of chemical additives, such as hot dogs, bacon, soft drinks
Pre-cooked, packaged, fabricated, pseudo-foods
Foods high in animal fat and cholesterol.

Cut out unnecessary consumption of stimulants and irritants. These contribute towards stress, and although they are sometimes unavoidable they should be taken as seldom as possible. They include coffee, tea, alcohol, fizzy drinks, salt, tap water, aspirins and anti-histamines.

Sex

Spending time on sex or beauty makes many people feel vaguely guilty. But sex is one of the best and cheapest of all beauty treatments. So get over the guilt and enjoy it.

Real beauty comes from confidence and from being in

touch with your own body. It is natural, not narcissistic, to like and enjoy your body, and any movement that gives you sensual pleasure helps to increase your awareness of yourself. Dancing, swimming, stretching, running – all of these give us the opportunity to be in touch with our own physicality. And only by appreciating our own bodies can we really enjoy other people's.

This does not mean that you have to strive for the perfect physical ripeness of cover girls and models – such perfection remains the prerogative of only a few. But you must realize that your body is beautiful in its own way: it is unique and individual, just as you are. To feel self-conscious in sex because of what you think are physical flaws is a sure way to sow the seeds of unease and embarrassment that will negate what should be a fulfilling experience.

A healthy sex life that gives you pleasure is an important part of feeling and looking great. It's an old cliché but true, that sex makes your skin glow and your eyes sparkle. It also makes you less edgy and nervous. And one of the greatest beauty treatments in the world is being in love – by which I mean the state of total euphoria that comes in the early stages of a romance or involvement. (There is also an unusual lack of appetite which is great for the figure!)

New romance is wonderful and spine-tingling and thrilling, but old romance is good too – and a happy marriage better still. In fact any kind of emotion that involves total care and commitment to another human being, be it baby or boyfriend, is beneficial to your looks.

Smoking and alcohol

The danger of smoking has been rammed down our throats a zillion times, and it's now a proven fact. So try to cut down even if you can't kick the habit. Each cigarette is like the bullet in a gun playing a game of Russian roulette: you never know which one could trigger off a dormant disease in your body.

Smoking is supposed to encourage the formation of wrinkles and although there is no proof of this, it is a fact that each cigarette uses up 25mg of Vitamin C in your body. Anyone who smokes heavily is almost certain to be short of this important vitamin and should take extra Vitamin C.

What smoking definitely does is contribute to lung cancer. Now that more women are smoking, many more incidents of lung cancer are being found in women. People who smoke are also more susceptible to heart palpitations, coughs, colds and respiratory conditions such as emphysema, and influenza. Nicotine is a potent drug which affects every cell in your body; it also dulls the hair and skin.

Alcohol not only uses up the B vitamins which play a major role in beauty but it also encourages the appearance of threadlike veins on cheeks and nose which are almost impossible to eradicate and very ugly. If you like drinking, drink wine. A wine spritzer (with soda or mineral water and ice) is even better. Whisky, gin and vodka are particularly bad for the thread–vein condition.

Drugs

Finally, my particular *bête noire* and what I (and many doctors) now consider to be one of the most totally destructive substances we can put into our bodies.

So–called soft drugs such as marijuana (pot or grass) and hashish are just as detrimental to your health in the long term as the hard drugs (cocaine and heroin). The taking of drugs has become almost socially acceptable in some quarters today and although marijuana is now legal in America, it does not mean that the cumulative effects are not really bad for you – after all cigarettes are also legal and we are all aware how dangerous they can be.

It has now been proven that smoking marijuana destroys brain cells, impairs the ability of the body to function properly, slows down bodily reactions, decreases sex drive (although initially it may increase it), changes body metabolism, makes it difficult to concentrate and finally *is* addictive (in spite of what the 'experts' say). For young people and teenagers it can destroy their lives. As far as looks go for women it is nothing less than disastrous. It causes premature wrinkling of the facial skin, a dull muddy complexion, bloodshot yellowing eyes and lacklustre hair.

The other insidious thing about smoking marijuana or hashish is that it often results in experimentation with hard drugs such as cocaine and heroin. I reluctantly sniffed some cocaine in St Tropez about twelve years ago when the 'jet set' were considering it the new chic thing to do. I couldn't sleep for 48 hours, and had a sore throat and post nasal drip for three weeks. Needless to say I haven't gone near it since. As for heroin it is one of the most utterly destructive things to a human being, mentally, physically and emotionally. Eventually those who snort it will inject, and that is the beginning of the end. It is unbelievably addictive, causing people to become almost zombies if they don't take it, and they begin to *need* it to function even half properly.

So my advice is to keep clear of all drugs, or if you've got the habit – break it before it breaks you.

From
The Joan Collins Beauty Book

<hr>

Miriam Stoppard
The Beauty Game

<hr>

Like most people I have a basic distrust of over-kill, and I shrink from anything which is being oversold. Consumer advertising is peppered with both, unlike medical advertising which must conform to an enforced ethical code. In consumer advertising, no product carries more appealing messages and promises than the beauty product.

The reality behind beauty advertisements

Every time I see an advertisement for a cosmetic claiming that if I use it for three or four days I shall be able to 'see' and 'feel' the 'difference', I feel angry and insulted, especially if the product makes a claim to remove wrinkles or change the texture of the skin. Nothing applied to the skin can remove

wrinkles and nothing applied to the skin can change its
texture. Such an advertisement stretches the credibility at the
level of basic common sense. But to anyone who knows
anything about the physiology of the skin it is an insult.
There is no basis yet known to science to justify the claims.
Furthermore, it is well nigh impossible to get hold of the
evidence on which the claims are based for independent
scientific scrutiny.

Beauty advertisements make me angry because they are
seducing the public into the purchase of products on the basis
of an unproven claim. The seduction often turns out to be an
extremely expensive one. That should come as no surprise
because the cost of the advertisement must be covered in the
price of the product, and the price is further inflated by the
cost of the glamorous packaging. In the end, only a fraction
of the good money we pay goes on what has been so
extravagantly packaged and glossily advertised.

Beauty advertisements make me angry because changing
the natural constitution of your skin is no more possible than

is changing the colour of your eyes. To all intents and purposes you are bequeathed your skin by your parents. Its
quality is genetically determined as are its faults. By far the
most important factor in determining a predisposition to
acne, wrinkles or any other defect, or the acquisition of an
unblemished skin, or one which remains unwrinkled into
middle age, or one which looks ten years younger than you
do, is *what sort of skin your mother and father had*.

Beauty advertisements make me angry because the
physiology of the skin (the way it works) and the anatomy of
the skin (its structure) do not permit anything from the
outside to affect the health of the skin on the inside. The way
the skin looks and feels on the outside can only be changed
from the inside. For the skin grows from within outwards,
and to affect the health of the skin we must affect the health of
the person wearing the skin. The skin is nourished from
within, it is fed from within, and the only way that you can
change it is by changing it from within.

So even if product X can change the skin in any measurable
way it can only change it transiently and this is never stated in
the advertisement. And transiently, in terms of the skin, is no
more than a few hours. Scientists know of no way in which
cosmetics, particularly those containing so-called hormones
and collagen, can penetrate to the single layer of living cells
deep in the skin and affect them in any way. Collagen, for
instance, is too large a molecule to penetrate even the upper
layers of the skin. Hormones, by law, cannot be sold over the
counter in quantities which are active. In such quantities they
must be sold under prescription. It follows that if you can buy
a product containing 'hormones' without a prescription it
does not have any hormonal effect.

Cosmetic routines

Having understood some of the basic physiology of the skin
we can make certain judgements about cosmetics and the
cosmetic routines laid down by beauty experts as though they
were written in tablets of stone. Beauty routines, while good
in themselves, need not be rigidly adhered to as though they
were the *sine qua non* of looking after the skin. While they may
have merit, there is no special magic about cleansing, toning
and nourishing. Beauticians' programmes are not the be-all

and end-all of keeping your skin in good condition. Nor is using expensive products necessarily any better than using cheap ones.

Do, by all means, cleanse your skin, but not necessarily last thing at night and not necessarily with a specially designed cleanser. There is nothing better than a wash with mild baby soap for people who have an oily skin, and for those with drier skins, baby lotion will cleanse, nourish and moisturize your skin if you put it on after you remove your make-up and underneath a new one. There is no law which says you must remove your make-up at night, though some women feel unclean if they do not. On the contrary, it is unphysiological to clean and nourish your skin at night because the skin is virtually dormant in the evening. The skin grows during the mid morning and the mid afternoon. It would therefore make much more sense to undertake your beauty routine at either or both of these times. Besides, why should your husband be the only man in your life who sees you without any make-up at all?

Moisturizers

I am not a proponent of beauty treatments which have a transient effect on the skin, e.g. face-packs, but I think it is worth making particular mention of moisturizing the skin. Beauticians have a tendency to make this a complicated business but it is very simple. There are only two ways to moisturize the skin: either you can put water into the skin, or you can prevent water being lost from the skin. The first is usually done by applying a cream formulated from oil and water in such a way that the oil can cling to the skin and thereby hold water on its surface. The second is done by applying a more greasy cream similar to the natural sebum produced by sebaceous glands in the skin. This greasy substance forms a film over the skin which prevents water from getting out. The water content in the skin temporarily rises and the skin becomes moisturized.

The second method is by far the more efficient and by far the longer lasting. It is possible to buy fairly inexpensive creams which mimic natural sebum and when applied to the skin will trap moisture for several hours. These latter creams are usually applied under make-up and their barrier effect can last until you remove it. The first type of moisturizer, those that put water into the skin, have a very transient effect. Some of them may last only minutes, rarely longer than a couple of hours. These creams are light and fluffy and when smoothed on the skin give it a soft, pliable feel and disappear in a few minutes.

Hazards of cosmetics

Cost aside, there are good reasons for using simple, pure, inexpensive cosmetics. One is that cosmetics can produce allergies. The more complicated the recipe for any particular cosmetic, the greater the chance of developing an allergy to it and the more difficult to track down the offending substance. A fairly common ingredient of cosmetics is known to be a potent allergen. (A potent allergen causes skin sensitivities and skin allergies in a large number of people.) This is lanolin or wool alcohol which is the base of many creams. A study done at the allergy clinic in St John's Hospital for Skin Diseases in London showed that forty-five per cent of women who come into the clinic with dermatitis are sensitive to lanolin. Many of these allergies are low grade and not easily detected. Some women who are suffering from lanolin allergy may buy more of the cosmetic in the hope that it will make their skin better, whereas it can only make their skin worse.

Allergies to cosmetics are many and varied – as different as allergy to mascara and allergy to nail varnish. These two very different allergies may show themselves in exactly the same way. Puffiness of the eyelids and swelling round the eyes are common expressions of an allergy to mascara and unlikely though it may seem, they are just as frequently seen in patients with an allergy to nail varnish. In nail varnish allergy, rashes and hives (nettle rash) can develop wherever the skin is touched by the polish. You are not always conscious of it but you are constantly putting your fingers to your mouth, nose and eyes. In the delicate skin around the eyes the allergic substances in nail varnish can excite redness, swelling and itching. Many women coming into an allergy clinic complaining of swellings round the eyes are surprised to be told they are allergic to their nail varnish. .

Cosmetics can also cause allergies due to the perfume they

contain. In some people perfume irritates the skin so that it produces more pigment than normal and brown patches appear. It is most common down the side of the face, near the forehead and over the cheekbone, but it may extend on to the neck. It can take up to a year to disappear and you must avoid the sun if you do not want the patches to go darker.

You will not go far wrong if you stick to cosmetics that are pure, simple and inexpensive. This does not mean joining the fashion for products which claim to be made entirely from natural extracts. Objective evidence is yet to be seen for the magic properties of zest of lemon, juice of cucumber or oil of avocado. If baby lotion is good enough for baby skin, it follows that it should be good enough for adult skin.

Just as important as what you put on your skin is the way you put it on. Every day of your life from the age of say, sixteen, you put on and take off make-up maybe three times a day. Cumulatively, that is an awful lot of massage and you can do your skin a lot of good by massaging it properly and a lot of harm by doing it badly. You should always massage your face in a way that minimizes and counteracts the ageing effects of gravity's pull, by following the movements which are shown in the diagram below.

The directions your fingers should follow when applying or removing make-up.

The main point about beauty routines is that the fingers should move over the skin in an upward direction. Take great care when massaging particularly delicate skin, e.g. that around the eyes.

31

Hair and nails

The skin has two important appendages – the hair and the nails. Both have living and growing roots but at the point where we can see and treat the hair and nails their cells are dead. Long hair has been dead for three years or more. This fact goes a long way to explaining why potions applied to the hair cannot radically change its constitution, except transiently. The time when you can influence the health of your hair is while it is growing. It grows from the hair follicle at a rate of about 0.2 to 0.4 millimetres per week and its quality is a reflection of your state of general health and nutrition at that time. A diet for healthy hair and nails should be balanced and contain foods with plenty of vitamin A, such as liver, fish and milk.

We have several different types of hair: scalp hair, eyebrow and eyelash hair, beard hair, 'secondary sexual' hair – for example in the armpits, in the genital area and on the chest of men – and very small hairs that cover most parts of the skin except the palms of the hands and the soles of the feet. These hairs grow away from the midline. Given a solitary finger you can tell if it is from the right or left hand by examining the direction of the hair growth; looking at the finger with the fingernail pointing towards you, it is a right finger if the hair is growing towards your left, and vice versa.

The growth of these types of hair is controlled in different ways. It is interesting that male hormones are responsible for both hair growth in the beard area and lack of growth (baldness) on the scalp. Hair growth, particularly of the scalp, goes through cycles of activity and rest, but synchronously, so that some hairs are growing while others are resting. This means that hair loss is hardly noticeable, except if an event pushes all the hair into one phase as pregnancy does. Many women notice that at any time between three and eighteen months after their baby is born they suffer frightening hair loss. This is normal and the thickness of the hair will return in due course, though it may take as long as two or three years.

There are a few myths about hair which should be dispelled:
DANDRUFF: Dandruff is the natural scaling of the scalp as it sheds its dead uppermost layers. The hair strands tend to trap the scales and they may pile up. It is not therefore either a

disease or an infection but merely a variation of normal. It follows that you need not use a medicated shampoo to get rid of it. Anything which irritates the scalp like vigorous brushing and massaging will only encourage more dandruff as producing scales faster is the only way that the scalp can protect itself.

SHAMPOOS: Some of the anti-dandruff shampoos contain an ingredient which is irritating if used too frequently so this kind of shampoo should be restricted to once a fortnight. The basic rule with shampoos is to use the mildest one you can find – a baby shampoo is very suitable. In a dermatology clinic in which I worked we used a carpet shampoo: whereas most people are prepared to take risks with their hair, they are not prepared to take the same risk with their best worsted Wilton carpet, nor were the manufacturers, so it was an extremely mild shampoo. We used to recommend a teaspoonful of the shampoo in a glassful of water used once on the hair.

CONDITIONERS: Conditioners of any kind, no matter how effective they may appear to be immediately after washing, can only have a temporary softening effect on dead hair.

WASHING THE HAIR: Most hair, even if it is fine and dry, benefits from being washed fairly frequently. Most dermatologists advocate washing the hair every three or four days or so. The hair and scalp should not be vigorously rubbed. Rubbing the scalp only irritates it and stimulates the production of grease and dandruff. The shampoo should be gently massaged into the hair, left in contact with it for no more than two minutes, then rinsed off. Hair, if anything, should be underwashed, never overwashed. Usually one wash is enough regardless of manufacturers' instructions. Any serious scalp or skin problem should of course be treated by your doctor.

The nails grow from the live nail-plate at the rate of 1 to 2 millimetres per month and are dead by the time they emerge from the cuticle. They are even more sensitive barometers of physical and emotional health than hair. A crisis of any sort, be it a serious illness or period of stress, can show up in the nails as a transverse ridge in their horny surface. Several illnesses leave tell-tale signs in the nails and a favourite examination topic for medical students is the diseases that may be diagnosed by examination of the nails – psoriasis, iron-deficiency anaemia and liver disease being but three.

Cellulite

Cellulite is a subject often written and talked about. Having studied very carefully a monumental Swiss document about cellulite, I am none the wiser. Cellulite is not a medical term, it describes no medical condition known to doctors, and I have yet to see a description of it that explains it in medically accepted terms.

Cellulite is the word that has been coined to describe dimpling of fat. It is seen most often on the thighs, but it can appear wherever there is too much fat under the skin, like the upper arm. It is confined to females and occurs rarely in young ones and rarely in thin ones. It is a condition, generally speaking, of obese middle-aged women, and is variously described as being due to abnormalities of fat metabolism or abnormal collections of fluid. The use of the word abnormal suggests that normality might be reinstated by some form of treatment, and such is female vanity that treatment is demanded. An irresistible demand will always find suppliers, hence the numerous offers of numerous treatments.

Dimpling of the skin over excessive layers of fat is not, however, abnormal, it is a variant of normal. No amount of massage, electrical stimulation or medication will correct it. It can often disappear though, if the cellulite lady loses sufficient weight to slim down her thighs and upper arms. But this too often requires more perseverance than most cellulite sufferers possess.

pH-controlled beauty aids

One new idea that has been introduced into the beauty business in the last few years and is scientifically very attractive, is the idea of pH control. The 'pH' is a measure of the acidity or alkalinity of things. The natural pH of the skin is well on the acid side. The acidity results from the secretion of sebum which contains several natural acids, and it is necessary for the skin's health, growth, smooth surface and for the suppression of bacterial multiplication. This applies to hair too. Nearly all the substances used to wash the skin and hair contain detergents which are strongly alkaline and this profoundly disturbs the health, ecology, appearance and feel of the skin. Any cleanser which has a similar pH to the skin and hair (often described as 'pH buffered') is therefore preferable to a strongly alkaline one.

Electrolysis

Electrolysis can be used in the treatment of facial and unwanted body hair. The aim of electrolysis is to kill the growing hair root. During treatment a fine needle carrying an electric current results in the shrivelling of the hair root. Usually only a few hairs are treated at a time – according to your stoicism. In good hands the treatment should be virtually painless. Only seek treatment from an accredited practitioner – in the wrong hands scarring can occur. Electrolysis is available on the National Health for some patients through your local GP and consultant dermatologist.

Massage and electrical stimulation

If you have a massage to make you feel good then you probably will not be disappointed, but if you have a massage to lose weight I can guarantee that you will. Your masseur may lose weight, not you. Fat cannot be rubbed away by hands, machines, moving belts or bumping rollers. Nor can it be removed, as though by magic, with electrical stimulating pads that make the muscles contract. A muscle has to contract many times against a force for a considerable period of time to use up sufficient energy to show as weight loss. Exercise, while essential for keeping you fit, is a very inefficient way of burning off excess calories: it takes over an hour digging in the garden or two hours walking to burn up the calories in a four-ounce bar of chocolate. The best answer is not to take them in.

I am opposed to all forms of apparatus or techniques which claim to make you lose weight while you do nothing yourself. The quickest way to show a drop in your weight is to lose water. You can achieve this with drugs (diuretics) or by wearing a garment which makes you sweat or by lowering your intake. As soon as you go back to normal your body will restore its natural water balance over the next few days and you will put on those pounds you took off without being able to do anything about it.

The beauty game is encouraged because people are made to feel inadequate for not looking the way the ad-men would have them believe they ought to look, so the search is on for easy ways out, for short cuts, for overnight solutions and miracle changes. Well, they do not exist. The maintenance of a slim figure needs constant vigilance, keeping a good skin in good condition means regular care. Like all other aspects of staying fit and healthy, it requires effort, not from others or machines or bottles or jars, but from *you*. You have to work at it. If you cannot be bothered, keep your expectations low and confine them to your own, not the advertisers'.

From
Healthcare

Michel de Montaigne
Women and Men

The men whose society and intimacy I seek are those who are called well-bred and talented men; and the thought of these gives me a distaste for others. Their kind is, rightly considered, the rarest that we have, a kind that owes almost everything to nature. The purpose of our intercourse is simply intimacy, familiarity, and talk; the exercise of the mind is our sole gain. In our conversations all subjects are alike to me. I do not care if there is no depth or weight in them; they always possess charm, and they always keep to the point. All is coloured by a ripe and steady judgement, blended with kindness, candour, gaiety, and friendship. It is not only on questions of succession and the affairs of kings that our wit displays its strength and beauty; it displays it just as much in intimate chat. I know my kind even by their silences and their smiles, and discover them more easily, perhaps, at the dining-table than in the council room. Hippomachus said truly that he knew a good wrestler simply by seeing him walk in the street.

If learning be pleased to take part in our talk, it will never be refused, so long as it is not schoolmasterly, imperious, and tiresome, as it usually is, but meek and ready to take a lesson.

We are only seeking to pass the time; when the hour comes to be instructed and preached to, we will go to seek learning on its throne. Let it descend to our level for the moment, if it will. For, however useful and desirable it may be, I take it that we can, at a pinch, easily dispense with its presence, and manage our affairs without it. The mind of a well-bred person, familiar with the world of men, can be sufficiently agreeable in itself. Art is nothing else but the register and record of the works of such minds.

The companionship of beautiful and virtuous women is also pleasing to me: 'for we too have eyes learned in such matters'. If the mind derives less enjoyment from such company than from that of men, the bodily senses, besides having a greater share in it, also succeed in raising it to a level almost as high, although, in my opinion, it still falls a little short. But this is a relationship in which men have to remain slightly on their guard, especially those, like myself, over whom the body exercises great sway. I scalded myself in my youth, and suffered all the torments that poets say come upon those who abandon themselves to it without sense or discipline. It is true that this whipping has since been a lesson to me,

> Quicunque Argolica de classe Capharea fugit,
> semper ab Euboicis vela retorquet aquis.*

It is folly to fix all one's thoughts upon relationship with a woman, and to become involved in a furious and reckless passion. But, on the other hand, to enter into it without any love or bond of affection; to play, as actors do, the common and customary role of the age, and to put in nothing of oneself but the words: that is indeed to keep on the safe side, but in a very cowardly fashion, like a man who forswears his honour, his profit, or his pleasure for fear of danger. For those who enter into it in this way can never expect it to bring any result capable of moving or satisfying a noble mind.

One must have desired a thing in all seriousness, if one wishes to take serious pleasure in it. This I say even though fortune may undeservedly favour our play-acting, as often happens, since there is no woman, however ill-favoured, who

* 'Anyone in the Argolid fleet who has escaped the Capharean rocks will always turn his sails away from the Euboean seas.' Ovid, *Tristia*, I, i, 83.

does not think herself quite attractive, and who has not something to recommend her, her youth, her smile, or her graceful bearing. For there is no absolutely plain woman any more than there are any absolutely beautiful; Brahmin girls who lack any other attractions go into the market-place, where the people have been expressly assembled by the public crier, and display their connubial parts, to see if these at least will not serve to get them a husband.

Consequently, there is no woman who does not easily let herself be persuaded by the first vow that a man swears to be her slave. Now the necessary result of those betrayals that are the common and ordinary practice of present-day men is, as experience has already shown us, either that women unite and fall back on themselves, banding together to avoid us, or that they conform to the example which we set them, play their part in the farce, and lend themselves to the business without passion, without concern or love. 'Untouched by passion, either in themselves or in another' they think that, as Lysias argued in Plato, the less we love them the more profitably and advantageously they may surrender to us. The result will be the same as in the theatre; the public will take as much or more pleasure in the play than the actors.

For my part, I can no more recognize Venus without Cupid than motherhood without offspring; these are things that lend and owe their essential character to one another. So this deception recoils on the man who practises it. It costs him little, but he gains nothing of value by it. Those who made Venus a goddess observed that her chief beauty was incorporeal and spiritual; but the desires that such men pursue are not only subhuman, they are not even animal.

The animals will not have things so crude and so earthy. We see that imagination and desire often inflame and invite them before the body does. We observe that in the herd both sexes pick and choose the object of their affection, and that they maintain long and kindly companionship together. Even those to whom old age denies bodily vigour still tremble, neigh, and quiver with love. We see them before the act full of hope and ardour; and when the body has had its sport, they are still gratified by the sweetness of recollection. Some even swell with pride as they walk away, and, weary and sated as they are, give voice to their joy and triumph. A creature who has only to relieve the body of a natural urge has no reason to trouble others with such elaborate preparations; love is no meat for a coarse and greedy appetite.

As I do not ask to be taken for any better than I am, I will say this of the errors of my youth. Not only because of the danger to my health – and yet I could not contrive so well as not to have had a couple of touches, though both slight and transitory – but also out of contempt for the practice, I have seldom had recourse to venal and public intimacies. I preferred to enhance my pleasure by difficulty, by desire, and by some measure of glory. I shared the taste of the Emperor Tiberius who, in his love-affairs, was as much captivated by modesty and noble birth as by any other quality; and the whim of the courtesan Flora, who never gave herself to anyone below the rank of dictator, consul, or censor, and took delight in the dignity of her lovers. Doubtless pearls and brocade contribute something in such cases, as well as titles and retinue.

For the rest, I used to set great store by the mind, but only on condition that there were no defects in the body. Indeed, to speak in all conscience, if one or the other of these attractions must perforce be lacking, I would rather have renounced the spiritual; since it can be employed on better things. For in the business of love, which is principally a matter of sight and touch, one can do something without the charms of the mind, nothing without the charms of the body. The true advantage of the ladies lies in their beauty; and beauty is so peculiarly their property that ours, though it demands somewhat different features, is at its best when, boyish and beardless, it can be confused with theirs. They say that at the court of the Grand Turk, those youths who are chosen for his service on the score of beauty, and the number is enormous, are dismissed at the age of 22, at the latest.

Reason, wisdom, and the offices of friendship are more easily found among men; that is why they govern the affairs of the world.

These two kinds of relationship are fortuitous and depend upon others. The first is disappointingly rare; the second withers with age. So they have been incapable of providing adequately for the needs of my life. The companionship of books, which is the third, is much more certain and more our own. It yields all other advantages to the first two, but it has on its side the constancy and facility with which it serves us. It has accompanied me all along my way, and assists me everywhere. It comforts me in my old age and solitude. It frees me from the weight of a tedious idleness, and releases me at any moment from disagreeable company. It dulls the pangs of any grief that is not intense and overmastering. To distract myself from tiresome thoughts, I have only to resort to books; they easily draw my mind to themselves and away from other things. And yet they show no resentment when they see that I only turn to them through lack of those other more real, lively, and natural satisfactions; they always receive me with the same welcome.

A man may well go on foot, as the saying is, if he is leading his horse by the bridle; and our contemporary James, King of

Naples and Sicily, who, though handsome, young, and sound in health, had himself carried about the country on a stretcher, lying on a wretched feather pillow, dressed in a grey cloth coat with a cap to match, but followed nevertheless by a great regal train, by litters, by led horses of all kinds, and by gentlemen and officers, presented a picture of an austerity still tender and wavering. A sick man is not to be pitied if he has a cure in his sleeve. In the experience and application of this maxim, which is a very true one, lies all the profit that I have derived from books. As a matter of fact, I hardly make more use of them than those who do not know them. I enjoy them as misers do their treasures, by knowing that I can enjoy them when I please; my mind is fully satisfied and contented by this right of possession.

I never travel without books either in peace or in war. Yet many days or months will go by without my using them. Very soon, I say to myself, or tomorrow, or when I feel like it. Meanwhile time runs by and is gone, and I am none the worse. For you cannot imagine how much ease and comfort I draw from the thought that they are beside me, to give me pleasure when I choose, and from the feeling that they bring great help to me in my life. They are the best provision I have found for this human journey, and I am extremely sorry for any intelligent man who is without them. I am the readier to accept any other sort of entertainment, however trivial, for knowing that this one can never fail me.

When at home, I turn a little more often to my library, from which I can easily overlook my whole household. There I am above the gateway, and can see below me my garden, my farmyard, my courtyard, and most parts of my house. There I turn the pages now of one book, now of another, without order and without plan, reading by snatches. Sometimes I reflect, and sometimes I compose and dictate my reflections, walking up and down, as at present.

My library is in the third story of a tower; on the first is my chapel, on the second a bedroom with ante-chambers, where I often lie to be alone; and above it there is a great wardrobe. Formerly, this was the most useless part of the house. But now I spend most of the days of my life there, and most of the hours of the day. I am never there at night. Adjoining my library is a very neat little room, in which a fire can be laid in winter, and which is pleasantly lighted by a window. And if I were not more afraid of the trouble than of the cost – trouble which deters me from every kind of business – I could easily join to each side a gallery a hundred paces long and twelve paces wide on the same level. For I have found the necessary walls built for another purpose to the requisite height. Every place of retirement requires a room for walking. My thoughts go to sleep if I sit still. My mind does not work if my legs do not shake it up. Those who study without books are all in this plight.

My library is circular in shape, with no flat wall except that taken up by my table and chair; and, being rounded, it presents me with all my books at once, arranged about me on five tiers of shelves. From this room I have three open views, and its free space is sixteen paces across. In winter I am there less continually, for my house is perched on a hill, as its name implies, and there is no room more exposed to the winds than this. It is a little difficult of access and out of the way, but this I like, both for the benefit of the exercise and for its keeping people away from me. It is my throne, and I try to rule here absolutely, reserving this one corner from all society, con-jugal, filial, and social. Everywhere else I have just a verbal authority, which is essentially doubtful. Miserable, to my mind, is the man who has no place in his house where he can be alone, where he can privately attend to his needs, where he can conceal himself! Ambition fitly requites her servants by keeping them always on show, like a statue in a market-place; 'a great fortune means great bondage'. They can have no privacy even in the privy. I consider nothing so harsh in the life of austerity followed by our religious orders, as the rule which I found in one of their communities, by which they are required perpetually to be in company, and to have numerous persons with them whatever they do. I find it rather more bearable always to be alone than never to have the power to be so.

If anyone tells me that it is degrading to the Muses to use them only as a plaything and a pastime, he does not know, as I do, how valuable pleasure, sport, and amusement are. I am almost prepared to say that any other aim is ridiculous. I live from day to day and, with reverence be it said, live only for myself; my purposes go no further. In my youth I studied out of ostentation; later a little to gain wisdom; now for pleasure; but never for the sake of learning. The idle and extravagant hobby I once had of collecting books as a kind of furniture, not merely enough to fill my needs but rather more for decoration and wall-lining, I gave up long ago.

Books have many pleasing qualities for those who know how to choose them. But nothing good is without its evil side; this pleasure is no purer or more unmixed than any other. It has its disadvantages, and very grave ones. Books exercise the mind, but the body, whose interests I have never neglected either, remains meanwhile inactive, and grows heavy and dull. I know of no excess that does me more harm, or that I should avoid more strictly in these my declining years.

Fashion

My early fashion photographs were quite simply . . . *bad*. Taken for the *Tatler* and *Sketch*, they were hopelessly awkward and stilted. Models used to do their own make-up and hair and even supplied their own accessories. The clothes never fitted, so to make the shape remotely right you stuffed socks down the front of their 'frocks', used bulldog clips at the waist and Scotch tape at the hem. And you retouched like crazy.

For some reason when I started working regularly for *Vogue*, Audrey Withers, the editor, thought she could switch me from the feature pages and make me into a fashion photographer. So I tried. I was at least determined to have fun for myself and hopefully for the reader as well. The models were made to move and react, either by putting them in incongruous situations or by having them perform unlikely and irresponsible feats. I made them run, dance, kiss – anything but stand still. Each sitting became a short story or miniature film strip. To liven up one sitting we invited the cast of *Irma la Douce* to join us. The comedian Ronnie Barker found himself in a lift with one of the fashion editors. 'Hello,' she said brightly. 'I'm Unity.' 'Well,' replied Ronnie Barker, clearly a union member, 'I'm Equity.'

I liked deceiving the reader's eye. Nylon thread became a favourite device, used to suspend a glass or hold up a house of cards. I would nail the girl's shoes to the floor to defy gravity and suspend her escort with a rope from the ceiling. Air tickets were frequently exchanged for publicity, which explains why nearly every fashion story abroad started with models climbing the stairs into the aeroplane. I just did it without the stairs.

Maybe the *Vogue* readers stopped to look, but I doubt if it helped to sell the clothes one bit. The only thing that could be said is that the photographs didn't imitate those elegant pictures by Irving Penn which I admired so much and which showed the clothes with such style.

I went to New York for the first time on a fashion trip with Penelope Gilliatt who was *Vogue*'s features editor, and

of course not remotely interested in fashion. We were amazed by the energy and style of New York. I held the door open for a lady on my first day and she said, 'Gee, you must be English.' When I asked a taxi driver, 'I wonder if you'd be so kind as to take me to 163 East 70th Street?' he said 'I'd *what*? What's the address?'

What hit me most was the brashness of the colours; the light seemed harder, the car dumps were like skyscrapers, people walked like a speeded-up movie. I asked Hermione Gingold, who was working in New York at the time, why all that steam came out of the manholes in the street. She said, 'I don't know darling. It's either an Indian reservation, or else they're trying to elect a new Pope.'

I stayed on for a bit, working in the New York theatre, and for American *Vogue*, doing beauty shots for one of their formidable editors, Margaret Case. Now you absolutely can't work for American *Vogue* and not have your own telephone, and Miss Case asked me for my number. Two weeks before I had photographed fifty Father Christmases having breakfast together in the Bowery, so I had the number of the Santa Claus at Macy's department store, which I gave to Margaret Case. She would ring it up and bark 'Mr Jones, where are you? You're late for an assignment.' The answer she'd get was a voice saying 'Ho, ho, ho, little girl, now what would *you* like Santa to bring you?' And she'd say 'Mr Jones, would you mind sobering up, we have a *very* important sitting in ten minutes.'

I had never been in a skyscraper before so when I had a session with Mrs William Paley, who appeared endlessly in *Vogue* sitting on a sofa, I had her leaning out of one window miles up, and I was leaning out of another. Margaret Case exploded: 'I don't understand you, Mr Jones, all this leaning out of windows; you can't treat *personalities* like this. When Cecil takes a photograph he just sits people down.' In the end I persuaded Miss Case to provide the smoky background I wanted. I got her first to stand behind Mrs Paley, then to kneel, and eventually to lie under the bed puffing at a cigar. After that we were inseparable and I got a telephone.

From
Personal View

Peter York
Style Wars

Styles were constantly described as schizophrenic in the seventies, meaning it wasn't clear what they were saying about their owners. There were too many styles, *too many options . . .* too much *repertoire.* I knew one fashion editor who went right off her head. She started saying fashion was irrelevant, left her job and described herself as *anti-fashion.* She got involved, so she said, with *politics* in 1977, style as a *statement*; into this eclectic trip where she'd be expressing her creativity by juxtaposing those legwarmers, different colours, with the shoes (like the black kids wore in Harlem), with Vivienne Westwood's bondage suits, and the whole big thing became not just making herself an art object but one that meant something. In the 1970s, fashion became *very* intellectual, ironic, political and Artistic and fragmented. Quite ordinary fashion editors and buyers generally had a crisis of confidence. Where was it? How to cover it? Who was it for? Oh, for an A-line, a sack . . . Courrèges!

Along with this came the development of the human theme parks that started to blossom in the late seventies, particularly the new Gossip World and Punk World, both of which had essentially *middle-class* déraciné origins in the first place (the real thing came later) and represented middle-class fantasy ideas of what it was, on the one hand, to be rich and smart and, on the other, to be a rough working-class person. They both dramatized ironic ideas. Not the real class war – not yet – but the Phoney One. In the first place, there weren't real aristos – except commercial ones – in the gossip world of *Ritz*; it was a Seventh Avenue idea of class, and there was little enough Social Realism in punk, which started off as an Art Idea.

Punk World and Gossip World were both dead risky because they played with some *heavy* things, things which used to mean something and were exciting precisely because they were so far off to the *right* and the *left* of the post hippy mainstream consensus. *Try it.* I remember John Ingham, one of the first journalists to really work up the original rhetoric of punk, telling me that the thing that really summed it all up for him was the famous picture which went the rounds of Sid Vicious chain whipping this hippy in the front row of the Nashville in 1976. I'd seen the picture a few months earlier when Vivienne Westwood had been telling me about that night when Sid had *stepped out of the performance* to give this poor dork a going over. That was a cause.

And there was all the playing about with the *Doc Martens* – the big boots – which was the biggest race memory of real heavy styles. In 1976 you didn't actually see skins around that much, they were only just beginning to filter back. You'd see more of the skinhead style in those macho gay magazines ('Sam, hot and heavy') where it was reckoned as one of the *traditional* costumes. And, of course, there were the punk Swastikas which faded out when punk bore left the following year and people were shamed out of it. John Krevine, who had the Boy shop on the King's Road, had skinhead and schlock horror tableaux which was a funny mix. Part of it came from the old New York Mutilation Art style, pushing the boat out; some of it was more home-grown memories of ironists in their late twenties, the kind of people who would have a complete set of the Richard Allen books – *Skinhead, Suedehead, Terrace Terrors*.

The big incentive then was *Liberal baiting* which by 1976 had become a major hobby, you only had to talk about a *social worker* or an *ethnic print dress* or any kind of Liberal stereotype figure to get a laugh. It was a lot of fun baiting the sixties Liberal consensus styles and it was dead easy. The main thing was to be a bit extreme. As for sex, drugs or rock and roll, *leave it out*, aggression was this year's model. That was when all the styles got really tight and aggressive, all the big floppy shambolic post-hippie styles started to disappear from 1975 on. *Tighten up.* At the same time, the Conservative radicals were sounding really sharp. On the right (or the hard-nut left right), that was where the action was. *Try it.* Margaret Thatcher, who liked to call people 'wet', was definitely in for the Liberal baiting. The Thatcher government – the British Experiment – was *definitely* an act of faith in the hard style. Might work, *try it*.

All this moving off to the 'right' and the 'left', this *polarizing*, made you wonder if you could carry anything through on the right style, like those experiments where the subjects had to administer successively higher doses of electric shocks to people who screamed and writhed. The thing that so excited the journalists who wrote the experiments up was just how far these mainstream mothers and fathers were prepared to go – hate to do it but . . .

They put on the cocktail kitsch cruelty wear, the Doc Martens, and the Swastika T-shirts in the name of irony. In the mid-seventies the signs didn't mean anything any more, so the party line went, rather like the uneasy old game – passé now – of joshing the black guys with a few race jokes to show you're relaxed about it all.

The coolest thing around was the *class* issue. The old class number had been an absolutely no-go territory in the media, with people drabbing off their accents or cleaning them up and *aiming for the middle*, the Parkinson territory, N.W.1, the *Time Out* Poly left. A touch of class was really the most exciting thing ever – given you couldn't get much going on the old sex, drugs or rock and roll. After ten years of official classlessness, it was meaty and risky, but safe because, like all those other exhumations, it suggested the old conflicts were thoroughly dead at the roots so you could muck around now and then, just like putting on the leathers.

A piece I wrote for *Harpers & Queen* called 'Sloane Rangers' provided a lot of funny responses that gave one a clue. I'd written it very much as a bit of fun, about what I thought was an historical aside, a traditional style *tightening up* to cope with the new world, pulling together for comfort and starting to look a little uniform. But one was definitely keeping a light tone. Some people took it very seriously though. First, I met one of the famous Tangier Queens at a party – the kind whose houses get written up in *House and Garden* magazines as 'in a house belonging to', meaning these people have houses like you and I have shoes – and he got really serious about Sloane Rangers.

He said it was *dangerous* sending up these poor upper middle-class girls with their precious little totems, a nice scarf or one or two Georgian bits. He'd been in Italy and he knew what could happen. He thought it was stirring things up. A few months later Thames did a T.V. documentary based on Sloane Rangers and really pushed the boat out, laying on the accents and the shooting parties and putting in a scene where one of the girls goes into Hèrmes in Bond Street and looks at £*800* bags. Of course, those girls – the real thing – wouldn't have done that in a million years, they'd make a £40 job do five years. After that people used to ask me, perfectly seriously, etiquette questions – Mitford questions – as to whether a *true* Sloane would do this or that and – here was the really heavy-breathing part – was this girl or that a *true* Sloane or a Sub-Sloane. There was a lot of harping on it. While people would keep the tone light you could see they really wanted to know. It was after that Gossip World really started to take off in a big way. They were pretty vacant and they didn't care. Gossip World was *Ritz* – absolutely anyone could be in *Ritz*. It was straight down the line vanity publishing, and most of the names were just people working in the trade. In the wings, however, there was a raft of people who took it all dead straight, the cocktail kitsch swanning and the Doc Martens, without a touch of irony. You had all these suburban middle-class Fleet Streeters getting *absolutely fixated* on the high society idea, the kind of girls who five years before would have been up to their necks in the Monsoon Indian print three-piece doing a little story on a play group were on to Roddy this and Di that and Mynah and Bryan and *Margaret Argyll* (never say die). One was asked to do pieces on *the Season* and where the Smart money was going and what it was really like at Annabel's or Tramp and the most amazing set of Rome's Burning ideas you ever heard.

A bit later the class war business began to show through in publishing with the new snob publishing, which was for the same market as the new snob accessories with the initials. It started off a bit tentatively with the little Debrett books, which were in a very fifties mould – keep the tone light and jokey little line drawings – but then it got going seriously with State secrets never before revealed. The Mitford line, hitherto somewhat private, developed into a big market with things like Jilly Cooper's *Class* book, which was a tourist guide with the same jokey line drawings, but also a piece of romantic *propaganda* for the old régime which would have been Breaking Faith ten years before.

You found people who had seemed to be tinkering about with this very stylized interest in luxury as kitsch – and were therefore O.K. – were playing it absolutely straight. The direction in 1975 was – *up-market*; so many people were going up-market you couldn't make out where all the business would be coming from. You saw all these old hippie retreads going full tilt for the Savoy Cocktail book and the patent shoes. *Try it*. Then in a little while you found they were turning really Right – like those progressive rock groups who said they were voting Tory in 1979.

The way the gays moved gave one a clue, from tentative camp to Lumberjack clone, so that was what it had been about all along (my body, your body, any body). With all the minorities out and running you felt safe to despise everybody. Everybody had had their break, 1967, 1971, etc., the blacks were out, the gays were out, so you didn't need to observe any of the little Liberal niceties. On the Punk World front come 1977 you started to see some extraordinary reactions around, particularly with the skinhead revival developing in a serious way – the hard-nut baldies. When the baldies came round again – any time from Manson to the Krishna Kids to the Deerhunter – you knew you were in for trouble.

Come Easter 1980 and the Seaside battles and you could see what had been going on in 1976 and how all the little kids who were ten and twelve then had taken it in. The mid-seventies Phoney War. The journalists who went down to cover the mods and rockers reruns got themselves tied in knots, because they found these battles, these Style wars, with four or five different armies pitching in – skins, rude boys and punks and teds and rockers and rockabillies – they couldn't sort them out. The *Mirror*'s centre spread, 'disturbing truth about the cults that breed on violence, see centre pages', came out of the Fleet Street Wax Museum since it was pretty much line for line Marjorie Proops talks to a mod girl (1964) save for a few smart 1980s touches like *class*. There was a nice little secondary piece on a disco in Manchester, however, where they almost caught the tone. The disco manager explained how they followed the same principle as tripling and quadrupling in cinemas – he had a room for the Bowie freaks and New Wavers, one for the soulies, one for the discos and another for the Two-Tones. 'The youngsters', he said, 'go into the rooms where their kind of music is being played and we have very little trouble.'

From
Style Wars

The Class System

About three years ago, when I rather tentatively suggested writing a book about the English class system, people drew away from me in horror.

'But that's all finished,' they said nervously, 'no-one gives a hoot any more. Look at the young.' They sounded as if I were intending to produce a standard work on coprophilia or child-molesting. It was plain that since the egalitarian shake-up of the sixties and early seventies, class as a subject had become the ultimate obscenity.

Three years of research later, I can assure you that the class system is alive and well and living in people's minds in England. There may have been an enormous shift of wealth between rich and poor. Every day Jack may be getting nearer his master financially, but social stratification remains incredibly resistant to change. It takes more than jeans and a taste in pop music to make even the young all one class. In fact after a period of enforced egalitarianism in the sixties when pop culture and socialism were in the ascendant, a whole new generation have appeared, who want the boundaries re-defined. This perhaps explains the popularity of Nigel Dempster's column in the *Daily Mail*, and such books as *The English Gentleman* by Douglas Sutherland and the recently published *U and Non-U Re-visited* edited by Richard Buckle.

Added to this is the colossal success of all those television serials and plays about the higher classes: *Upstairs Downstairs*, *Thomas and Sarah*, *Flambards* and *Rebecca*, not to mention the royal sagas. The fact that they have all been set in the past – because nostalgia excuses everything, enabling people to click their tongues over the out-dated inequalities, yet guiltily enjoy the sense of hierarchy – must mean a hankering after some kind of social pecking order.

What struck me, however, as soon as I started the book, was the enormity of the task I had taken on. It was like trying to catalogue the sea. For the whole system, despite its stratification, is constantly forming and re-forming like coral. 'Even a small town like Swansea,' said Wynford Vaughan Thomas, 'has as many layers as an onion, and each one of them reduces you to tears.' To me, the system seemed more like a huge striped rugger shirt that had run in the wash, with each layer blurring into the next one, and snobbery being the fiercest at the place where one stripe merged with another.

I found, too, that people were incredibly difficult to pin down into classes. John went to a more famous boarding school than Thomas, who has a better job than Charles, who's got smarter friends than Harry, who lives in an older house with a bigger garden than David, who's got an uncle who's an earl, but whose children go to a comprehensive school. Who is then the gentleman?

A social class can perhaps be rather cumbersomely described as a group of people with certain common traits: descent, education, accent, similarity of occupation, wealth, moral attitudes, friends, hobbies, accommodation; and with generally similar ideas, and forms of behaviour, who meet each other on equal terms, and regard themselves as belonging to one group. A single failure to conform would certainly not exclude you from membership. Your own class tend to be people you feel comfortable with – 'one of our sort' – as you do when you are wearing old flat shoes, rather than teetering round on precarious five-inch heels. Aristocrats, for example, feel at home with aristocrats: 'The nice thing about the House of Lords,' explained one peer, 'is that you can have incredibly snobbish conversations without feeling snobbish. Yesterday I admired a chap's wife's diamonds: he said they came from Napoleon's sword, and before then from Louis XIV.'

When people consider they are not of the same class it becomes more complicated. 'Who knows,' wrote Montaigne, 'when I play with my cat, whether I do not make her more sport than she makes me.' In the same way, quite often you think you are being terribly democratic talking to some vulgar little man at a party, while he at the same time is thinking how decent he is wasting time on some one as socially insignificant as you.

Another charge has been levelled at me. What right, I am asked, have *I* to hold forth on the subject of the English class system? Most people who have tried in the past – Nancy Mitford, Christopher Sykes, Angus Maude – have been members of the upper classes. The answer is no right at all; all I can claim is a passionate interest in the subject, and that, being ashamedly middle class, I am more equidistant from the bottom and the top.

It is perhaps important to point out here, the various definitions of class which have been in use in England over the past twenty-five years. Principally there is the Census: *Classification of Occupations*, which is published every ten years or so (the latest was in 1970), which classifies everyone by the occupation of the head of the household of which they are members, irrespective of all other circumstances. This arbitrary categorisation is used as 'gospel' in most social surveys. Secondly there is 'U and Non-U,' a distinction invented by Professor Alan S. C. Ross in an essay first published in a learned Finnish periodical in 1954, which divided English people into 'U' (upper class) and 'Non-U' (non-upper class), mostly by the way they spoke and by the vocabulary they used. And finally comes the classification: 'A, B, C1 and C2, D and E', which is used by the media and by advertising, but which is basically the same as that of the Census.

What follows is the idiosyncratic view of someone bred in Yorkshire who has lived most of her life in London. If it reveals an obsessive interest in the classes nearest to the one in which I put myself, showing envy of those just above me in the hierarchy, scorn of those just below, and a slightly romanticized fantasy of those most far from my own experience, this will surely only confirm what is most typical of attitudes to class. An interest in social mobility and an obsession with class are, after all, thoroughly middle-class characteristics.

It might therefore be appropriate here to digress a little to explain what my own origins are. My paternal grandfather was a wool-merchant, but my maternal grandmother's family were a bit grander. They owned newspapers, and were distinguished Whig M.P.s for Leeds during the nineteenth century. My mother's side were mostly in the church, her father being Canon of Heaton near Bradford. Her mother was a beauty. Both sides had lived in the West Riding of Yorkshire for generations. They were very very strait-laced; to this day there has never been a divorce in the family.

My father went to Rugby, then to Cambridge, where he got a first in two years, and then into the army. After getting married, he found he wasn't making enough money, and joined Fords, and he and my mother moved somewhat reluctantly to Hornchurch, where I was born. At the beginning of the second world war he was called up, and became one of the army's youngest brigadiers. After the war, we moved back to Yorkshire, living first in a large Victorian house. I was eight, and I think for the first time became aware of class distinction. Our next-door neighbour was a newly rich and very ostentatious wool manufacturer, of whose sybaritic existence my parents disapproved. One morning he asked me over to his house. I had a heavenly time, spending all morning playing the pianola, of which my mother also disapproved – too much pleasure for too little effort – and eating a whole eight-ounce bar of black market milk chocolate, which, just after the war, seemed like stumbling on Aladdin's cave. When I got home I was sick. I was aware that it served me right both for slumming and for over-indulgence.

Soon after that we moved into the Hall at Ilkley, a splendid Georgian house with a long drive, seven acres of fields for my ponies, a swimming pool, and tennis and squash courts. From then on we lived an élitist existence: tennis parties with cucumber sandwiches, large dances, and fêtes in the garden. I enjoyed playing little Miss Muck tremendously. I had a photograph of the house taken from the bottom of the drive on my dressing-table at school, and all my little school friends, and later my boy-friends, were very impressed when they came to stay.

My brother, however, still had doubts about our life-style: it was too bourgeois, too predictable and restricted, he thought. One wet afternoon, I remember him striding up and down the drawing-room, going on and on and on about our boring middle-class existence.

Suddenly my mother, who'd been trying to read a detective story, looked over her spectacles, and said with very gentle reproof: 'Upper middle-class, darling.'

Occasionally we were taken down a peg by a socialist aunt who thought we'd all got too big for our boots. One day my mother was describing some people who lived near York as being a very 'old' family.

'Whadja mean old?' snorted my aunt. 'All families are old.'

On another occasion when my mother was grumbling about her char not turning up, my aunt suddenly snapped: 'And who are you to demand service?' Both became family catch-phrases.

There were very few eligible young men for me in Ilkley. The glamorous hard-drinking wool merchants' sons with their fast cars, teddy-bear coats, and broad Yorkshire accents were as above me sexually as they were below me, I felt, socially. But when I was about eighteen, two Old Etonians came to live for a year in the district. They were learning farming before going back to run their estates. They were both very attractive and easy-going, and were consequently asked everywhere, every mum with a marriageable daughter competing for their attention. I was terribly disconcerted when, after a couple of visits to our house and one of them taking me out once, they became complete habitués of the house of a jumped-up steel merchant across the valley. Soon they were both fighting for the hand of his not particularly good-looking daughter. But she's so much commoner than me – I remember thinking in bewilderment, why don't they prefer my company and our house? I realise now that they far preferred the easy-going atmosphere of the steel merchant's house, with its lush hospitality, ever-flowing drink, and poker sessions long into the night, to one glass of sherry and self-consciously intelligent conversation in ours. I had yet to learn, too, that people invariably dislike and shun the class just below them, and much prefer the class below that, or even the one below that.

I was further bewildered when, later in the year, I went to Oxford to learn to type, and shared a room with an 'Hon.' who said 'handbag'. This seemed like a blasphemy. Nancy Mitford's *The Pursuit of Love* had been my bible as a teenager. I knew peers' daughters, whom she immortalised as 'Hons', said 'bag' rather than 'handbag'. At that time, aware, too, of a slowly emerging sexuality and away for once from parental and educational restraint, I evolved a new way of dressing: five-inch high-heeled shoes, tight straight skirts, very very tight cheap sweaters, and masses of make-up to cover a still rather bad skin. I looked just like a tart. People obviously took me for one too. For when the room-mate who was an Hon. introduced me to all her smart friends at Christchurch, one young blood promptly betted another young blood a tenner he couldn't get me into bed by the end of the week. Before he had time to lay siege, the story was repeated back to me. I was shattered: shocked and horrified to my virginal middle-class core; I cried for twenty-four hours. My would-be-seducer, who had a good heart, on hearing of my misery, turned up at my digs, apologised handsomely, and suggested, by way of making amends, rather than me, that he take me to the cinema. On the way there, he stopped at a sweet shop and bought a bar of chocolate. Breaking it, he gave me half, and started to eat the other half himself.

'But you can't eat sweets in the street,' I gasped, almost more shocked than I had been by his intended seduction.

'I,' he answered, with the centuries of disdain in his voice, 'Can do anything I like.'

Hons that talked about handbags, lords who ate chocolate in the streets like the working classes, aristocrats who preferred the jumped-up to the solidly middle class: I was slowly learning that the class system was infinitely more complicated than I had ever dreamed.

It takes many years, writes Jonathan Gathorne Hardy in *The Rise and Fall of the British Nanny*, for the outsider to master those complex, subtle distinctions, the nuances of accent, attitudes and behaviour that went, indeed which go, into that living, changing thing – English upper-class snobbery. He might have added that this is true of any class's snobbery.

The whole thing is relative. Freddie Trueman, who was certainly born working-class, defined a gentleman as someone who gets out of his bath 'to go t' toilet.' George IV said you could recognise the people who weren't gentlemen by the way they divide their coats when they sit down. The Queen Mother used to listen to *Mrs Dale's Diary* to find out how life went on in a 'middle-class' family. But most people who consider themselves middle-class, would regard Mrs Dale's life-style as flagrantly 'lower middle'.

When I went on Yorkshire Television with Jean Rook of the *Daily Express* a few years ago, the interviewer began most embarrassingly by saying: 'Now here you are, two columnists from Yorkshire, but from very different backgrounds. You're working-class, aren't you Jean, and, Jilly you're upper-class.'

We both shrieked with horror.

'I'm middle, not upper,' I muttered, going scarlet.

'I'm upper middle,' said Miss Rook witheringly. 'I know lots of duchesses.'

Conversely when I go to very grand parties, my hostess invariably excuses my commonness and polyester cleavages by saying: 'D'you know Jilly? She's rather famous.'

Every court, I suppose, needs its jester.

But even in an egalitarian age, when it's no longer done to despise someone of a different class – (although the chippy working classes don't make much effort not to) it's very difficult not to adjust your behaviour according to the company you are in.

Shopping in Harrods with a peer's daughter recently, I actually found myself buying a little white dress with blue snowdrops for a boy baby rather than a Baby-Gro, because I'd read the week before in *Harper's* that the upper classes thought Baby-Gros were common. Next day I was lunching in a restaurant with a working-class writer and I found myself, who never touch pudding, saying I'd love some because he was, and I didn't want to appear snooty.

I heard also of a psychiatrist who was treating an aristocrat for depression. A month went by, and they seemed to be making little progress.

'I want you to be completely honest,' said the psychiatrist at the next session, 'And tell me exactly what's in your mind at the moment.'

'I was thinking,' said the aristocrat apologetically, 'What a vulgar little man you were.'

It was their final session. The psychiatrist was unable to go on, because he'd completely lost any feeling of ascendancy.

'And so,' as John Coleman once wrote in the *Sunday Times*, 'the old movements of social advance and recoil go on, just as much as they always did. It is the perpetual inaccuracy of imitation that makes up the English social comedy and tragedy.'

But there is plenty of comedy. As a small boy at my son's last school pointed out in an essay, 'All people should be gentlemen except ladies, but it puts a bit of variety into life if some are not.'

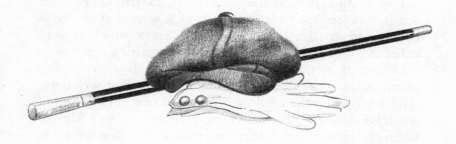

From
Class

Ralph Waldo Emerson
On Aristocracy

The existence of an upper class is not injurious, as long as it is dependent on merit. For so long it is provocation to the bold and generous. These distinctions exist, and they are deep, not to be talked or voted away. If the differences are organic, so are the merits, that is to say the power and excellence we describe are real. Aristocracy is the class eminent by personal qualities, and to them belongs without assertion a proper influence. Men of aim must lead the aimless; men of invention the uninventive. I wish catholic men, who by their science and skill are at home in every latitude and longitude, who carry the world in their thoughts; men of universal politics, who are interested in things in proportion to their truth and magnitude; who know the beauty of animals and the laws of their nature, whom the mystery of botany allures, and the mineral laws; who see general effects and are not too learned to love the Imagination, the power and the spirits of Solitude; – men who see the dance in men's lives as well as in a ballroom, and can feel and convey the sense which is only collectively or totally expressed by a population; men who are charmed by the beautiful Nemesis as well as by the dire Nemesis, and dare trust their inspiration for their welcome; who would find their fellows in persons of real elevation of whatever kind of speculative or practical ability. We are fallen on times so acquiescent and traditionary that we are in danger of forgetting so simple a fact as that the basis of all aristocracy must be truth, – the doing what elsewhere is pretended to be done. One would gladly see all our institutions rightly aristocratic in this wise. . . .

The ancients were fond of ascribing to their nobles gigantic proportions and strength. The hero must have the force of ten men. The chief is taller by a head than any of his tribe. Douglas can throw the bar a greater cast. Richard can sever the iron bolt with his sword. The horn of Roland, in the romance, is heard sixty miles. The Cid has a prevailing health that will let him nurse the leper, and share his bed without harm. And since the body is the pipe through which we tap all the succors and virtues of the material world, it is certain that a sound body must be at the root of any excellence in manners and actions; a strong and supple frame which yields a stock of strength and spirits for all the needs of the day, and generates the habit of relying on a supply of power for all extraordinary exertions. When Nature goes to create a national man, she puts a symmetry between the physical and intellectual powers. She moulds a large brain, and joins to it a great trunk to supply it; as if a fine alembic were fed with liquor for its distillations from broad full vats in the vaults of the laboratory. . . .

An aristocracy could not exist unless it were organic. Men are born to command, and – it is even so – 'come into the world booted and spurred to ride.' The blood royal never pays, we say. It obtains service, gifts, supplies, furtherance of all kinds from the love and joy of those who feel themselves honored by the service they render.

Dull people think it Fortune that makes one rich and another poor. Is it? Yes, but the fortune was earlier than they think, namely, in the balance or adjustment between devotion to what is agreeable to-day and the forecast of what will be valuable to-morrow.

Certainly I am not going to argue the merits of gradation in the universe; the existing order of more or less. Neither do I wish to go into a vindication of the justice that disposes the variety of lot. I know how steep the contrast of condition looks; such excess here and such destitution there; like entire chance, like the freaks of the wind, heaping the snow-drift in gorges, stripping the plain; such despotism of wealth and comfort in banquet-halls, whilst death is in the pots of the wretched, – that it behooves a good man to walk with tenderness and heed amidst so much suffering. I only point in passing to the order of the universe, which makes a rotation, – not like the coarse policy of the Greeks, ten generals, each commanding one day and then giving place to the next, or like our democratic politics, my turn now, your turn next, – but the constitution of things has distributed a new quality or talent to each mind, and the revolution of things is always bringing the need, now of this, now of that, and is sure to bring home the opportunity to every one.

The only relief that I know against the invidiousness of superior position is, that you exert your faculty; for whilst each does that, he excludes hard thoughts from the spectator. All right activity is amiable. I never feel that any man occupies my place, but that the reason why I do not have what I wish, is, that I want the faculty which entitles. All spiritual or real power makes its own place.

We pass for what we are, and we prosper or fail by what we are. There are men who may dare much and will be justified in their daring. But it is because they know they are in their place. As long as I am in my place, I am safe. 'The best lightning-rod for your protection is your own spine.' Let a man's social aims be proportioned to his means and power. I do not pity the misery of a man underplaced: that will right itself presently: but I pity the man overplaced. A certain quantity of power belongs to a certain quantity of faculty. Whoever wants more power than is the legitimate attraction of his faculty, is a politician, and must pay for that excess; must truckle for it. This is the whole game of society and the politics of the world. Being will always seem well; – but whether possibly I cannot contrive to seem, without the trouble of being? Every Frenchman would have a career. We English are not any better with our love of making a figure. 'I told the Duke of Newcastle,' says Bubb Doddington in his Memoirs, 'that it must end one way or another, it must not remain as it was; for I was determined to make some sort of a figure in life; I earnestly wished it might be under his protection, but if that could not be, I must make some figure; what it would be I could not determine yet; I must look round me a little and consult my friends, but some figure I was resolved to make.'

It will be agreed everywhere that society must have the benefit of the best leaders. How to obtain them? Birth has been tried and failed. Caste in India has no good result. Ennobling of one family is good for one generation; not sure beyond. Slavery had mischief enough to answer for, but it had this good in it, – the pricing of men. In the South a slave was bluntly but accurately valued at five hundred to a thousand dollars, if a good field-hand; if a mechanic, as carpenter or smith, twelve hundred or two thousand. In Rome or Greece what sums would not be paid for a superior slave, a confidential secretary and manager, an educated slave; a man of genius, a Moses educated in Egypt? I don't know how much Epictetus was sold for, or Æsop, or Toussaint l'Ouverture, and perhaps it was not a good market-day. Time was, in England, when the state stipulated beforehand what price should be paid for each citizen's life, if he was killed. Now, if it were possible, I should like to see that appraisal applied to every man, and every man made acquainted with the true number and weight of every adult citizen, and that he be placed where he belongs, with so much power confided to him as he could carry and use.

In the absence of such anthropometer I have a perfect confidence in the natural laws. I think that the community, – every community, if obstructing laws and usages are removed, – will be the best measure and the justest judge of the citizen, or will in the long run give the fairest verdict and reward; better than any royal patronage; better than any premium on race; better than any statute elevating families to hereditary distinction, or any class to sacerdotal education and power. The verdict of battles will best prove the general; the town-meeting, the Congress, will not fail to find out legislative talent. The prerogatives of a right physician are determined, not by his diplomas, but by the health he restores to body and mind; the powers of a geometer by solving his problem; of a priest by the act of inspiring us with a sentiment which disperses the grief from which we suffered. When the lawyer tries his case in court he himself is also on trial and his own merits appear as well as his client's. When old writers are consulted by young writers who have written their first book, they say, Publish it by all means; so only can you certainly know its quality.

Piers Paul Read
Reading

They returned to the Rectory for lunch and sat around the kitchen table once again – the eccentric brigadier, his heroic wife, fashionable daughter, slobbish son, moody son-in-law and fidgeting grandchildren. Food. Drink. Shepherd's pie. Cider. Stewed plums. Thoughts. And some conversation.

Then the longueur of the afternoon stretched before them. Eustace went to read and sleep in the drawing-room. Clare and her mother prepared to take the children to the beach. Guy set out to take his motor-bicycle to the garage, while John went into the library to smoke a Dutch cigar, re-read the *Guardian*, and wonder what the Mascalls would give them for dinner the next day. Twenty minutes later, when he had finished both the cigar and the paper, he decided to read a book. He rose from his chair, yawned, and staggered scratching his stomach towards the mahogany bookshelves. There a thousand books were set out at random, including uniform editions of Dickens, Scott, Dumas and Wilkie Collins, but there was no question now of embarking upon a fat work of fiction. In his last years at school, and throughout his time at university, John had been a periodic reader of French and Russian novels, but later his preoccupation with his work as a barrister, and the demands made upon him by marriage and family life, had led him to confine his reading to *The Times*, the *Economist*, the *Evening Standard*, a few Sunday newspapers and, of course, his briefs and law books. If he ever returned to fiction it was only when he was on holiday, and even then over the years he had developed a certain philistinism and was inclined to confine himself to biography and memoirs. He took the almost common view that no one reads novels any more, or that if they do it is only for distraction and never affects their lives.

His eye now was on the lookout for something new and it fell upon the spine of a book entitled *The Death of Ivan Ilych*. The name Ivan Ilych meant something to him: he thought perhaps that he was a Soviet dissident writer or a vegetarian guru in Mexico, so he pulled the volume from the shelf, looked at the front cover, and saw to his disappointment that it was the title story of a small collection by Leo Tolstoy.

He had read books by Tolstoy in his time – *War and Peace*, *Anna Karenina*, even *Resurrection* – and he had no intention now of re-reading a major work of Russian literature; but since these were only short stories, and it was some time since he had read any fiction, he thought he might as well look at one of them which would carry him through until tea.

The first in the collection was called 'Family Happiness' – an optimistic title which suited his present mood. He settled down in a brown, loose-covered armchair by the window and started to read. *We were in mourning for my mother, who had died in the autumn, and I spent all that winter alone in the country with Katya and Sonya* . . . It took him a certain time to get into the story. His mind kept wandering onto this and that – the shepherd's pie which they had eaten at lunch, the safety of the children on the beach – but he had covered thirty pages, and had reached the marriage of the narrator heroine to Sergey Mikhaylych, before falling asleep. He dozed contentedly, for while he could not quite see himself as the 'tall, robust, middle-aged' hero, he could well imagine Clare as the heroine. *In my heart there was happiness, happiness* . . .

He awoke after sleeping for half an hour or so and resumed reading the story. The sky had grown overcast, so the room darkened as the story darkened too. The marriage which had started so well turned sour. There were scenes between husband and wife which reminded John of unpleasant exchanges he had had with Clare – and he realized with growing annoyance that the title of the story was ironic. He felt almost angry with Tolstoy: he would never have started the story if he had known it was pessimistic.

On the other hand he had been brought up always to finish what he had started, so he hurried through the final pages – quite detached now from the narrative. Clare and he may have had their differences but there had never been any melodrama: nor did she resemble the heroine of the story. He could hardly imagine her trembling as a Frenchman whispered *'je vous aime'* in her ear, or being tempted to *throw herself headlong into the abyss of forbidden delights*. The ending, in which Marenchka declares *a new feeling of love for my children and the father of my children*, did nothing to redeem what he concluded to be an entirely disagreeable story.

The women and children returned for tea. The family gathered yet again around the kitchen table. Eustace talked about cricket. Guy stirred four spoonfuls of sugar into each of his four cups of tea. The children bickered. Helen sighed. Family happiness.

It was only after a game of chess with Tom, and then racing demon with Anna, that John returned to the library and once again picked up his book. The next story in the collection was the title story, 'The Death of Ivan Ilych', and since this had a decidedly mournful sound to it John was about to shut the book and return it to the shelves when certain words jumped out from the first few lines which aroused his curiosity – *trial, Law Courts, Public Prosecutor*. It struck him that if this story was about barristers in Tsarist Russia then it might well be of some documentary interest, so he made up his mind to give it a try.

This novella, for those who have not read it, is about an amiable, intelligent young man – *le phénix de la famille* – who through the cultivation of the right people rises to the post of Public Prosecutor in a Russian provincial city. He leads a contented life. *The pleasures connected with his work were the pleasures of ambition ; his social pleasures were those of vanity ; but Ivan Ilych's greatest pleasure was playing bridge.* Then, at the age of forty-five, after an accident on a step-ladder during the decoration of his large new house, Ivan Ilych begins to have *a queer taste in his mouth* and *feels some discomfort in his left side.* The pain grows worse. Different doctors diagnose different conditions, but nothing they prescribe prevents his decline. Worse, however, than the deterioration of his body is the effect of the disease on his mind. *Ivan Ilych saw that he was dying and he was in continual despair.* He is terrified of death. He loathes his healthy family which while he is dying continues to live as before. Their life seems as futile as his own. *Life, a series of increasing sufferings, flies further and further towards its end – the most terrible suffering . . . There is no explanation. Agony, death . . . what for?*

By the time he had reached this point in the story, John Strickland was totally possessed by his fellow-lawyer, Ivan Ilych. He ceased to notice the room in which he was sitting or the passing of time. When he was called through to the drawing-room for a drink before dinner, and then to dinner itself, he obeyed automatically: he talked and listened as if some small tape-recorder were fixed in his larynx, playing pre-programmed replies to predictable questions – leaving his conscious mind in the suffering body of Ivan Ilych.

As soon as dinner was over John returned to the library to finish the story. The sufferings of Ivan Ilych increased: so too did his hatred for his bland, complacent wife. *Go away,* he shouts at her, *Go away and leave me alone. From that moment the screaming began that continued for three days, and was so terrible that one could not hear it through two closed doors without horror.*

By the time John had finished this story Clare and her parents, who had been watching television, were already in bed. John went upstairs still clutching the book and placed it on his bedside table. There was a curious expression in his eyes as he looked at Clare, but since she was absorbed by a Trollope novel she did not see it. She paid no attention to him as he took off his clothes, went to take his tepid bath, and returned to climb into bed in his pyjamas. It was only when he was lying beside her that she looked up from her book.

'Shall we sleep?' she asked.

'Yes.'

They switched off their bedside lamps and then embraced under the blankets as they had embraced every night since they had married – a gesture which served not just to express a residual affection for one another but to demonstrate by its intensity whether one or other or both were in the mood to make love. It had been evolved after those crises in the early years of their marriage when Clare, bored by the monotonous and mechanical expression of his so-called love, had refused his advances – leaving him baffled and humiliated. Later, of course, she had grown out of her illusions, and that night at Busey it was she who placed one of her long legs over his body and kissed him with soft lips and a half-open mouth. But still possessed by Ivan Ilych, John's body remained rigid beside hers. He gave her an abrupt kiss with pursed lips, so she turned to face away, wished him good night, and in a short time was asleep.

John was not so fortunate, for unlike the fictional Ivan Ilych who dies repentant on the last page of Tolstoy's story, John remained alive, awake, and in much the same state of terror and despair. The certainty of death now combined with the ache in his back to convince him that he too was dying; and even if a reasonable voice within him expressed the opinion that the pain came from a sprained muscle rather than cancer of the spine – even that sensible faculty could not deny that agony and death were as certainly the inevitable destiny of John Strickland as they had been of Ivan Ilych.

Looking forward to death in this way was only half of what led to his sleepless despair. To look back was worse. Like Ivan Ilych he asked himself: *Maybe I did not live as I ought to have done?* – and it was as inadequate for him as it had been for Ivan Ilych to reply: *But how could that be when I did everything properly?* For lying in that sagging bed he could remember quite well the ambitions he had once had to dedicate his life to something more than his own material interests – to serve, indeed, the old ideals of liberty, equality and fraternity in their new guise of socialism. At the age of twenty-five he had assumed that by forty he would be a Member of Parliament in the Labour interest – perhaps a Cabinet Minister – so how had it happened that he found himself instead the leading junior licensing counsel, pleading the interests of the very men who with beer and bingo take from the poor what little they possess? Why did he not defend the drunks, prostitutes, pimps and thieves whom he had once seen as the guiltless dross left after the harvesting of profit by impersonal capitalist combines?

For a moment the face of the young garage mechanic reappeared to torment him; then, as the clock of Busey Church struck one, he opened in his own defence. He specialized in licensing, he argued, because the clerks gave him the work; and they gave him the work because they knew that he was good at the job and needed the money. But why did he need the money? Others did with less. They lived quite happily in Ealing or Croydon, returning home each day to eat their tea, read their briefs, watch television and go to bed; while he had to have a house in Holland Park and dine with merchant bankers – men with grotesque salaries as well as private means – or was obliged to invite them back to elaborate, expensive dinner parties in his own home. But why these friends? Why this way of life? Because he had married Clare.

It suddenly became quite clear to him that if his life had gone wrong it was from the moment he had married Clare, and for the first time in his life John felt that he hated his wife. Terror of disease and death was replaced by a venomous aversion for the woman lying beside him. Her regular, complacent breathing sounded to him like the grunts of a pig. She smelt like an old woman. The smiling, trembling girl he had married had imperceptibly disappeared like a smouldering log, and a hard, middle-aged housewife had risen from the ashes – *le phénix de la famille!*

He smiled now into his pillow at the thought of the small revenge he had taken that night for the countless times when she had been the one to refuse to make love. Even now he suspected that she had only wanted to reassure herself that he still found her attractive – her whose body had borne two children and had become like a sucked-out grape. He now felt only repugnance and loathing for Clare, not just because she had spoilt his past life but for the role she would play in the future. He knew from statistics that she would outlive him, and he could well imagine how she who was so squeamish would detest his final suffering – retching at his incontinence, cowering from his pain. His children might be sorry, but their expectations would console them – just as the Constable or the Turner watercolour would console Clare. As with Ivan Ilych, John's family would watch him die, wishing that he would hurry up and praying to God to dispatch him.

The thought of their God as it pranced into his insomniac mind angered him so much that he ground his teeth together. Not only would Clare outlive him, but when she died she would believe she was going to Heaven whereas John, an agnostic, had no faith whatsoever in an afterlife; so while she could look forward to eternal bliss he lay dreading the empty unknown.

From
A Married Man

John Updike
Guilt-Gems

Ferris, a divorced, middle-aged man, discovered in the blue ground of his midnight brain certain bright moments that never failed to make him feel terrible. Guilty. The treasure was of inestimable value.

One gem showed his younger son, at that time about fourteen, in tearful exasperation throwing two cats down the cellar stairs. The enveloping situation was this: Ferris's doctor had strongly advised him, for the sake of his asthma, to get rid of the cats. 'But they're the children's pets,' Ferris had said. 'We can't just get rid of them.'

'Get rid of them,' his doctor had said. 'Those cats are suffocating you.'

'They don't mean to,' Ferris had pointed out. 'They can't help making dander.'

'Tell Eileen to get rid of them. Tell Eileen it's either you or those cats.'

'I've told her, and she says the children love the cats. She's right. She's always right. What can we do?'

His doctor then had peered at him through the upper half of his bifocals. Returning his eyes to the record he was making of this visit, he muttered, 'It would help to keep them down in the cellar.'

But the cats had been used to the run of the house and always found ways to evade their confinement. They would writhe out through a loose cellar window and come in through the kitchen door with the milkman, or a visiting child, or with Eileen when she had her hands full. Ferris's asthma continued bad. He was clogging his lungs with the Medihaler; his hands always trembled. Only his younger son recognized the emergency: it was his father or the cats. Since the cats could be neither killed nor controlled, Ferris would have to leave. He had already made his decision when, one day otherwise altogether forgotten, he saw the boy so desperately trying to keep the animals in the cellar and his father in the house.

Had Ferris imagined his son's tears of despairing fury? He thought not; there has to be some shine of the extreme, to make a guilt-gem.

Months later, he had left, and one of the duties that had fallen to him in the breakup was the driving of his older son back to his boarding school, in southern New Hampshire. It was usually a Sunday night, and the night he remembered must have been in winter, for there seemed to be ice everywhere. In the car, they had tried to talk; Ferris had tried to thank the boy, for continuing to go to his classes, to pass his exams, to play on the hockey team, to grow. For Ferris's dereliction loomed to him so large that he saw it as a blanket permission for all the derelictions in the world. The boy had listened in a silence that became wet and warm and heavy-breathing, and when Ferris began to touch, he thought delicately, upon the reasons that had led him to leave the child's mother, the boy said 'Yeah' with the quickness of a sucked breath. He knew enough and wanted to know no more: it was the kind of signal one man gives another.

Yet at the destination, in the dark cold spaces of the

campus, after unloading from the car some piece of the bulky equipment – ski boots, or a guitar – essential to an American male adolescent, his son kissed him goodbye. The lit windows of the dormitories glowed all about them. The kiss was like a little spot warmed through a frosty windowpane. Through it Ferris saw how the boy's room felt to him, as haven – haven, amid the Escher prints and motorcycle posters, the hi-fi sets and horseplay-scarred walls, from the horror of having parents, of family.

Also in this period, his younger daughter, his baby, announced across the net from him at tennis, as she hit the ball with a clumsy forehand, 'I think you're very *self*ish.' The 'self' stood out twangingly in the memory, the sweet spot of the sentence. The ball was out. He called it in. It was this false call, oddly, that had crystallized. Her accusation had the flaw that it was *meant* to make him feel guilty; and such a moment is to the real thing as a cultured pearl is to the found pearl.

His older daughter had married soon after his divorce, as if to keep a marriage in the family. She had been his child longer than any; she had taken the full brunt of his parental ineptitude. Once, he had twirled her by the hands so hard that her little wristbones audibly snapped, though X-rays at the hospital showed no fracture. On another occasion of acrobatic foolery, she had bitten him on the leg to get him to stop holding her upside down. Worse than these shameful incidents, however, loomed a childish softball game he had played as pitcher for two teams of children, his own and a neighbor's. For some reason, the neighbor's children feasted off his underhand offerings, pounding hit after hit into the tall grass of the outfield. His own children chased the ball until they were red in the face, while those loathsome little opponents jeeringly rounded the bases.

When at last the young Ferrises' turn at bat came, the very intensity of their father's wish to serve up fat pitches must have put something baffling on the ball, for they unaccountably hit pop-ups and dribblers. A ball bounced out to the mound and Ferris had no choice but to field it and chase down his older daughter as she raced from first to second. The child didn't have a chance; his legs were longer. He could think of no way not to make the play. In the moment before the tag, she looked at him with a smile, a smile preserved as in amber by a childish wild plea on her face. She w‿‿ out.

And now, though all the other players of that day had grown much larger, and whatever expression *he* had worn in that moment had faded forever from his daughter's mind, her bright helpless face hovering above her hurrying body had lost none of its lustre for Ferris, none of its edge, and immutably invested him with shame, with an urgent futile need to *undo*, whenever he held this moment up against the blue light of midnight.

Guilt, for those prone to it, need not attach to conduct generally judged reprehensible. Had Ferris deliberately dropped the ball, had he *not* tagged his daughter out, that would have been reprehensible. In himself he detected, like the background radio noise that underlies the universe and apparently is still transmitting the big bang of its creation, a pervasive ceaseless guilt in regard to his children for having called them into being at all. Just to see one of them walk across a high-school stage to receive a diploma, or up a church aisle to get married, or into the thick of a college soccer game on an overcast November Saturday, was to spangle his insides with terror.

Contrariwise, while it was widely agreed he had treated his ex-wife reprehensibly, her image shed his guilt as a seal sheds droplets of water. In his dreams she floated lithe and uncomplaining, and about ten years younger than she really was. He did remember this: at some point in their separation, Eileen had put her arms around him in their old kitchen, overcome by the sight of him once more leaving, and had sobbed; and by sympathetic pumping action her belly beat against his like a heart. Like a heart: more background noise, momentarily amplified by a defect in his automatic deafener.

His mother, now old, and he, now single, had flown to England together for a trip; she had always wanted to see Tintern Abbey. But she lived in southern New Jersey and he had holed up in Boston, so from Kennedy Airport she had to drive home alone, while he took a shuttle flight in the opposite direction. Worse, he drove himself in her car to LaGuardia, giving her the wheel with all of Queens and

Brooklyn between her and the route home. Could she make it, in the Sunday traffic of megalopolis, tired as she was from the trip? As when he had fielded the softball and his daughter was racing from first to second, he couldn't think what else to do. But tag her. But abandon her.

It was a darkling spring evening in the eastern United States. Rain bejewelled the windshield and there was just enough light left for her to make the Verrazano Bridge. Ferris studied the map. '278, Mother,' he said. 'Just stay on 278 South, no matter what.'

'278 South,' she said faintly, from a great distance away, behind the wheel. The distance between them, after their week together, had suddenly become the distance between one who must fly and one who must drive, between one who must submit and one who must steer. She was seventy-two. A sea of damp metal surrounded her. It had been sunny – that golden, almost mintable sunshine of poems – at Tintern Abbey.

'Stay in your lane,' he told her. 'If anybody honks, ignore them.'

'They might be trying to tell me something.'

'They have nothing to tell you,' he told her. 'Don't change lanes without looking, is all.'

'Once I get to the turnpike, I'll be all right,' she insisted.

'278 South will take you there,' he said. 'Mother, maybe you should stay in a motel. Maybe I should drive with you and fly from Philly.'

'Don't be silly,' she said. 'The light's fading. I can do it. My goodness. I just stay on 278.'

'South,' he said.

Sitting behind the wheel, she was trembling; more than trembling, she was filling the interior of the car with the anticipatory vibrations of a girl before a dance – a prom, the dance of a lifetime. He imagined a corsage on her chest. Her cheek, as he leaned over to kiss it, was stretched smooth by fear, and he could smell perfume, the perfume our nerves give off above a certain pitch of tension. He pulled his suitcase out of the car and slammed the door. As she haltingly pulled into the roadway, in the dusk, in the rain, a car honked, and then another.

How young her face had become at the last! Smooth and

oval, with a half-laugh on her lips. That same half-laugh was in her voice when, three hours later, she had called Boston. 'No mishaps,' she told him. 'Just a thunderstorm over Newark. It got so dark I thought my eyesight was failing. I felt my age.'

'How do you like it?' Ferris had asked, of feeling one's age. He was genuinely curious. He saw her now as his forward scout in the wilderness of time.

With a lilt quite unexpected, dipping into some spring of girlish enthusiasm predating his birth, she answered, 'I *hate* it!' and did laugh.

Her face, the parting kiss, his sense of perfume remained to torment him. His constant guilt had here compressed, her about-to-be-abandoned face a crystallization of the seducer's shame he had failed to feel on other, more appropriate occasions.

A guilt-gem is a piece of the world that has volunteered for compression. Those souls around us, living our lives with us, are gaseous clouds of being awaiting a condensation and preservation – faces, lights that glimmer out, somehow not seized, save in this gesture of remorse. Sifting them through his brain, Ferris would grow dulled to their glitter, indifferent to life and able to sleep. He had been a bully since his first cry for milk, and had continued a tyrant. He had tripped an infant playmate so the boy's head struck a radiator and gushed blood. He had told lies, about an imaginary pet dog, in Sunday school. He had teased his father, once pretending to start the car while the old man was putting a tire in the trunk, making the crowd of kids on the luncheonette steps laugh. Lord, what a treasure! Greater than Fafner's, a lode that goes down and down. Ferris was further soothed by this discovery: in amassing these guilt-gems, in reducing the matrical terror and grave displacement of his existence to a few baubles he could, as it were, put in his pocket and jingle, he was, doubly, guilty.

—Isaiah Berlin—
An
Encounter with Pasternak

A few days later, accompanied by Lina Ivanovna Prokofiev, the composer's estranged wife, I took the train to Peredelkino. Gorky, I was told, had organised this colony to provide recognised writers with an environment in which they could work in peace. Given the temperament of creative artists, this well-intentioned plan did not always lead to harmonious co-existence: some of the personal and political tensions could be sensed even by an ignorant stranger like myself. I walked down the tree-lined road which led to the houses inhabited by the writers. On the way there, we were stopped by a man who was digging a ditch; he climbed out of it, said his name was Yazvitsky, asked after our names, and spoke at some length about an excellent novel that he had written called *The Fires of the Inquisition*; he warmly recommended it to us and told us that we should read an even better novel he was in the course of writing about Ivan III and medieval Russia. He wished us Godspeed and returned to his ditch. My companion thought it all somewhat uncalled-for, but I was charmed by this unexpected, direct, open-hearted and utterly disarming monologue; the simplicity and immediacy, even when it was naïve, the absence of formalities and small talk which seemed to hold everywhere outside official circles, was, and is, wonderfully attractive.

It was a warm, sunlit afternoon in early autumn. Pasternak, his wife and his son Leonid were seated round a rough wooden table in the tiny garden at the back of the dacha. The poet greeted us warmly. He was once described by his friend the poetess Marina Tsvetaeva as looking like an Arab and his horse: he had a dark, melancholy, expressive, very *racé* face, now familiar from many photographs and his father's paintings; he spoke slowly, in a low tenor monotone, with a continuous, even sound, something between a humming and a drone, which those who met him almost always remarked; each vowel was elongated as if in some plaintive, lyrical aria in an opera by Tchaikovsky, but with more concentrated force and tension. With an awkward gesture I offered him the parcel that I was holding in my hands, and explained that I had brought him a pair of boots sent him by his sister Lydia. 'No, no, what is all this?' he said, visibly embarrassed, as if I were offering him a charitable gift: 'It must be a mistake, this must be for my brother.' I, too, became acutely embarrassed. His wife, Zinaida Nikolaevna, tried to put me at my ease and asked me whether England was recovering from the effects of the war. Before I could answer, Pasternak broke in: 'I was in London in the 30s – in 1935 – on my way back from the Anti-Fascist Congress in Paris. Let me tell you what happened. It was summer, I was in the country, when two officials, probably from the N.K.V.D. – not, I think, the Writers' Union – called – we were not quite so afraid of such visits then, I suppose – and one of them said "Boris Leonidovich, an Anti-Fascist Congress is taking place in Paris. You have been invited to it. We should like you to go tomorrow. You will go via Berlin: you can stay there for a few hours and see anyone you wish: you will arrive in Paris on the next day and will address the Congress in the evening." I said that I had no suitable clothes for such a visit. They said that they would see to that. They offered me a formal morning coat and striped trousers, a white shirt with stiff cuffs and a wing collar, a magnificent pair of black patent leather boots which, I found, fitted perfectly. But I somehow managed to go in my everyday clothes. I was later told that pressure had been brought to bear at the last minute by André Malraux, one of the chief organisers of the Congress, to get me invited. He had explained to the Soviet authorities that not to send me and Babel' might cause unnecessary speculation, since we were very well known in the west, and there were, at that time, not many Soviet writers to whom European and American liberals would be so ready to listen. So, although I was not on the original list of Soviet delegates – how could I possibly be? – they agreed.'

He went via Berlin, as arranged, where he met his sister Josephine and her husband, and said that when he arrived at the Congress many important and famous people – Dreiser, Gide, Malraux, Forster, Aragon, Auden, Spender, Rosamond Lehmann and other celebrities – were there. 'I spoke. I said "I understand that this is a meeting of writers to organise resistance to Fascism. I have only one thing to say to you about that. Do not organise. Organisation is the death of art. Only personal independence matters. In 1789, 1848, 1917, writers were not organised for or against anything; do not, I implore you, do not organise." I think they were very surprised. But what else could I say? I thought I would get into trouble at home after that, but no one ever said a word to me about it, then or now. I went on from Paris to London, where I saw my friend Lomonosov, a most fascinating man, like his namesake, a kind of scientist – an engineer. Then I travelled back to Leningrad in one of our boats, and shared a cabin with Shcherbakov, then the Secretary of the Writers' Union, who was tremendously influential. I talked without ceasing, day and night. He begged me to stop and let him sleep. But I went on and on. Paris and London had awoken me, I could not stop. He begged for mercy, but I was relent-less. He must have thought me quite deranged; it may be that I owe a good deal to his diagnosis of my condition.' Pasternak did not explicitly say that what he meant was that to have been thought a little mad, or at least very eccentric, might have helped to save him during the Great Purge; but the others present told me that they understood this all too well, and explained it to me later.

Pasternak asked me whether I had read his prose – in particular *The Childhood of Lüvers*, which I greatly admired. I said that I had. 'I can see by your expression', he said, quite unjustly, 'that you think that these writings are contrived, tortured, self-conscious, horribly modernist – no, no, don't deny it, you do think this and you are absolutely right. I am ashamed of them – not of my poetry, but of my prose – it was influenced by what was weakest and most muddled in the symbolist movement, which was fashionable in those years, full of mystical chaos – of course Andrey Bely was a genius – *Petersburg*, *Kotik Letaev* are full of wonderful things – I know that, you need not tell me – but his influence was fatal – Joyce is another matter – all I wrote then was obsessed, forced, broken, artificial, no good [*negodno*]; but now I am writing something entirely different: something new, quite new, luminous, elegant, harmonious, well-proportioned [*stroinoe*], classically pure and simple – what Winckelmann wanted, yes, and Goethe; and this will be my last word, and most important word, to the world. It is, yes, it is, what I wish to be remembered by; I shall devote the rest of my life to it.'

I cannot vouch for the accuracy of all these words, but this is how I remember them and his manner of speaking. This projected work later became *Doctor Zhivago*.

From
Personal Impressions

Boris Pasternak
Autumn

I have allowed my family to scatter,
All my dear ones are dispersed.
A life-long loneliness
Fills nature and my heart,

And here I am with you, in a small house.
Outside, the forest is unpeopled like a desert.
As in the song, the drives and footpaths
Are almost overgrown.

The log walls are sad,
Having only us two to gaze at.
But we never undertook to leap the barriers.
We will perish honestly.

At one o'clock we shall sit down to table,
At three we shall rise,

I with my book, you with your embroidery.
At dawn we shan't remember
What time we stopped kissing.

Leaves, rustle and spill yourselves
Ever more splendidly, ever more recklessly,
Fill yesterday's cup of bitterness
Still more full with the pain of to-day.

Let devotion, desire, delight,
Be scattered in the uproar of September:
And you, go and hide in the crackling autumn,
Either be quiet or be crazy.

You fling your dress from you
As the coppice flings away its leaves.
In a dressing-gown with a silk tassel
You fall into my arms.

You are the good gift of the road to destruction
When life is more sickening than disease
And boldness the root of beauty.
This is what draws us together.

From
Doctor Zhivago

────John Le Carré────
Karla on the Bridge

For those unfamiliar with the characters in Le Carré's cast of spies and spy-catchers, it is impossible to summarize the cold world they inhabit. In this scene George Smiley and his colleagues are waiting to see if Karla, a senior KGB officer and life-long adversary of Smiley's, will 'come over' – defect to the West – in response to a convoluted plan to persuade him to do so.

It's like putting all your money on black, thought Guillam, staring out of the window of the café: everything you've got in the world, your wife, your unborn child. Then waiting, hour by hour, for the croupier to spin the wheel.

He had known Berlin when it was the world capital of the cold war, when every crossing point from East to West had the tenseness of a major surgical operation. He remembered how on nights like these, clusters of Berlin policemen and Allied soldiers used to gather under the arc lights, stamping their feet, cursing the cold, fidgeting their rifles from shoulder to shoulder, puffing clouds of frosted breath into each other's faces. He remembered how the tanks waited, growling to keep their engines warm, their gun barrels picking targets on the other side, feigning strength. He remembered the sudden wail of the alarm klaxons and the dash to the Bernauerstrasse or wherever the latest escape attempt might be. He remembered the fire brigade ladders going up; the orders to shoot back; the orders not to; the dead, some of them agents. But after tonight, he knew that he would remember it only like this: so dark you wanted to take a torch with you into the street, so still you could have heard the cocking of a rifle from across the river.

'What cover will he use?' he asked.

Smiley sat opposite him across the little plastic table, a cup of cold coffee at his elbow. He looked somehow very small inside his overcoat.

'Something humble,' Smiley said. 'Something that fits in. Those who cross here are mostly old age-pensioners, I gather.' He was smoking one of Guillam's cigarettes and it seemed to take all his attention.

'What on earth do pensioners want here?' Guillam asked.

'Some work. Some visit dependents. I didn't enquire very closely, I'm afraid.'

Guillam remained dissatisfied.

'We pensioners tend to keep ourselves to ourselves,' Smiley added, in a poor effort at humour.

'You're telling me,' said Guillam.

The café was in the Turkish quarter because the Turks are

now the poor whites of West Berlin, and property is worst and cheapest near the Wall. Smiley and Guillam were the only foreigners. At a long table sat a whole Turkish family, chewing flat bread and drinking coffee and Coca-Cola. The children had shaven heads and the wide, puzzled eyes of refugees. Islamic music was playing from an old tape-recorder. Strips of coloured plastic hung from the hardboard arch of an Islamic doorway.

Guillam returned his gaze to the window, and the bridge. First came the piers of the overhead railway, next the old brick house that Sam Collins and his team had discreetly requisitioned as an observation centre. His men had been moving in surreptitiously these last two days. Then came the white halo of sodium arc lights, and behind it lay a barricade, a pillbox, then the bridge. The bridge was for pedestrians only, and the only way over it was a corridor of steel fencing like a bird walk, sometimes one man's width and sometimes three. Occasionally one crossed, keeping a meek appearance and a steady pace in order not to alarm the sentry tower, then stepping into the sodium halo as he reached the West. By daylight the bird walk was grey; by night for some reason yellow, and strangely bright. The pillbox was a yard or two inside the border, its roof just mastering the barricade, but it was the tower that dominated everything, one iron-black rectangular pillar at the bridge's centre. Even the snow avoided it. There was snow on the concrete teeth that blocked the bridge to traffic, snow swarmed round the halo and the pillbox and made a show of settling on the wet cobble; but the sentry tower was immune, as if not even the snow would go near it of its own free will. Just short of the halo, the bird walk narrowed to a last gateway and a cattle pen. But the gateway, said Toby, could be closed electrically at a moment's notice from inside the pillbox.

The time was ten-thirty but it could have been three in the morning, because along its borders, West Berlin goes to bed with the dark. Inland, the island-city may chat and drink and whore and spend its money; the Sony signs and rebuilt churches and conference halls may glitter like a fair-ground; but the dark shores of the borderland are silent from seven in the evening. Close to the halo stood a Christmas tree, but only the upper half of it was lit, only the upper half was visible from across the river. It is a place of no compromise, thought Guillam, a place of no third way. Whatever reservations he might occasionally have about the Western freedom, here, at this border, like most other things, they stopped dead.

'George?' said Guillam softly, and cast Smiley a questioning glance.

A labourer had lurched into the halo. He seemed to rise into it as they all did the moment they stepped out of the bird walk, as if a burden had fallen from their backs. He was carrying a small briefcase and what looked like a rail man's lamp. He was slight of build. But Smiley, if he had noticed the man at all, had already returned to the collar of his brown overcoat and his lonely, far-away thoughts. 'If he comes, he'll come on time,' Smiley had said. Then why do we get here two hours early? Guillam had wanted to ask. Why do we sit here, like two strangers, drinking sweet coffee out of little cups, soaked in the steam of this wretched Turkish kitchen, talking platitudes? But he knew the answer already. Because we *owe*, Smiley would have said if he had been in a talking mood. Because we owe the caring and the waiting, we owe this vigil over one man's effort to escape the system he has helped create. For as long as he is trying to reach us, we are his friends. Nobody else is on his side.

He'll come, Guillam thought. He won't. He may. If this isn't prayer, he thought, what is?

'More coffee, George?'

'No, thank you, Peter. No, I don't think so. No.'

'They seem to have soup of some sort. Unless that was the coffee.'

'Thank you, I think I've consumed about all I can manage,' said Smiley, in quite a general tone, as if anyone who wished to hear was welcome.

'Well, maybe I'll just order something for rent,' said Guillam.

'Rent? I'm sorry. Of course. God knows what they must live on.'

Guillam ordered two more coffees and paid for them. He was paying as he went, deliberately, in case they had to leave in a hurry.

Come for George's sake, he thought; come for mine. Come for all our damn sakes, and be the impossible harvest we have dreamed of for so long.

'When did you say the baby was due, Peter?'

'March.'

'Ah. March. What will you call it?'

'We haven't really thought.'

Across the road, by the glow of a furniture shop that sold reproduction wrought iron and brocade and fake muskets and pewter, Guillam made out the muffled figure of Toby Esterhase in his Balkan fur hat, affecting to study the wares. Toby and his team had the streets, Sam Collins had the observation post: that was the deal. For the escape cars, Toby had insisted on taxis, and there they stood, three of them, suitably shabby, in the darkness of the station arches, with notices in their windscreens saying 'OUT OF SERVICE,' and their drivers standing at the *Imbiss*-stand, eating sausages in sweet sauce out of paper dishes.

The place is a total minefield, Peter, Toby had warned. *Turks,*

Greeks, Yugoslavs, a lot of crooks – even the damn cats are wired, no exaggeration.

Not a whisper anywhere, Smiley had ordered. *Not a murmur, Peter. Tell Collins.*

Come, thought Guillam urgently. We're all rooting for you. Come.

From Toby's back, Guillam lifted his gaze slowly to the top-floor window of the old house where Collins' observation post was sited. Guillam had done his Berlin stint, he had been part of it a dozen times. The telescopes and cameras, the directional microphones, all the useless hardware that was supposed to make the waiting easier; the crackle of the radios, the stink of coffee and tobacco; the bunk-beds. He imagined the co-opted West German policeman who had no idea why he had been brought here, and would have to stay till the operation was abandoned or successful – the man who knew the bridge by heart and could tell the regulars from the casuals and spot the smallest bad omen the moment it occurred: the silent doubling of the watch, the Vopo sharpshooters easing softly into place.

And if they shoot him? thought Guillam. If they arrest him? If they leave him – which they would surely like to, and had done before to others – bleeding to death, face downward in the bird walk not six feet from the halo?

Come, he thought, less certainly, willing his prayers into the black skyline of the East. Come all the same.

A fine, very bright pin-light flitted across the west-facing upper window of the observation house, bringing Guillam to his feet. He turned round to see Smiley already half-way to the door. Toby Esterhase was waiting for them on the pavement.

'It's only a possibility, George,' he said softly, in the tone of a man preparing them for disappointment. 'Just a thin chance, but he could be our man.'

They followed him without another word. The cold was ferocious. They passed a tailor's shop with two dark-haired girls stitching in the window. They passed wall posters offering cheap ski holidays, death to Fascists, and to the Shah. The cold made them breathless. Turning his face from the swirling snow, Guillam glimpsed a children's adventure playground made of old railway sleepers. They passed between black, dead buildings, then right, across the cobbled road, in pitch-frozen darkness to the river bank, where an old timber bullet-shelter with rifle-slits offered them the whole span of the bridge. To their left, black against the hostile river, a tall wooden cross, garnished with barbed wire, bore memory to an unknown man who had not quite escaped.

Toby silently extracted a pair of field-glasses from his overcoat and handed them to Smiley.

'George. Listen. Good luck, okay?'

Toby's hand closed briefly over Guillam's arm. Then he darted away again, into the darkness.

The shelter stank of leaf-mould and damp. Smiley crouched to the rifle slit, the skirts of his tweed coat trailing in the mud, while he surveyed the scene before him as if it held the very reaches of his own long life. The river was broad and slow, misted with cold. Arc lights played over it, and the snow danced in their beams. The bridge spanned it on fat stone piers, six or eight of them, which swelled into crude shoes as they reached the water. The spaces between them were arched, all but the centre, which was squared off to make room for shipping, but the only ship was a grey patrol boat moored at the Eastern bank, and the only commerce that it offered was death. Behind the bridge, like its vastly bigger shadow, ran the railway viaduct, but like the river it was derelict, and no trains ever crossed. The warehouses of the far bank stood monstrous as the hulks of an earlier barbaric civilisation, and the bridge with its yellow bird walk seemed to leap from half-way up them, like a fantastic light-path out of darkness. From his vantage point, Smiley could scan the whole length of it with his field-glasses, from the floodlit white barrack house on the Eastern bank, up to the black sentry tower at the crest, then slightly downhill again towards the Western side: to the cattle pen, the pillbox that controlled the gateway, and finally the halo.

Guillam stood but a few feet behind him, yet Guillam could have been back in Paris for all the awareness Smiley had of him: he had seen the solitary black figure start his journey; he had seen the glimmer of the cigarette-end as he took one last pull, the spark of it comet towards the water as he tossed it over the iron fencing of the bird walk. One small man, in a worker's half-length coat, with a worker's satchel slung across his little chest, walking neither fast nor slowly, but walking like a man who walked a lot. One small man, his body a fraction too long for his legs, hatless despite the snow. That is all that happens, Smiley thought; one little man walks across a bridge.

'Is it him?' Guillam whispered. 'George, tell me! Is it Karla?'

Don't come, thought Smiley. *Shoot*, Smiley thought, talking to Karla's people, not to his own. There was suddenly something terrible in his foreknowledge that this tiny creature was about to cut himself off from the black castle behind him. Shoot him from the sentry tower, shoot him from the pillbox, from the white barrack hut, from the crow's-nest on the prison warehouse, slam the gate on him, cut him down, your own traitor, kill him! In his racing imagination, he saw the scene unfold: the last-minute discovery by Moscow Centre of Karla's infamy; the phone calls to the frontier – 'Stop him at any cost!' And the shooting, never too much – enough to hit a man a time or two, and wait.

'It's him!' Guillam whispered. He had taken the binoculars from Smiley's unresisting hand. 'It's the same man! The photograph that hung on your wall in the Circus! George, you miracle!'

But Smiley in his imagination saw only the Vopo's search-lights converging on Karla as if he were like a hare in the headlights, so dark against the snow; and Karla's hopeless old man's run before the bullets threw him like a rag doll over his own feet. Like Guillam, Smiley had seen it all before. He looked across the river into the darkness again, and an unholy vertigo seized him as the very evil he had fought against seemed to reach out and possess him and claim him despite his striving, calling him a traitor also; mocking him, yet at the same time applauding his betrayal. On Karla has descended the curse of Smiley's compassion; on Smiley the curse of Karla's fanaticism. I have destroyed him with the weapons I abhorred, and they are his. We have crossed each other's frontiers, we are the no-men of this no-man's-land.

'Just keep moving,' Guillam was murmuring. 'Just keep moving, let nothing stop you.'

Approaching the blackness of the sentry tower, Karla took a couple of shorter steps and for a moment Smiley really thought he might change his mind and give himself up to the East Germans. Then he saw a cat's tongue of flame as Karla lit a fresh cigarette. With a match or a lighter? he wondered. *To George from Ann with all my love.*

'Christ, he's cool!' said Guillam.

The little figure set off again, but at a slower pace, as if he had grown weary. He is stoking up his courage for the last step, thought Smiley, or he is trying to damp his courage down. He thought of Vladimir and Otto Leipzig and the dead Kirov; he thought of Haydon and his own life's work ruined; he thought of Ann, permanently stained for him by Karla's cunning, and Haydon's scheming embrace. He recited in his despair a whole list of crimes – the tortures, the killings, the endless ring of corruption – to lay upon the frail shoulders of this one pedestrian on the bridge, but they would not stay there: he did not want these spoils, won by these methods. Like a chasm, the jagged skyline beckoned to him yet again, the swirling snow made it an inferno. For a second longer,

Smiley stood on the brink at the smouldering river's edge.

They had started walking along the tow-path, Guillam leading, Smiley reluctantly following. The halo burned ahead of them, growing as they approached it. *Like two ordinary pedestrians*, Toby had said. *Just walk to the bridge and wait, it's normal.* From the darkness around them, Smiley heard whispered voices and the swift, damped sounds of hasty movement under tension. 'George,' someone whispered. 'George.' From a yellow phone box, an unknown figure lifted a hand in discreet salute, and he heard the word 'triumph' smuggled to him on the wet freezing air. The snow was blurring his glasses, he found it hard to see. The observation post stood to their right, not a light burning in the windows. He made out a van parked at the entrance, and realised it was a Berlin mail van, one of Toby's favourites. Guillam was hanging back. Smiley heard something about 'claiming the prize.'

They had reached the edge of the halo. An orange rampart blocked the bridge and the chicane from sight. They were out of the eye-line of the sentry-box. Perched above the Christmas tree, Toby Esterhase was standing on the observation scaffold with a pair of binoculars, calmly playing the cold-war tourist. A plump female watcher stood at his side. An old notice warned them they were there at their own risk. On the smashed brick viaduct behind them Smiley picked out a forgotten armorial crest. Toby made a tiny motion with his hand: *thumbs up, it's our man now*. From beyond the rampart, Smiley heard light footsteps and the vibration of an iron fence. He caught the smell of an American cigarette as the icy wind wafted it ahead of the smoker. There's still the electric gateway, he thought; he waited for the clang as it slammed shut, but none came. He realised he had no real name by which to address his enemy: only a code-name and a woman's at that. Even his military rank was a mystery. And still Smiley hung back, like a man refusing to go on stage.

Guillam had drawn alongside him and seemed to be trying to edge him forward. He heard soft footsteps as Toby's watchers one by one gathered to the edge of the halo, safe from view in the shelter of the rampart, waiting with bated breath for a sight of the catch. And suddenly, there he stood, like a man slipping into a crowded hall unnoticed. His small right hand hung flat and naked at his side, his left held the cigarette timidly across his chest. One little man, hatless, with a satchel. He took a step forward and in the halo Smiley saw his face, aged and weary and travelled, the short hair turned to white by a sprinkling of snow. He wore a grimy shirt and a black tie: he looked like a poor man going to the funeral of a friend. The cold had nipped his cheeks low down, adding to his age.

They faced each other; they were perhaps a yard apart, much as they had been in Delhi jail. Smiley heard more footsteps and this time it was the sound of Toby padding swiftly down the wooden ladder of the scaffold. He heard soft voices and laughter; he thought he even heard the sound of gentle clapping, but he never knew; there were shadows everywhere, and once inside the halo, it was hard for him to see out. Paul Skordeno slipped forward and stood himself one side of Karla; Nick de Silsky stood the other. He heard Guillam telling someone to get that bloody car up here before they come over the bridge and get him back. He heard the ring of something metal falling onto the icy cobble, and knew it was Ann's cigarette-lighter, but nobody else seemed to notice it. They exchanged one more glance and perhaps each for that second did see in the other something of himself. He heard the crackle of car tyres and the sounds of doors opening, while the engine kept running. De Silsky and Skordeno moved towards it and Karla went with them, though they didn't touch him; he seemed to have acquired already the

submissive manner of a prisoner; he had learned it in a hard school. Smiley stood back and the three of them marched softly past him, all somehow too absorbed by the ceremony to pay attention to him. The halo was empty. He heard the quiet closing of the car's doors and the sound of it driving away. He heard two other cars leave after it, or with it. He didn't watch them go. He felt Toby Esterhase fling his arms round his shoulders, and saw that his eyes were filled with tears.

'George,' he began. 'All your life. Fantastic!'

Then something in Smiley's stiffness made Toby pull away, and Smiley himself stepped quickly out of the halo, passing very close to Ann's lighter on his way. It lay at the halo's very edge, tilted slightly, glinting like fool's gold on the cobble. He thought of picking it up, but somehow there seemed no point and no one else appeared to have seen it. Someone was shaking his hand, someone else was clapping him on the shoulder. Toby quietly restrained them.

'Take care, George,' Toby said. 'Go well, hear me?'

Smiley heard Toby's team leave one by one until only Peter Guillam remained. Walking a short way back along the embankment, almost to where the cross stood, Smiley took another look at the bridge, as if to establish whether anything had changed, but clearly it had not, and though the wind appeared a little stronger, the snow was still swirling in all directions.

Peter Guillam touched his arm.

'Come on, old friend,' he said. 'It's bedtime.'

From long habit, Smiley had taken off his spectacles and was absently polishing them on the fat end of his tie, even though he had to delve for it among the folds of his tweed coat.

'George, you won,' said Guillam as they walked slowly towards the car.

'Did I?' said Smiley. 'Yes. Yes, well I suppose I did.'

From
Smiley's People

King Claudius

My mind moves to distant places.
I'm walking the streets of Elsinore,
through its squares, and I recall
the very sad story –
that unfortunate king
killed by his nephew
because of some fanciful suspicions.

In all the homes of the poor people
secretly (because they were afraid of Fortinbras)
he was mourned. A quiet, gentle man;
a man who loved peace
(his country had suffered much
from the wars of his predecessor).
He behaved graciously towards everyone,
the humble and the great alike.
Never high handed, he always sought advice
in the kingdom's affairs
from serious and experienced persons.

Just why his nephew killed him
was never satisfactorily explained
The prince suspected him of murder;
and the basis of his suspicion was this:
walking one night along an ancient battlement
he thought he saw a ghost
and with this ghost had a talk
what he heard from the ghost supposedly
were certain accusations against the king.

It must have been a fit of fancy
and an optical illusion
(the prince was nervous in the extreme;
while studying at Wittenberg
many of his fellow students thought him a maniac).

A few days later he went
to his mother's chambers to discuss
some family affairs. And suddenly,
while he was talking, he lost his self-control
and started shouting, screaming,
that the ghost was there in front of him.
But his mother saw nothing at all.

And that same day, for no apparent reason
he killed an old gentleman of the court.
Since the prince was due to sail for England
in a day or two,
the king hustled him off posthaste
in order to save him.

But the people were so outraged
by the monstrous murder
that rebels rose up
and tried to storm the palace gates,
led by the dead man's son,
the noble lord Laertes
(a brave young man, and also ambitious;
in the confusion, some of his friends called out:
'Long live King Laertes!').

Some time later, once the kingdom had calmed down
and the king lay resting in his grave,
killed by his nephew
(the prince never went to England;
he escaped from the ship on his way there),
a certain Horatio came forward
and tried to exonerate the prince
by telling some stories of his own.
He said that the voyage to England
had been a secret plot, and orders
had been given to kill the prince there
(but this was never clearly ascertained).
He also spoke of poisoned wine –
wine poisoned by the king.
It's true that Laertes spoke of this too.
But couldn't he have been lying?
Couldn't he have been mistaken?
And when did he speak of this?
While dying of his wounds, his mind reeling,
and seeming to talk deliriously.
As for the poisoned weapons,
it was shown later that the poisoning
had not been done by the king at all:
Laertes had done it himself.
But Horatio, whenever pressed,
would produce even the ghost as a witness:
the ghost said this and that,
the ghost did this and that!

Because of all this, though hearing him out,
most people in their hearts
pitied the poor king,

who, with all these ghosts and fairy tales,
was unjustly killed and disposed of.

Yet Fortinbras, who profited from it all
and so easily won the throne,
gave full attention and weight
to every word Horatio said.

Translated by Edmund Keeley and George Savidis

Fay Weldon
Breakages

'We blossom and flourish
Like leaves on a tree,
And wither and perish
But nought changeth thee.'

... sang David's congregation in its laggardly, quavery voice.
Some trick of acoustics made much of what happened in the
Church audible in the vicarage kitchen, where tonight, as so
often, Deidre sat and darned socks and waited for Evensong
to end.

The vicarage, added as a late-Victorian afterthought,
leaned up against the solidity of the Norman church. The
house was large, ramshackle, dark and draughty, and prey to
wet rot, dry rot, woodworm and beetle. Here David and
Deidre lived. He was a vicar of the established church; she
was his wife. He attended to the spiritual welfare of his
parishioners: she presided over the Mothers Union and the
Women's Institute, and ran the Amateur Dramatic Society.
They had been married for twenty-one years. They had no

children, which was a source of acute disappointment to them and to Deidre's mother, and of understandable disappointment to the parish. It is always pleasant, in a small, stable and increasingly elderly community, to watch other people's children grow up, and sad to be deprived of that pleasure.

'Oh no, please,' said Deidre, now, to the Coronation Mug on the dresser. It was a rare piece, produced in anticipation of an event which had never occurred: the coronation of the Duke of Windsor. The mug was, so far, uncracked and unchipped, and worth some £300, but had just moved to the very edge of its shelf, not smoothly and purposively, but with an uneven rocking motion which made Deidre hope that entreaty might yet calm it, and save it from itself. And indeed, after she spoke, the mug was quiet, and lapsed into the ordinary stillness she had once always associated with inanimate objects.

> 'Immortal, invisible,
> God only wise . . .
> In light inaccessible . . .'

Deidre joined in the hymn, singing gently and soothingly, and trying to feel happy, for the happier she felt the fewer the breakages there would be and perhaps one day they would stop altogether, and David would never, ever find out; that, one by one, the ornaments and possessions he most loved and valued were leaping off shelves and shattering, to be secretly mended by Deidre with such skills as she remembered from the early days, before marriage had interrupted her training in china restoration, and her possible future in the Victoria and Albert Museum.

Long ago and far away. Now Deidre darned. David's feet were sensitive to anything other than pure, fine wool. Not for him the tough nylon mixtures that other men wore. Deidre darned.

The Coronation Mug rocked violently.

'Stop it,' said Deidre, warningly. Sometimes to appear stern was more effective than to entreat. The mug stayed where it was. But just a fraction further, and it would have fallen.

Deidre unpicked the last few stitches. She was in danger of cobbling the darn, and there is nothing more uncomfortable to sensitive skin than a cobbled darn.

'You do it on purpose,' David would complain, not without reason. Deidre's faults were the ones he found most difficult to bear. She was careless, lost socks, left lids unscrewed, taps running, doors open, saucepans burning: she bought fresh bread when yesterday's at half price would do. It was her nature, she maintained, and grieved bitterly when her husband implied that it was wilful and that she was doing it to annoy. She loved him, or said so. And he loved her, or said so.

The Coronation Mug leapt off its shelf, arced through the air and fell and broke in two pieces at Deidre's feet. She put the pieces at the very back of the drawer beneath the sink. There was no time for mending now. Tomorrow morning would have to do, when David was out parish-visiting, in houses freshly dusted and brightened for his arrival. Fortunately, David seldom inspected Deidre's drawer. It smelt, when opened, of dry rot, and reminded him forcibly of the large sums of money which ought to be spent on the repair of the house, and which he did not have.

'We could always sell something,' Deidre would sometimes venture, but not often, for the suggestion upset him.
David's mother had died when he was four; his father had
gone bankrupt when he was eight; relatives had reared him
and sent him off to boarding school where he had been
sexually and emotionally abused. Possessions were his
security.

She understood him, forgave him, loved him and tried
not to argue.

She darned his socks. It was, today, a larger pile than usual.
Socks kept disappearing, not by the pair, but singly. David
had lately discovered a pillowslip stuffed full of them pushed
to the back of the wardrobe. It was his wife's deceit which
worried him most, or so he said. Hiding socks! That and the
sheer careless waste of it all. Losing socks! So Deidre tried
tying the socks together for the wash, and thus, in pairs, the
night before, spun and dried, they had lain in the laundry
basket. In the morning she had found them in one ugly,
monstrous knot, and each sock oddly long, as if stretched by
a hand too angry to know what it was doing. Rinsing had
restored them, fortunately, to a proper shape, but she was
obliged to darn where the stretching had worn the fabric thin.

It was always like this: always difficult, always upsetting.
David's things were attacked, as if the monstrous hand were
on her side, yet it was she, Deidre, who had to repair the
damage, follow its source as it moved about the house,
mending what it broke, wiping tomato purée from the
ceiling and toothpaste from the lavatory bowl, replanting
David's seedlings, rescrewing lids, closing doors, refolding
linen, turning off taps. She scarcely dared leave the house for
fear of what might happen in his absence, and this David
interpreted as lack of interest in his parish. Disloyalty, to God
and husband.

Times were bad between them. Yet they loved each other.
Man and wife.

Deidre's finger was bleeding. She must have cut it on the
sharp edge of the broken Coronation Mug. She opened the
table drawer, took out the first piece of cloth which came to
hand, and wrapped her finger. The cold tap started to run of
its own accord, but she ignored it. Blood spread out over the
cloth but presently, fortunately, stopped.

Could you die from loss of blood, from a small finger cut?

The invisible hand swept the dresser shelf, knocking all sorts of treasures sideways but breaking nothing. It had never touched the dresser before, as if awed, as Deidre was, by the ever-increasing value of its contents – rare blue and white pieces, frog mugs, barbers' bowls, lustre cups, a debatedly Ming bowl, which a valuer said might well fetch five thousand pounds.

Enough to paint the vicarage, inside, and instal central heating, and replaster walls and buy a new vacuum cleaner.

The dresser rattled and shook: she could have sworn it slid towards her.

David did not give Deidre a housekeeping allowance. She asked for money when she needed it, but David seldom recognised that it was in fact needed. He could not see the necessity of things like washing-up liquid, sugar, toilet rolls, new scourers. Sometimes she stole money from his pocket: once she took a coin out of the offertory on Sunday morning instead of putting a coin in it.

Why did she stoop to it? She loved him.

A bad wife, a barren wife, and a poor sort of person.

David came home. The house fell quiet, as always, at his approach. Taps stopped running and china stopped rattling. David kissed her on her forehead.

'Deidre,' said David, 'what have you wrapped around your finger?'

Deidre, curious herself, unwrapped the binding and found that she had used a fine lace and cotton handkerchief, put in the drawer for mending, which once had belonged to David's grandmother. It was now sodden and bright, bright red.

'I cut my finger,' said Deidre, inadequately and indeed foolishly, for what if he demanded to know what had caused the wound? But David was too busy rinsing and squeezing the handkerchief under the tap to enquire. Deidre put her finger in her mouth and put up with the salt, exciting taste of her own blood.

'It's hopelessly stained,' he mourned. 'Couldn't you just for once have used something you wouldn't spoil? A tissue?'

David did not allow the purchase of tissues. There had been none in his youth: why should they be needed now, in his middle age?

'I'm sorry,' said Deidre, and thought, as she spoke, 'I am always saying sorry, and always providing cause for my own remorse.'

He took the handkerchief upstairs to the bathroom, in search of soap and a nailbrush. 'What kind of wife are you, Deidre?' he asked as he went, desperate.

What kind, indeed? Married in a Register Office in the days before David had taken to Holy Orders and a Heavenly Father more reliable than his earthly one. Deidre had suggested that they re-marry in church, as could be and had been done by others, but David did not want to. Hardly a wife at all.

A barren wife. A fig-tree, struck by God's ill-temper. David's God. In the beginning they had shared a God, who was bleak, plain, sensible and kind. But now, increasingly, David had his own jealous and punitive God, whom he wooed with ritual and richness, incense and images, dragging a surprised congregation with him. He changed his vestments three times during services, rang little bells to announce the presence of the Lord, swept up and down aisles, and in general seemed not averse to being mistaken for God.

The water pipes shrieked and groaned as David turned on the tap in the bathroom, but that was due to bad plumbing rather than unnatural causes. She surely could not be held responsible for that, as well.

When the phenomena – as she thought of them – first started, or rather leapt from the scale of ordinary domestic carelessness to something less explicable and more sinister, she went to the doctor.

'Doctor,' she said, 'do mumps in adolescence make men infertile?'

'It depends,' he said, proving nothing. 'If the gonads are affected it well might. Why?'

No reason had been found for Deidre's infertility. It lay, presumably, like so much else, in her mind. She had had her tubes blown, painfully and unforgettably, to facilitate conception, but it had made no difference. For fifteen years twenty-three days of hope had been followed by five days of disappointment, and on her shoulders rested the weight of David's sorrow, as she, his wife, deprived him of his earthly immortality, his children.

'Of course,' he said sadly, 'you are an only child. Only children are often infertile. The sins of the fathers . . .' David regarded fecundity as a blessing; the sign of a woman in tune with God's universe. He had married Deidre, he vaguely let it be known, on the rebound from a young woman who had gone on to have seven children. Seven!

David's fertility remained unquestioned and unexamined. A sperm count would surely have proved nothing. His sperm was plentiful and he had no sexual problems that he was aware of. To ejaculate into a test-tube to prove a point smacked uncomfortably of Onanism.

The matter of the mumps came up during the time of Deidre's menopause, a month or so after her, presumably, last period. David had been in the school sanitorium with mumps: she had heard him saying so to a distraught mother, adding, 'Oh mumps! Nothing in a boy under fourteen. Be thankful he has them now, not later.'

So, he was aware that mumps were dangerous, and could render a man infertile. And Deidre knew well enough that David had lived in the world of school sanatoria after the age of fourteen, not before. Why had he never mentioned mumps? And while she wondered, and pondered, and hesitated to ask, toothpaste began to ooze from tubes, and rose-trees were uprooted in the garden, and his seedlings trampled by unseen boots, and his clothes in the wardrobe tumbled in a pile to the ground, and Deidre stole money to buy mending glue, and finally went to the doctor.

'Most men,' said the doctor, 'confuse impotence with infertility and believe that mumps cause the former, not the latter.'

Back to square one. Perhaps he didn't know.

'Why have you *really* come?' asked the doctor, recently back from a course in patient-doctor relations. Deidre offered him an account of her domestic phenomena, as she had not meant to do. He prescribed valium and asked her to come back in a week. She did.

'Any better? Does the valium help?'

'At least when I see things falling, I don't mind so much.'

'But you still see them falling?'

'Yes.'

'Does your husband see them too?'

'He's never there when they do.'

Now what was any thinking doctor to make of that?

'We could try hormone replacement therapy,' he said.

'No,' said Deidre. 'I am what I am.'

'Then what do you want me to do?'

'If I could only feel angry with my husband,' said Deidre, 'instead of forever understanding and forgiving him, I might get it to stop. As it is, I am releasing too much kinetic energy.'

There were patients waiting. They had migraines, exzema and boils. He gave her more valium, which she did not take.

Deidre, or some expression of Deidre, went home and churned up the lawn and tore the gate off its hinges. The other Deidre raked and smoothed, resuscitated and blamed a perfectly innocent child for the gate. A child. It would have taken a 40-stone giant to twist the hinges so, but no-one stopped, fortunately, to think about that. The child went to bed without supper for swinging on the vicar's gate.

The wound on Deidre's finger gaped open in an unpleasant way. She thought she could see the white bone within the bloodless flesh.

Deidre went upstairs to the bathroom, where David washed his wife's blood from his grandmother's hankie. 'David,' said Deidre, 'perhaps I should have a stitch in my finger?'

David had the toothmug in his hand. His jaw was open, his eyes wide with shock. He had somehow smeared toothpaste on his black lapel. 'The toothmug has recently been broken, and very badly mended. No-one told me. Did you do it?'

The toothmug dated from the late eighteenth century and was worn, cracked and chipped, but David loved it. It had been one of the first things to go, and Deidre had not mended it with her usual care, thinking, mistakenly, that one more crack amongst so many would scarcely be noticed.

'I am horrified,' said David.

'Sorry,' said Deidre.

'You always break my things, never your own.'

'I thought that when you got married,' said Deidre, with the carelessness of desperation, for surely now David would start an inspection of his belongings and all would be discovered, 'things stopped being yours and mine, and became ours.'

'Married! You and I have never been married, not in the sight of God, and I thank Him for it.'

There. He had said what had been unsaid for years, but there was no relief in it, for either of them. There came a crash of breaking china from downstairs. David ran down to the kitchen, where the noise came from, but could see no sign of damage. He moved into the living room. Deidre followed, dutifully.

'You've shattered my life,' said David. 'We have nothing in common. You have been a burden since the beginning. I wanted a happy, warm, loving house. I wanted children.'

'I suppose,' said Deidre, 'you'll be saying next that my not having children is God's punishment?'

'Yes,' said David.

'Nothing to do with your mumps?'

David was silent, taken aback. Out of the corner of her eye Deidre saw the Ming vase move. 'You're a sadistic person,' said David eventually. 'Even the pains and humiliations of long ago aren't safe from you. You revive them.'

'You knew all the time,' said Deidre. 'You were infertile, not me. You made me take the blame. And it's too late for me now.'

The Ming vase rocked to the edge of the shelf: Deidre moved to push it back, but not quickly enough. It fell and broke.

David cried out in pain and rage. 'You did it on purpose,' he wept. 'You hate me.'

Deidre went upstairs and packed her clothes. She would stay with her mother while she planned some kind of new life for herself. She would be happier anywhere in the world but here, sharing a house with a ghost.

David moved through the house, weeping, but for his treasures, not for his wife. He took a wicker basket and in it laid tenderly – as if they were the bodies of children – the many broken and mended vases and bowls and dishes which he found. Sometimes the joins were skilful and barely detectable to his moving forefinger: sometimes careless. But everything was spoilt. What had been perfect was now second-rate and without value. The finds in the junk-shops, the gifts from old ladies, the few small knick-knacks which had come to him from his dead mother – his whole past destroyed by his wife's single-minded malice and cunning.

He carried the basket to the kitchen, and sat with his head in his hands.

Deidre left without saying another word. Out of the door, through the broken garden gate, into the night, through the churchyard, for the powers of the dead disturbed her less than the powers of the living, and to the bus station.

David sat. The smell of rot from the sink drawer was powerful enough, presently, to make him lift his head.

The cold tap started to run. A faulty washer, he concluded. He moved to turn it off, but the valve was already closed. 'Deidre!' he called, 'what have you done with the kitchen tap?' He did not know why he spoke, for Deidre had gone.

The whole top of the dresser fell forward to the ground. Porcelain shattered and earthenware powdered. He could hear the little pings of the Eucharist bell in the church next door, announcing the presence of God.

He thought perhaps there was an earthquake, but the central light hung still and quiet. Upstairs heavy feet bumped to and fro, dragging, wrenching and banging. Outside the window the black trees rocked so fiercely that he thought he would be safer in than out. The gas taps of the cooker were on and he could smell gas, mixed with fumes from the coal fire where Deidre's darning had been piled up and was now smouldering. He closed his eyes.

He was not frightened. He knew that he saw and heard these things, but that they had no substance in the real world. They were a distortion of the facts, as water becomes wine in the Communion service, and bread becomes the flesh of the Saviour.

When next he opened his eyes the dresser was restored, the socks still lay in the mending basket, the air was quiet.

Sensory delusions, that was all, brought about by shock. But unpleasant, all the same. Deidre's fault. David went upstairs to sleep but could not open the bedroom door. He thought perhaps Deidre had locked it behind her, out of spite. He was tired. He slept in the spare room, peacefully, without the irritant of Deidre's warmth beside him.

In the morning, however, he missed her, and as if in reply to his unspoken request she reappeared, in the kitchen, in time to make his breakfast tea. 'I spent the night in the hospital,' she said. 'I went to casualty to have a stitch put in my finger, and I fainted, and they kept me in.'

Her arm was in a sling.

'I'm sorry,' he said. 'You should have told me it was a bad cut and I'd have been more sympathetic. Where did you put the bedroom key?'

'I haven't got it,' she said, and the teapot fell off the table and there was tea and tealeaves everywhere, and, one-armed, she bungled the business of wiping it up. He helped.

'You shouldn't put breakables and spillables on the edge of tables,' he reproached her. 'Then it wouldn't happen.'

'I suppose not.'

'I'm sorry about what I may have said last night. Mumps are a sore point. I thought I would die from the itching, and my friends just laughed.'

Itching? Mumps?

'Mumps *is* the one where you come out in red spots and they tie your hands to stop you scratching?'

'No. That's chicken-pox,' she said.

'Whatever it was, if you're over fourteen you get it very badly indeed and it is humiliating to have your hands tied.'

'I can imagine.'

He wrung out the dish-cloth. The tap, she noticed, was not dripping. 'I'm sorry about your things,' she said. 'I should have told you.'

'Am I such a frightening person?'

'Yes.'

'They're only things,' he said, to her astonishment. The house seemed to take a shift back into its ordinary perspective. She thought that, though childless, she could still live an interesting and useful life. Her friends with grown-up children, gone away, complained that it was as if their young had never been. The experience of child-rearing was that, just that, no more, no less. An experience without much significance, presently over; as lately she had experienced the behaviour of the material world.

David insisted that Deidre must surely have the bedroom key, and was annoyed when she failed to produce it. 'Why would I lock you out of the bedroom?' she asked.

'Why would you do anything!' he remarked dourly. His

gratitude for her return was fading: his usual irritation with her was reasserting itself. She was grateful for familiar ways, and as usual animated by them.

He went up the ladder to the bedroom window, and was outraged. 'I've never seen a room in such a mess,' he reported, from the top of the ladder, a figure in clerical black perched there like some white-ruffled crow. 'How you did all that, even in a bad temper, I can't imagine.'

The heavy wardrobe was on its side, wedged against the door; the bed was upside down; the chairs and light bulb broken; the bedclothes, tumbled and knotted, had the same stretched and strained appearance as David's socks; and the carpet had been wrenched up, tossing furniture as it lifted, and wrung out like a dishcloth.

When the wardrobe had been moved back into place, the door was indeed found to be locked, with the key on the inside of the door, but both preferred not to notice that.

'I'm sorry,' said Deidre, 'I was upset about our having no children. That, and my time of life.'

'All our times of life,' he said. 'And as to your having no children, if it's anyone's fault, it's God's.'

Together they eased the carpet out of the window and down onto the lawn, and patiently and peaceably unwrung it. But the marks of the wringing stayed, straying for ever across the bedroom floor, to remind them of the dangers of, for him, petulance, and for her, the tendency to blame others for her own shortcomings.

Presently the Ming vase was mended, not by Deidre but by experts. He sold it and they installed central heating and had a wall knocked out there, a window put in here, and the washer on the kitchen tap mended, and the dry rot removed so that the sink drawer smelled like any other, and the broken floorboard beneath the dresser replaced. The acoustics in the kitchen changed, so that Deidre could no longer hear David's services as she sat by the fire, so she attended church rather more often; and David, she soon noticed, dressed up as God rather less, and diverted his congregation's attention away from himself and more towards the altar.

Hans Küng
God in China

The whole complexity of the religious, theological and
political problems presented by the world religions in their
relationship to Christianity is reflected in the one apparently
simple question: *How is God's name to be translated?* It is a
question that first became an important issue at the time of the
great controversy about translating the name of the Christian
God for a different cultural background – that of China – at
the dawn of the modern age (the period of Descartes and
Pascal, from which we started out) and has remained relevant
up to the present time. History itself has made the Chinese
religion a typical case (in this connection we might also have
discussed Hinduism or Buddhism).

Western Europe and Eastern Asia were scarcely known to
one another until well into modern times and were able to
interpret anything alien only in terms of their own self-
understanding. For China, which regarded and still regards
itself even geographically as 'Land of the Center,' everything
Western was described as 'Buddhist' and the Portuguese
settlers in Macao in the sixteenth century were seen as
'Buddhist sects.' Conversely, Nestorian Christians in the
seventh and ninth centuries and Franciscan missionaries who
travelled to China by the continental route in the thirteenth
century scarcely noticed China's own original philosophical
and religious tradition. Marco Polo also, on his Chinese
journey in the same century, described the Chinese simply as
'pagans.' It was the Jesuit missionaries of the sixteenth and
seventeenth centuries who first discovered Confucianism for
Europe and brought its meaning home to the European mind.
At first, as they went around preaching, they even dressed and
behaved like Buddhist monks. Popular Buddhism, with its
particular doctrines and deified beings, its ethic of compassion,
its monastic asceticism and belief in a life after death, seemed
at first closer to Christianity than Confucianism, which had
grown out of the earlier Chinese religion and which concentrated more pragmatically on interpersonal relationships,
saying little about man's relationship to a superhuman reality.

The founder of the modern mission to China, the Italian Jesuit *Matteo Ricci*, worked there from 1583 onward and from 1601 was allowed to stay even in Peking, the imperial city. As a result of conversations with people and the study of the Confucian classical writers, he came to the conclusion that the dominant Chinese world view was not Buddhism but Confucianism, which, precisely because of its lack of dogma, its lofty ethic and its reverence for a supreme being (without a heaven inhabited by gods and without fables about the gods), might be a better ally for Christianity than popular Buddhism, with its belief in idols and problematic doctrine of transmigration. In his famous catechism 'The True Idea of God' (*T'ien-chu shih-i*), Ricci explained that the original Confucian texts, not yet influenced by Buddhism or anti-Buddhism, contained in a very rudimentary form concepts analogous to those of God and life after death. But Ricci's interpretation and adoption of traditional Chinese cultural and ethical values was soon to lead to a violent controversy with the institutional Church and official theology. This was known as the 'rites controversy,' although in reality the controversy was less about rites than about names.

Today research by scholars has shown that the ancient Chinese actually believed in a personal God whom they venerated under two names: 'Supreme Lord' and 'Heaven.' Presumably this *duality of names for God* – analogous to that in the Old Testament ('Yahweh' and 'Elohim') – which there provides a basis for the distinction of sources in the Pentateuch, the five books of Moses – emerged from two cultic traditions, behind which were two ethnic groups:
'Supreme Lord' ('Shang-ti') is the God of the Shang dynasty (from about 1766 BC).
'Heaven' ('T'ien') – originally written as an ideograph of a man with a large head – is the God of the Chou dynasty, which came from the West and conquered the Shang state (about 1111–249 BC).

The mingling of the two cults was reflected in the Confucian classics, especially in the *Book of Odes* and the *Book of Records*, where the two names alternate in the same prayers. But, in the course of time, the term *'heaven'* acquired *also other ethical and ontological meanings*. It could be used for the dualistic view of a Yin-Yang universe (with feminine and masculine principles representing earth and heaven); and it could also be used for a pantheistic or panentheistic view of the Absolute as expressed in the 'Tao' of Lao-tse or in the 'Li' ('principle') and 'T'ai-chi' (the ultimate reality) of neo-Confucian philosophy. In addition, there were also undoubtedly atheistic interpretations, denying any sort of religious significance to 'heaven.'

All this complicated the situation for the Jesuit missionaries, since they arrived in China at a time when neo-Confucianism had reached its zenith and was regarded generally as the orthodox interpretation of the early classics. What was to be done in view of the diverse conceptions of God or the Absolute among the classical writers themselves and their later commentators? Ricci and the Jesuits declared themselves in favor of a return to the former Chinese idea of a personal God. But, at the same time, they kept to the practice of Christian missionaries from apostolic times and used such heavily loaded terms as *Theos, Deus,* 'God,' for Yahweh, the one true God of Israel and of Jesus Christ. So they adopted the usual Chinese terms for the Deity: 'Shang-ti' ('Supreme Lord,' then used only in the annual imperial cult of heaven) and the (admittedly ambiguous) term 'T'ien' ('Heaven'); an additional expression came into use; 'T'ien-chu' ('Lord of Heaven').

Matteo Ricci, in the course of a decade, with his mathematical and astronomical studies in Peking, had attracted numerous leading mandarins and intellectuals. In 1610, at the age of fifty-eight, he collapsed prematurely under the strain of his missionary work and was honored by the Emperor with a solemn state funeral. It was only after his death that the tragedy began that eventually, a hundred years later, led to the prohibition of his missionary methods and thus for a long time blocked the way for Christianity to the soul of Asiatic man.

From
Does God Exist?

Arthur Koestler
East and West

In his recent book Bricks to Babel, *Koestler has reprinted, with linking commentary, a wide range of passages from his own work. Among them is the following excerpt, which he describes as 'truculent', from* The Lotus and the Robot.

Lilies that fester smell far worse than weeds: both India and Japan seem to be spiritually sicker, more estranged from a living faith than the West. They are at opposite ends of the Asian spectrum, whose centre is occupied by the vastness of China, one of the world's oldest cultures; yet it proved even less resistant against the impact of a materialistic ideology. The Chinese nation which had held fast for two and a half millennia to the teachings of Confucius, Lao-Tse and the Buddha, succumbed to the atheistic doctrine formulated by the son of a German lawyer, and has become the most accomplished robot state this side of science fiction. To look to Asia for mystic enlightenment and spiritual guidance has become as much of an anachronism as to think of America as the Wild West.

Asians have a tendency to lay the blame for this decline on the soul-destroying influence of the West, and Western intellectuals are inclined to accept the blame. 'As pupils we were not bad, but hopeless as teachers' – Auden's *mea culpa* might serve as a motto for the Western guilt complex towards Asia. Like other complexes, it consists of a mixture of fact and fantasy. The factual elements belong to a chapter of history – imperialist expansion and colonial exploitation – which, as far as Asia is concerned, is now closed. It was, no doubt, an ugly chapter of predatoriness combined with hypocrisy. But, of course, the history of Asiatic nations is an equally unedifying tale of invasions, conquests and oppression – right up to the Moslem-Hindu massacres after Independence; and it could be cynically argued that the seafaring invaders of modern times were merely returning the visit of the Mongol invaders of Europe in earlier days. If the past were admitted to weigh on its conscience, every nation would be compelled to commit hara-kiri. Instead of nursing a guilt-complex derived from the crimes of our forebears, the duty of the West is to give material help to the 'underprivileged' Asian nations; and that is now being done on a larger scale than ever before in history.

Let us turn, then, to another aspect of the complex: the psychological ravages which our materialistic civilisation is supposed to have caused among the spiritual values of the traditional Asiatic cultures.

An apparent digression might help to clarify the problem. On a similar scale, but in a more concentrated form, a similar process is now taking place closer to us. One might call it the coca-colonisation of Western Europe, and in this respect I feel the same resentment as the Asian traditionalist. I loathe processed bread in cellophane, processed towns of cement and glass, and the Bible processed as a comic-strip; I loathe crooners and swooners, quizzes and fizzes, neon and subtopia, the Organisation Man and the *Reader's Digest*. But who coerced us into buying all this? The United States do not rule Europe as the British ruled India; they waged no Opium War against us to force their revolting 'coke' down our throats. Europe bought the whole package because it wanted it. The Americans did not americanise us – they were merely one step ahead on the road towards a global civilisation with a standardised style of living which, whether we like it or not, is beginning to emerge all over the world. For we live in a state of cultural osmosis where influences percolate across the porous frontiers, native traditions wane, and the movement towards a uniform, mechanised, stereotyped culture-pattern has become irresistible. What makes it irresistible are the new media of mass-communication; and what makes the emerging pattern so vulgar is the emergence of the under-privileged classes with their undeveloped tastes as consumers of mass-culture. The result is that inevitable levelling-down of standards to the lowest common denominator, which accompanied every revolution in the past.

But this process of cultural osmosis started long before the media of mass-communication were invented – it started with Alexander, it continued in the Mogul invasion of India, and it gained a new impetus with the opening up of sea communications. European rule in Asian countries was based on force, but its cultural influence was not. They bought our culture because they wanted it; because their own cultures had lost their vigour, and succumbed to European influence – as Europe succumbed in the twentieth century to American influence. The Japanese bought European Renaissance learning from the Dutch traders in Nagasaki; then nineteenth-century Science during the Meiji reform; then the robot civilisation after the Second World War. The Indian élite became anglicised because Hindu philosophy, science and literature had come to a standstill a long time ago, and had nothing to offer to them. We ruled by rape, but influenced by seduction. And a saint who lets herself be seduced willingly and asks for more, cannot be much of a saint.

The native customs and crafts were certainly damaged in the process. There is a tribe in Assam, the Khasis, who used to weave beautiful coloured fabrics; they also used to sacrifice little boys to the gods by pushing a two-pronged stick up their nostrils and into the brain. Now they buy hideous mass-produced textiles – and sacrifice no more little boys. It would have been better if they had accepted one half of the offer without the other. But these patterns of living hang together, they go, as the Americans say, by package deal. The Indian Government is now trying to revive the native crafts, but meets with little response. The reason, *mutatis mutandis*, is the same as in Europe: the produce of the cotton mills is cheaper than homespun *khadi*. It is, of course, also much uglier, and again for the same reason: the law of the lowest common denominator in taste. But this, too, may be a transitory phenomenon: some Indian factories are beginning to turn out remarkably attractive fabrics, printed in the traditional designs; and, sentimentality apart, only a few among the weavers, potters and cabinet-makers of the past were great artists.

If the Western cultural imports into Asia provide often no more than cheap, superficial frills, the reason is that the uneducated Asiatic masses are inevitably attracted by the trashiest influence and wares – as the previously underprivileged classes in Europe are attracted by the lures of coca-colonisation. If we are 'hopeless as teachers' both at home and abroad, it is because literacy, culture-hunger and leisure-time are increasing even more rapidly than the birth-rate. There have never been, relatively speaking, fewer creative talents facing a vaster audience of consumers.

All this does not prove that the material poverty of Asia is a sign of its spiritual superiority in the present or in the past. Materialism as a philosophy is less than two centuries old in Europe and now on the wane; 'materialism' in the sense of a mechanical, mindless sort of living is less than half a century old, though still on the increase. Before that, religion had been the dominant chord in European philosophy, art and social life, as far back into the past as historical comparisons are meaningful.

Asian history has been as bloody and cruel as ours; and the Buddhist-Hindu version of tolerance without charity produced as much suffering and misery as a Christian charity without tolerance did. Nonviolence was an abstract command, like turning the other cheek, until quite recent times when Gandhi's genius forged it into a political weapon. The great Hindu epics, the *Ramayana* and *Mahabharata*, are as full of savagery and gore as the Old Testament, and the first three chapters of the *Bhagavad Gita* – the nearest Hindu equivalent to the Gospels – are devoted to an eloquent refutation of the doctrine of nonviolence. The Lord Krishna in person appears on the battle-field as the charioteer of his friend Arjuna, and persuades him to drop his pacifist scruples – mainly on the grounds that the indestructible atma is embodied in both the slayer and the slain, who are One; therefore Arjuna must obey the law of Karma Yoga and fight. 'There is no higher good for a Kashatriya [member of the warrior class] than a righteous war. The truly wise mourn neither for the living nor for the dead.'

Gandhi himself was never an integral pacifist; he endorsed the Congress Resolution of 1940 that India would enter the war if granted Independence, and he gave his agreement to the invasion of Kashmir. Similarly, Vinoba Bhave in 1959 advocated armed resistance against Chinese infiltration in the Himalayas 'because India is not yet spiritually prepared for a wholly non-violent resistance'. Pacifism is a philosophy which, unfortunately, only appeals to pacifists. There is always that child bashed about by a brute, a Czechoslovakia or a Himalayan province invaded; and the dilemma between active intervention and passive complicity has never been solved, either by the East or by the West.

'You have developed the head; the heart did not keep pace. With us it was the opposite – it was with the development of the heart that we have been concerned in India.' When Vinoba said that to me, I accepted it as a truism, as most guilt-ridden Westerners do. The first half of the statement is certainly true; but what evidence is there for the second? If 'heart' refers to charity, the Oriental attitude to the sick and the poor is notoriously indifferent, because caste, rank, wealth and health are pre-ordained by the laws of Karma. Welfare work in the slums and care of the poor in general was, and still is, the monopoly of the Christian missions in Asia. Gandhi's crusade for the Untouchables and Vinoba's crusade for the landless are modern developments under Western influence – Gandhi himself acknowledged that he was inspired by Christianity, Tolstoy, Ruskin and Thoreau.

If by 'heart' Vinoba meant religion, it has been in steady

decline for the last fifteen hundred years. Buddhism, Confucianism and Taoism were all founded in the sixth pre-Christian century; their spiritual message is confined to the ancient texts and to the monumental works of art which they inspired. Religious thought in the East retained its archetypal character; it does not show that evolutionary progression, that combination of a firm basic doctrine with social plasticity, which lent Western monotheism its unique continuity and ethos. Each of the great Eastern religions represents a way of life rather than a self-contained metaphysical doctrine; and when that way of life is altered by changing circumstances, as in India and Japan, the spiritual values crumble away. The Sankaracharya insisted on the rigorous observance of the Hindu rites – because if the observances go, nothing of Hinduism is left. A Hindu who breaks caste, eats meat and forsakes his *lotha*, ceases, by definition, to be a Hindu. The industrial revolution in England caused a more violent uprooting of traditions than India is experiencing at present; yet the Church of England weathered the storm, while Hinduism is foundering. The only live religious tradition in India in the last thousand years was carried on by exceptional individuals – by its great swamis, from Sankara to Vinoba. But their contribution lay more in their personality than in their teaching, and they rarely left written works of value on which their successors could build.

In other words, I think that our cherished habit of contrasting the contemplative and spiritual East with the crude materialism of the West is based on a fallacy. The contrast is not between spirituality and materialism, but between two basically different philosophies; so different, in fact, that Haas, the German Orientalist, who wrote a thoughtful and stimulating book on the question, suggested a new word for the Eastern approach to life: 'philousia' as opposed to Western 'philosophy'. For all the historical evidence goes to show that the East is less interested in factual knowledge – *sophia* – of the external world than in *ousia* – essential Being; that it prefers intuition to reason, symbols to concepts, self-realisation through the annihilation of the ego to self-realisation through the unfolding of individuality. Obviously the two attitudes ought to complement each other like the principles of masculine logic and feminine intuition, the *yin* and *yang* in Taoist philosophy. And in the history of European thought they did indeed complement each other – either by simultaneously competing for supremacy or alternating in dominance. In every chapter of European history we can trace this creative polarity on various levels – the Dionysian and the Apollonian principles; the materialism of the Ionian philosophers and the mysticism of the Eleatics; Plato, Plotinus and Augustine negating the world of the senses, Aristotle, Albert and Aquinas reasserting it; Schopenhauer's Indian pessimism confronted by Nietzsche's arrogant superman; Jung's psychology of archetypes by Adler's psychology of power – through the ages the fertile opposition of *yin* and *yang* is reformulated under different aspects.

In the history of the great Asiatic cultures, the emphasis lay much more consistently on one side only – on the intuitive, subjective, mystical, logic-rejecting side. This attitude apparently arose out of the equally consistent refusal to recognise the independent reality of the external world. As a result, conceptual thinking could not develop, and *yin* had it all to herself against *yang*.

Thus the *hubris* of rationalism is matched by the *hubris* of irrationality, and the messianic arrogance of the Christian crusader is matched by the Yogi's arrogant attitude of detachment towards human suffering. Mankind is facing its most deadly predicament since it climbed down from the trees; but one is reluctantly brought to the conclusion that neither Yoga, Zen, nor any other Asian form of mysticism has any significant advice to offer.

From
The Lotus and the Robot

Islam and the West

*S. H. Nasr is a distinguished Iranian scientist and philosopher, who
has studied in the West (M.I.T. and Harvard), and is now
Professor of the History of Science and Technology at Tehran
University. This devoutly Islamic view of the conflict between the
material and the spiritual, as will be apparent, was written before
the overthrow of the Shah.*

The general tendency among Muslims affected by the
evolutionist mentality is to forget the whole Islamic conception of the march of time. The later Quranic chapters about
eschatological events and the latter days of mankind are
forgotten or passed over in silence. All the *hadīths* pertaining
to the last days and the appearance of the Mahdī are laid aside
or malconstrued, either through ignorance or by ill intention.
Just the one *hadīth* of the Prophet that asserts that the best
generation of Muslims are those who are his contemporaries,
then the generation after, then the following generation until
the end of time, is sufficient to nullify, from the Islamic point
of view, the idea of linear evolution and progress in history.
Those who think they are rendering a service to Islam by
incorporating evolutionary ideas, as currently understood,
into Islamic thought are, in fact, tumbling into a most
dangerous pitfall and are surrendering Islam to one of
modern man's most insidious pseudo-dogmas, one created in
the eighteenth and nineteenth centuries to enable men to
forget God.

Moreover, accepting the evolutionary thesis brings into
being overt paradoxes in daily life which cannot be easily
resolved. If things are going to evolve for the better, then why
bother to spend one's effort on improvement? Things are
going to get better by themselves anyway. The very
dynamism preached by modernists stands in opposition to the
usually accepted idea of evolution. Or, seen from another
point of view, it can be argued that if the effort, work,
movement and the like preached in the modern world are
effective, then man can influence his future and destiny. And
if he can affect his future then he can also affect it for the worse,

and there is no guarantee of an automatic progress and evolution to say the least. All of these and many other paradoxes are brushed aside in certain quarters because of an enfeebled intellectual attitude which has as yet to produce a serious and widely known Islamic response of a metaphysical and intellectual nature to the hypothesis of evolution. The challenge of evolutionary thought has been answered in contemporary Islam in nearly the same way as has the challenge of Marxism. There have been some religious replies based upon the Holy Book, but not an intellectual response which could also persuade the young Muslims whose faith in the Quran itself has been in part shaken by the very arguments of the evolutionary school. Meanwhile, works of evolutionary writers, even of the nineteenth century such as Spencer, who are no longer taught as living philosophical influences in their own homeland, continue to be taught in universities far and wide in the Islamic world, especially in the Indian subcontinent, as if they represented the latest proven scientific knowledge or the latest philosophical school of the West. Few bother even to study the recent anti-evolutionary developments in biology itself or the reassertion of the pre-evolutionary conception of man – views which are gaining ever greater adherence in many circles in the West itself today. And what is worse, there are too few efforts on the part of the Muslim intellectual élite to formulate from Islamic sources the genuine doctrine of man and his relation to the Universe which would act as a criterion for the judgment of any would-be theory of man and the cosmos, evolutionary or otherwise, and which would also provide the light necessary to distinguish scientific facts from mere hypotheses and scientific evidence from crass philosophical materialism parading in the dress of scientific fact or even religious belief.

Another important 'philosophical' challenge to the Islamic world concerns the Freudian and Jungian interpretation of the psyche. The modern psychological and psychoanalytical point of view tries to reduce all the higher elements of man's being to the level of the psyche, and moreover to reduce the psyche itself to nothing more than that which can be studied through modern psychological and psychoanalytical methods. Until now, this way of thinking, in its scientific form, has not affected the Islamic world as directly as has evolutionism, and we do not know of any important and influential Muslim writers who are Freudian or Jungian, but its effect is certain to increase soon. It must therefore be remembered that Freudianism, as well as other modern Western schools of psychology and psychotherapy, are the by-products of a particular society very different from the Islamic. It needs to be recalled also that Freud was a Viennese Jew who turned away from Orthodox Judaism. Few people know that he was connected to a messianic movement which was opposed by the Orthodox Jewish community of Central Europe itself, and that therefore he was opposed to the mainstream of Jewish life, not to speak of Christianity. Many study Freudianism but few delve into its deeper origins which reveal its real nature.

Recently one of the outstanding figures of Sufism from the East wrote a series of articles on Sufism and psychoanalysis in French, making a comparison between the two. With all due respect to him it must be said that he has been too polite and lenient towards psychoanalysis, which is truly a parody of the initiatic methods of Sufism. Fortunately for Muslims, until now the influence of psychoanalysis has not penetrated deeply among them, nor have they felt the need for it. This is due most of all to the continuation of the practice of religious rites such as the daily prayers and pilgrimage. The supplications, 'discourses' and forms of pleading that are carried out in religious centres by men, women and children open the soul to the influx of Divine Grace and are a most powerful means of curing the soul's ailments and untying its knots. These forms of prayer achieve a goal which the psychoanalyst seeks to accomplish without success and moreover often with dangerous results, for he lacks the power which comes from the Spirit and which alone can dominate and control the soul.

But psychoanalytical thought, which is agnostic or even in certain cases demonic, is bound to penetrate gradually into the Islamic world, probably mostly through the translation of Western literature into Arabic, Persian, Turkish, Urdu and other Islamic languages. The effect of such translations will be to bring into being, and in fact is already bringing into being, a so-called 'psychological literature' opposed to the very nature and genius of Islam. Islam is a religion which rejects individualistic subjectivism. The most intelligible material symbol of Islam, the mosque, is a building with a space in which all elements of subjectivism have been eliminated. It is an objective determination of the Truth, a crystal through which radiates the light of the Spirit. The spiritual ideal of Islam itself is to transform the soul of the Muslim, like a mosque, into a crystal reflecting the Divine Light.

Truly Islamic literature is very different from the kind of subjective literature we find in the writings of Franz Kafka or at best in Dostoevsky. These and similar writers are, of course, among the most important in modern Western literature, but they, along with most other modern Western literary figures, nevertheless present a point of view which is very different from, and usually totally opposed to, that of Islam. Among older Western literary figures who are close to the Islamic perspective, one might mention first of all Dante and Goethe who, although profoundly Christian, are in many ways like Muslim writers. In modern times, one could mention, on of course another level, T. S. Eliot, who, unlike most modern writers, was a devout Christian and possessed, for this very reason, a vision of the world not completely removed from that of Islam.

In contrast to the works of such men, however, the psychological novel, through its very form and its attempt to penetrate into the psyche of men without possessing any criterion with which to discern Truth as an objective reality, is an element that is foreign to Islam. Marcel Proust was, without doubt, a master of the French language and his *In Search of Time Past* is of much interest for those devoted to modern French literature, but this type of writing cannot under any conditions become the model for a genuinely Muslim literature. Yet it is this very type of psychological literature that is now beginning to serve as a 'source of inspiration' for a number of writers in Arabic and Persian. It is of interest to note that the most famous modern literary figure of Persia, Sadeq Hedayat, who was deeply influenced by Kafka, committed suicide because of psychological despair and that, although certainly a person of great literary talent, he was divorced from the Islamic current of life. Today, in fact, his ideas are opposed by Islamic elements within Persian society. Nevertheless, such writers, who often deal with psychological problems and disturbances found in

Western society, problems which the Muslims have not experienced until now, are becoming popular among the Muslim youth who thereby become acquainted, and even inflicted, with these new maladies.

One of the worst tragedies today in the Muslim world is that there has appeared recently a new type of person who tries consciously to imitate the obvious maladies of the West. Such people, for example, are not really in a state of depression but try to put themselves into one in order to look modern. They compose poetry that is supposed to issue from a tormented and depressed soul whereas they are not depressed at all. There is nothing worse than a state of nihilism except its imitation by someone who is not nihilistic but tries to produce nihilistic literature or art only to imitate the decadence of Western art. The influence of psychology and psychoanalysis, combined with an atheistic and nihilistic point of view and disseminated within the Islamic world through literature and art, presents a major challenge to Islam which can be answered only through recourse to traditional Islamic psychology and psychotherapy contained mostly within Sufism, and also through the creation of a genuinely Islamic literary criticism which would be able to provide an objective evaluation of so much that passes for literature today.

The degree of penetration of anti-Islamic psychological as well as philosophical Western ideas through literature into the Islamic World can be best gauged by just walking through the streets near universities in various Middle Eastern cities. Among the books spread on the ground or on stands everywhere one still observes traditional religious books, especially of course the Quran. But one observes also a larger number of works in Islamic languages dealing with subjects ranging all the way from Marxism and existentialism to pornography, presented usually as 'literature'. There are, of course, rebuttals and answers as well, for Islam and its spirituality are still alive. But the very presence of all this writing itself reveals the magnitude of the challenge.

As far as nihilism is concerned, the Islamic answer is particularly strong and, putting pretenders aside, the Muslims, even the modernized ones, have not experienced nihilism in the same way as have Westerners, for whom nihilism has become an experience of almost central importance. The main reason for this is that in Christianity the Spirit has been almost always presented in a positive form, as an affirmation, as the sacred art of Christianity reveals so clearly. The void or the *nihil* has not usually been given a spiritual significance in Christian theology and art, as it has been for example in Islam and also in the Far East. Therefore, as a result of the rebellion against Christianity, modern man has experienced the *nihil* only in its negative and terrifying aspect, while some have been attracted to Oriental doctrines especially because of the latter's emphasis upon the Void.

In contrast to Christianity, where the manifestation of the Spirit is identified always with an affirmation and a positive form, Islamic art makes use of the 'negative' or the 'Void' itself in a spiritual and positive sense in the same way that metaphysically the first part of the *shahādah* begins with a negation to affirm the vacuity of things *vis-à-vis* Allah. The space in Islamic architecture is essentially a 'negative space'. Space in Islamic architecture and city-planning is not the space around an object or determined by that object. Rather, it is the negative space cut out from material forms, as for example in traditional bazaars. When one walks through a bazaar one walks through a continuous space determined by the inner surface of the wall surrounding it, and not by some object in the middle of it. That is why what is happening architecturally in many Middle Eastern cities – such as the building of a large monument in the middle of a square to emulate what one finds in the West – is the negation of the very principles of Islamic art and is based on a lack of understanding of the positive role of negative space and the *nihil* in Islamic architecture.

From
Islam and the Plight of Modern Man

Freya Stark
A Letter from Persia

Hamadan
23 April 1930

Dearest Car,

It is wonderful to be writing from Persia. I wake up with that feeling every morning, and then feel how very like one's own country it is – not so much Scotland as North Italy – if one looks beyond the poplars to the snowy ridges: but if one looks out over the naked plain and the far bare ranges, it is just Persia, some high land in the centre of the world, getting near the very central table-land where all history began.

The tomb of Esther is here: a neglected dome in one corner of an untidy square where a few Persians slouch about in their absurd long frock coats and peaked caps, looking like people in a mid-Victorian farce. The tomb has a large stone door like those of the Jebel Druse, with a hole where the rabbi's arm goes through. We had an appointment with the rabbi at five o'clock and were waiting for him on the steps of the tomb when a Venerable Being with a Beard came up and took our proffered hands in both of his, pressing them gently between his grey cotton gloves: we were deeply impressed, till the real rabbi came, with a longer and broader beard and we found the other to be merely a Dervish of no importance. Inside the little vaulted room are the two carved wooden coffins, all swathed in damasks and brocades: Esther and Mordecai, side by side – and in a little room close by, a beautiful case with the rolls of the old Testament written on parchment in lovely lettering. And every Friday night the Jews of Hamadan (there are 5,000) gather here, and the book of Esther is read out to them. They seem to be on friendly terms now with the Moslems, but it is only quite recently. In fact as far as one can see everything is beautifully peaceful, and all the population intent only on picnics and motor cars, or little drives over the cobbly streets in a small 'fiacre' vividly upholstered with crimson velvets and flowers, and a hand for luck stamped in henna on the horse's back if it happens to be a white one.

Lionel Smith persuaded me to come up here with the matron of the hospital in Baghdad – and this has made me be welcomed as a respectable member of society by the British of Hamadan, though it was about twice as expensive as my own ideas of native travelling. Anyway it could not be pleasanter: the hotel garden has hoopoes and blackbirds and blossom of every kind, and the most amusing lot of non-descript passers-by, as Hamadan is a necessary stopping-place on the road. Very few English, and it is rather a pleasant feeling to be in a country which is living its own life, however it may be mismanaging it.

My Persian is getting on: I can get about the bazaars and shops. I have an old scamp of a teacher with a beard dyed in henna and a twinkle in his eye which doesn't quite disappear even when he tells me that he has twice seen the Hidden Imam. He got rather annoyed with me for asking for details of his costume and appearance – which appear to have been ordinary coat and trousers. Anyway he is an excellent teacher and comes two hours a day and promises to make me ready for talk with the Assassins by the middle of next month.

Your
Freya

From
The Furnace and the Cup

Alan Moorehead
The Mahdi

Even today the traveller on the Nile must be struck by the power of Islam in the North and Central Sudan. It would seem that there is little enough to thank God for in these appalling deserts, and yet the poorest and most wretched of the inhabitants will be seen throughout the day to prostrate themselves upon the sand with a simple concentrated fervour that is hardly known in the green delta of Egypt. No village lacks its minaret even if it be nothing more than a ramshackle scaffolding of poles, and the muezzin, calling the people to prayer, at once brings to a halt all sound and movement on the ground below. Here every precept of the Prophet, every injunction that governs the great fasts and feasts, appears to be observed to the letter.

Perhaps it is the very austerity of life in these arid wastes that predisposes the people to worship. Mecca lies only a short journey away across the Red Sea, and the Prophet Mohammed himself lived and received his inspirations in just such an

environment as this. An immense silence possesses the surrounding desert. The heat is so great it stifles the appetite and
induces a feeling of trance-like detachment in which
monotony dissolves into a natural timelessness, visions take
on the appearance of reality, and asceticism can become a
religious object of itself. These are ideal circumstances for
fanaticism, and a religious leader can arouse his followers with
a devastating effect. All at once the barriers are swept aside,
revolt becomes a holy duty, and it can be a shocking and
uprooting thing because it makes so sharp a break with the
apathy that has gone before. The long silence is broken, the
vision is suddenly translated into action, and detachment is
replaced by a fierce and violent concentration.

In the very nature of things, then, the revolt in the Sudan
was bound to be at once more drastic and more fundamental
than the rising in Egypt. It was a religious, rather than a
political, movement, and although the events in Egypt
undoubtedly affected the Sudan, it was a spontaneous
explosion. Had Gordon been able to continue as Governor-
General it might have been another story, but directly he
went the authority of the government disintegrated and
revolt became inevitable. Emin continued in Equatoria,
Slatin continued in Darfur, and Frank Lupton, the British
sailor, replaced Gessi in Bahr-el-Ghazal, but there was nothing
really effective these white men could do to hold the Sudan
together so long as an Egyptian Governor-General ruled in
Khartoum – and Raouf Pasha, the man who followed Gordon
in that office, was the worst possible choice. Gordon had
actually dismissed him from the Sudan service because of his
inhumanity to the Africans. Raouf, like a good party boss, lost
no time in restoring his old cronies to office, men of the
calibre of Abu Saoud, who had swindled both Baker and
Gordon in his day, and in very little time bribery once more
became the normal method of conducting business in
Khartoum, flogging and torture were resumed in the prisons,
and the slave-traders everywhere took heart again. In 1882
Abd-el-Kader, the soldier who had once commanded Baker's
Forty Thieves, succeeded Raouf as Governor-General, and he
was a better man. But by then it was too late: the Sudan was
ready for chaos.

Hatred of the Egyptians was the first motive of the rebellion.

There were about 28,000 of them stationed in the various garrisons throughout the country, and their behaviour towards the Sudanese had become unbearable. Taxes were gathered with extreme harshness, and every Egyptian official was known to be corrupt. A British officer sent up from Cairo to investigate the garrisons after Gordon left wrote in his report: 'Their general conduct and overbearing manner is almost sufficient to cause a rebellion. When to this conduct cowardice is added, it is impossible for me to avoid expressing my contempt and disgust.' Gordon himself had foreseen trouble, even as far back as 1879, when he wrote, '. . . If the present system of government goes on, there cannot fail to be a revolt of the whole country.'

Early in 1881 the general air of unrest in the Sudan began to crystallize around the name of a strange personality who had appeared on Abba Island in the Nile, about 150 miles upstream from Khartoum. This man was said to have set himself up as a new religious leader, a Mahdi. The Sudan, he declared, was to be purged of the corrupt Egyptians, and her people were to be brought back to the austerities of the true faith.

There was no great alarm at first. Abu Saoud and a force of 200 men were dispatched to Abba Island with instructions to bring the rebel into Khartoum for punishment. But it was soon apparent that the Mahdi was something more than another provincial fakir with visions of glory. His followers on the island obeyed him with a fanatical reverence. They butchered Abu Saoud's soldiers with terrible ease, and presently there was news that the Mahdi, retreating into the deserts of Kordofan, had raised the cry for a Jihad, a Holy War.

Mohammed Ahmed Ibn el-Sayyid Abdullah, the Mahdi, follows the true tradition of the warrior-priests of Islam. Like a sandstorm in the desert he appears, suddenly and inexplicably out of nowhere, and by some strange process of attraction generates an ever-increasing force as he goes along. Confused accounts were given of his origins: some said that he came from a family of boat-builders on the Nile, others that he was the son of a poor religious teacher, others again that he was the descendant of a line of sheikhs. It was generally accepted, however, that he was born in the Dongola province in the North Sudan in 1844 (which would make him 37 years of age at this time), and that quite early in life he had achieved a local reputation for great sanctity and for a gift of oratory that was quite exceptional. His effects, it seemed, were obtained by an extraordinary personal magnetism. To put it in Strachey's phrase: 'There was a strange splendour in his presence, an overwhelming passion in the torrent of his speech.' He was a man possessed. Mohammed had promised that one of his descendants would one day appear and re-animate the faith, and Abdullah now declared, with an unshakable conviction, that he himself was that man. His hatred of the Egyptians was intense.

We have several first-hand descriptions of the Mahdi, the best of which perhaps is that given by Father Joseph Ohr-walder, the Austrian priest who for seven years was his prisoner. 'His outward appearance,' Father Ohrwalder says, 'was strangely fascinating; he was a man of strong constitu-tion, very dark complexion, and his face always wore a pleasant smile.' He had 'singularly white teeth, and between the two upper middle ones was a vee-shaped space, which in the Sudan is considered a sign that the owner will be lucky. His mode of conversation, too, had by training become exceptionally pleasant and sweet.'

Slatin, the Governor of Darfur, who spent an even longer period as the Mahdi's prisoner, bears this description out. The Mahdi, he says, was a powerfully-built man, with broad shoulders, a large head, sparkling brown eyes, a black beard and three tribal gashes on his cheek. He was forever smiling. He smiled when he prescribed the most brutal tortures for some wretch who had blasphemed or had taken a glass of liquor. He was a smiler with a knife.

Wingate, the future Governor of the Sudan who made an exhaustive study of the subject, came to this conclusion: 'There is no doubt that until he was ruined by unbridled sensuality, this man had the strongest head and the clearest mental vision in the two million square miles of which he more or less made himself master before he died.'

There is an element of fantasy in the progress of this inspired and highly gifted man, and even now, after the passage of eighty years, it is difficult to assess him. Certainly he was not an adventurer in the ordinary sense. Even if it is assumed that he was not sincere, that his religious protestations were simply a bogus cover for his personal ambition, it still has to be admitted that his followers worshipped him; they never, now or later, questioned his authority, they thought him semi-divine, and from the most powerful Emir to the humblest water-carrier they were ready to die for him. He was lifted up on a wave of religious adoration, and he was able to exact from his wild followers a sense of duty and of discipline that was utterly lacking in the Egyptian ranks. His success was astonishing. To begin with, in Kordofan his men were hardly armed at all, except for spears and sticks, and yet they routed a column of Egyptian soldiers sent against them, and in August 1882 (the same month that the British landed on the Suez Canal) they laid siege to El Obeid, which was a town of 100,000 people, protected by a strong Egyptian garrison. The Egyptians knew that they could expect nothing but death from these madmen, and so they held on for six months. Famine defeated them in the end; it was so frightful that every rat and dog was eaten by the garrison, and a single camel fetched the price of two thousand dollars. In January 1883 the city fell, and when the ensuing massacre had subsided it was found that a large store of arms and a sum of money equal to about £100,000 had fallen into the Mahdi's hands. From this point onward the revolution became a civil war.

The tyranny of the Mahdi in the desert in the eighteen-eighties followed a pattern that was not altogether dissimilar from dictatorship in Europe in the nineteen-thirties. It was merely cruder and more violent; atrocities here were committed not in the name of patriotism, but of God.

At the centre stood the Mahdi, the new reincarnation of the Prophet, and he was attended by his inner ring of disciples: the three Khalifas who were his principal lieutenants. Beneath these were the Emirs, the Mukuddums, and the leaders of the tribes. Finally came the wild horde of tribesmen themselves, with their camp followers and their herds of domestic animals. They had their uniform – a *jibbeh* with square patches sewn on it as a mark of virtuous poverty, and a turban; their emblems – the flags of the Emirs inscribed with texts from the Koran, and the green flag of the Mahdi himself; and their military parades – usually a headlong cavalry charge across the open desert.

The following proclamation was published by the Mahdi

from his new residence at Government House in El Obeid:

'Let all show penitence before God, and abandon all bad and forbidden habits, such as the degrading acts of the flesh, the use of wine and tobacco, lying, bearing false witness, disobedience to parents, brigandage, the non-restitution of goods to others, the clapping of hands, dancing, improper signs with the eyes, tears and lamentations at the bed of the dead, slanderous language, calumny, and the company of strange women. Clothe your women in a decent way, and let them be careful not to speak to unknown persons. All those who do not pay attention to these principles disobey God and His Prophet, and they shall be punished in accordance with the law.

'Say your prayers at the prescribed hours.

'Give the tenth part of your goods, handing it to our Prince, Sheikh Mansour [the new governor of El Obeid], in order that he may forward it to the treasury of Islam.

'Adore God, and hate not each other, but assist each other to do good.'

These precepts were ferociously enforced. Flogging to death and the cutting off of the hands were the penalties for the most trivial offences. Marriage feasts and festivities of every kind were abolished. No man might swear, or take an alcoholic drink, or even smoke, unless he cared to face the instant pain of death. There was but one honourable way to die and that was in battle in the holy service of the Mahdi.

After the fall of El Obeid, Father Ohrwalder says that the Mahdi was venerated almost as the Prophet himself. The very water in which he washed was distributed to his followers who hoped in drinking it to cure themselves of their ills. No one doubted the success of his mission any longer, and his nightly dreams and visions were regarded as a direct revelation from God. When all the Sudan had fallen, the Mahdi declared, he would take Egypt and proceed to the bloodiest of all battles outside Mecca. Next he would advance on Jerusalem where Christ would descend from heaven to meet him, and Islam thereafter would conquer the whole world.

The Mahdi's notions of the world were extremely sketchy, but this was of no consequence in these early days of his crusade; the desert was the only world these people knew. The Mahdi smiled and a sublime confidence radiated from him. He was not at all dismayed when he heard, in the sum-mer months of 1883, that an Egyptian army commanded by a British general was advancing upon him from the Nile.

Egypt had taken a full year to bestir herself. From month to month it had been hoped that the Governor-General in Khartoum would have been able to handle the situation with the soldiers already under his command. But with the fall of Kordofan, the richest province in the Sudan, it had become plain that a military expedition would have to be sent from Cairo if the revolution was to be suppressed. But who was to raise this expedition? The British would have no part in it. In England a reaction had set in after the Battle of Tel-el-Kebir. Gladstone wanted no more conquests in Africa, and would no doubt have retired the British soldiers from Egypt had Baring been able to rule the country without them. It remained then for the Egyptian government to find the arms and the men, and in this, miraculously, they succeeded. The command was given to Colonel William Hicks of the Bombay Army, who was yet another of the footloose soldiers who had joined the Egyptian service, and he had with him a staff of over a dozen Europeans, including a correspondent of *The Times* and another from the London *Graphic*. When the force was finally assembled and despatched up the Nile to Khartoum it num-bered some 7,000 infantry, 1,000 cavalry, and the usual horde of camp followers. More than 5,000 camels were required to carry supplies into the desert, and the equipment included both mountain and machine guns with a million rounds of ammunition. On paper it was a formidable array, but there were ominous weaknesses. Many of the soldiers were men who were serving terms of imprisonment because they had taken part in the Arabi rebellion – they were actually sent off in chains to Khartoum – and Colonel Hicks was a long way from being another Gessi. He was a thorough-going British officer who was not at all lacking in courage, and he might have done very well had he been leading an expedition in Europe. But this was Africa. 'In three days,' the *Times* correspondent wrote from Khartoum, 'we march on a campaign that even the most sanguine look forward to with the greatest gloom.'

There is no need to linger over the painful details. After a series of preliminary skirmishes the expedition ascended the

Nile as far as el-Dueim, about 100 miles south of Khartoum, and then marched westward across the dry plains towards El Obeid. The guides either deliberately or through carelessness lost their way, the commissariat was hopeless, the soldiers unwilling, and the supply of water virtually non-existent. It was a wonderfully obsolete cavalcade. Despite the terrible heat some of the wretched soldiers were wearing chain armour and antique helmets, which looked as though they might have dated from the times of the Crusaders. In battle they were ordered to form a square with their guns pointing outwards from each corner while their camels were herded together with the baggage in the centre. Each soldier carried with him a contraption made of four iron spikes known as a crow's foot, and this he threw down in front of him on the sand so as to make a barrier against the charges of the enemy.

From El Obeid the Mahdi and his Khalifas watched the approach of this cumbersome and helpless column with a predatory joy. Long before the inevitable end there was a despairing note in the dispatches which Hicks sent back to Khartoum: the water has failed, in increasing numbers his men and his camels are dying every day, the Mahdi's horsemen have cut off his line of supply to the Nile and he does not know where he is. On November 5, 1883, the expedition was wandering in the depths of a dry forest thirty miles to the south of El Obeid when 50,000 Arab warriors burst upon it. No one knows the exact details of the battle, since the Arabs kept no written records and few if any prisoners were taken. Of the original ten thousand two or three hundred men may have survived, and Hicks and his European staff were not among them. Two weeks elapsed before the news of the disaster filtered through to Khartoum and the outside world, and months were to go by before its full implications were realized.

In the Sudan it was as though a dam had burst. In a tremendous wave the cult of Mahdism swept outward, and there was hardly a corner of the huge country that was not engulfed. In Khartoum a panic began and many of the wealthier families fled down the Nile to Egypt. In Darfur Slatin was completely cut off. He fought a series of hopeless battles with the Arabs and then surrendered. In Bahr-el-Ghazal Frank Lupton hung on desperately into the New Year, and then he too collapsed.

Emin in Equatoria retreated up the Nile. And far away to the east a Turkish-Sudanese slave-dealer named Osman Digna rose for the Mahdi on the Red Sea coast. Here and there, at strongholds like Sennar and Kassala, an Egyptian garrison remained like an island above the tide, but they were islands of sand rather than of rock.

At the end of 1883 it might then have been argued that the honours in the struggle between Islam and Christianity were fairly equal. The British had won Egypt but they had lost the Sudan. Gladstone no doubt would have been glad to have left the matter at that – in fact, he was determined to do no more. Khartoum, he declared, must look out for itself, and the Egyptians in the Sudanese garrisons must fend for themselves as best they could. But there were others in England who believed that nothing as yet had been settled, that all that had happened to date was merely a prelude to a much more intensive struggle on the Nile. These people believed that, having gone so far in Africa, England could not go back, and they began in the winter of 1883 to look about for a man who would force the government into action. They found him in General Gordon.

From
The White Nile

Philip Howard
Standard English

It is a truth universally acknowledged that the English
language is having one of its periodic fits of rapid change, as it
did after the Norman Conquest, and again after the invention
of printing. The new question is: is this change different in
kind as well as in scale from the changes that continually
adapt a living language to meet new needs and new generations? And even, if you are feeling pessimistic as well as

apocalyptic, is it terminal? Instead of becoming the world language, is English cracking up?

As we babble and scribble our way into the Eighties, worrying about the state of the language has become as fashionable as worrying about the state of one's own health, or the end of civilization as we know it. Like the last two, it is a self-fulfilling activity. The worrywart hypochondriac imagines aches and hears muffled knockings in the outlying provinces of his (or her) body at three in the morning. If he sets his mind doggedly to it, the determined doom-watcher can find the gloomy satisfaction of 'I told you so' in every issue of his newspaper, and every time he turns on the radio or television.

Similarly the eyes of the purist fretter about language pass over any virtues on a page without a flicker, and are drawn exclusively to misprint, catachresis, misspelling, solecism, barbarism, and other evidence that English ain't what it used to be. It never was. It is never clear when English was at that golden peak of perfection from which it is supposed to have declined. But it often seems to have been when the parents of the worried wordFowler were at school, being taught old-fashioned parsing and grammar (preferably the Latin sort) by Mr Chips or Miss Popham.

In extreme cases the worrier takes the alleged decadence of English as a cause and not just a symptom of our supposed general decline. As the Dark Ages roll over us, he/she and a small élite of literati who still use the Queen's English correctly will be besieged in their Gowers-towers, while outside the troops of Midian will prowl and prowl around, splitting infinitives and grunting 'hopefully' to each other.

The notion of correct (or Queen's, or standard) English has become a difficult one for our generation, which is correctly suspicious of authority. Like what we bees needin is beaucoup cognizance that brothers and sisters rappin on am not necessarily talkin a substandard creole, but don disprove that in living vibrant color.

That may be incorrect *Times* style, liable to make the chief sub-editor Gasp and Stretch his Eyes, and the night lawyer wake up with a start from dreams of juicy libels. But it is *correct* in Watts Country where the language of *The Times* would seem, if spoken, grotesquely stuffy, alien, and unintelligible.

Each of us uses many different dialects of English for different occasions (writing to one's bank manager, writing an informal letter, talking to a friend, talking to a stranger, talking to a child, talking to oneself, talking on the dreadful telephone . . .), and each dialect is 'correct' in its proper context. What goes wrong is not deviation from some notional absolute standard of correctitude, but the use of an inappropriate dialect in an incongruous context, as in, 'Ta-ta, Your Holiness, baby; see you soon, luv', or, 'With the completion of that progression of beverages may I hazard the opinion that it falls to me to procure the next one?'

One of the principal reasons for the present rapid change and expansion of English is that many more people of many more races and cultures are speaking it as a first or second language, introducing their own national idioms and idiosyncrasies.

Most Indians learn English not by the spoken word in their homes, but at school from books. So Indian English tends to be characteristically formal, even pedantic. An English-speaking father says to his son: 'You are advised to meet your mother.' A British father in the same circumstances would say: 'Why don't you ask your mother, darling?' Indians characteristically tag 'isn't it' on to the end of sentences, regardless of the number and gender of the subject: 'They went to the cinema, isn't it?' Australians, who are extremely inventive with the language, insert the Great Australian Adjective *passim* in their English: 'Cripes, Pommy, it sticks out like a bloody moment of fun at a Rolf Bloody Harris concert; I mean, we just don't speak the same bloody language.' Other national and regional groups of English-speakers have their own dialects. But they enrich rather than impoverish the central language. The centripetal forces of the printed word and other media of modern mass communication are stronger than the centrifugal forces of regional variation.

The proliferation of knowledge is another cause of the rapid change in English. It spawns new jargons that are often so far removed from everyday speech that they are unintelligible to those of us outside the Fancy. A philosopher writes; 'There is a number of kinds of sets of infinite numbers of nomological propositions to each of which we must attribute zero intrinsic probability.' His colleagues understand what he is saying. The eyes of the rest of us glaze over.

At the Ministry of Defence the ize have it. Here is a small sample of their current jargon for communicating with each other inside NATO: synopsize, prioritize, impossibilize, parameterize, architecture (no, not that meaning), techno-boggling, definitize, channelize. And here is an advertisement of 1980 by the Institute of the London Centre for Psychotherapy: 'The course will be experiential and can be used for self-exploration through role-playing and psychodrama in the context of an on-going group process.'

We may suspect that the last two clumps of jargon could be more simply expressed without losing precision. We may even suspect, if we are hardened and shameless cynics, that the last example is witch-doctor mumbo-jumbo designed principally to impress the gullible. But presumably mathematically-inclined philosophers, Royal Naval Captains on the make, and aspiring practitioners of psychotherapy understand their respective jargons and find them useful shorthand. If they do not, the jargons will rapidly die anyway.

The language is changing because there are more sources of new slang, and because slang spreads instantly around the world. Almost everybody has access to such media of mass communication as trannies. Slang has always been around. Most language starts as slang, the vernacular of ordinary people in the cave or on the Clapham omnibus, if they can catch one. If slang is successful, it is adopted into the language. It should therefore not vex us or worry us that the American young today use 'bad', pronounced 'ba-a-ad', to describe something or somebody easy on the eye; 'foxy' as a sexy compliment for a pretty girl; 'dynamite' to mean super; 'brick house' to mean a good-looking, well-stacked girl; and 'buns' to mean bum. No doubt young Brits, influenced by television, films, and magazines, will pick up the slang. But other terms will soon become fashionable, as the old ones become boring. Chesterton said that all slang was metaphor, and all metaphor is poetry.

English is changing because many more people are speaking it as a first or second language. The grammar is becoming simpler and coarser, as it is taught by teachers for whom it is not the native language. 'Whom' will be as old-fashioned as wing collars and corsets by the end of the century. The distinction between 'will' and 'shall' is dying. Under American influence the difference between 'I haven't got' and 'I don't have' is dead. 'I haven't got indigestion' means that I am not suffering from a belly-ache at the moment. 'I don't have indigestion' means that I am not dyspeptic. 'We haven't got any bananas' means that there happen to be none in the shop, but we usually have them. 'We don't have bananas' means that we don't stock them: blackberries and breadfruit yes; bananas never.

In these and other ways English is losing some useful distinctions. This weakens the language, because the more distinctions there are available in a language, the more power-ful and useful it is. There is nothing that we can do to halt this gradual simplification of English grammar, which is wel-comed by democratic levellers, except deplore it and perhaps slow down the process a little. It has been going on for centuries. Those who care for precision can carry on using 'whom', 'shall', and 'I haven't got' for the present, without appearing to be linguistic Luddites.

English is changing because people, some through ignorance, others deliberately in order to persuade or deceive, attach new meanings to old words. It does not much matter that many of us led by Ted Heath, now confuse 'flout' and 'flaunt', although it can lead us to say the opposite of what we mean: 'It sheds light on his character that he was willing to *flaunt* the conventions of his time.' But it is sinister when somebody calls his master's previous statement 'inoperative', when what he means is that it was a lie; or calls a dissident a psychiatric criminal; or uses 'pacification' as a whited sepulchre of a euphemism for killing everything that moves. But our generation did not invent such weasel words. According to Tacitus, the British chieftain Calgacus accused the Romans of inventing the last one: '*Ubi solitudinem faciunt, pacem appellant*'; they make a desolation, and call it pacification. Calgacus was not fooled; and nor are we, yet.

It may be true that English is under greater threat to its precision, versatility, and concreteness than it has been for some centuries. Relativists and exponents of structural linguistics rush to defend almost any solecism or neologism as an 'alternate mode of communicating'. Pessimists and purists reply that they are no more alternative modes of communicating than shooting the referee is an alternative way of playing football, or upsetting the board is an alternative way of playing chess.

But we are still a long way from Orwell's Newspeak of *1984*, when 'every concept that can ever be needed will be expressed by exactly *one* word, with its meaning rigidly defined and all its subsidiary meanings rubbed out and forgotten.' English in the Eighties is an exciting and deafening Babel of dialects. It has grown prodigiously since the war because of the vast increase in knowledge of all sorts, as well as the vast increase in numbers of people of all sorts speaking it as a first or second language. It makes little sense to talk about language being 'correct' or in decline. Eskimo may not suit our life, but the language is perfectly adapted to the material culture of the Eskimos. Latin did not 'decline' from golden into silver, and bronze after the fall of Rome. It was merely spoken by different chaps; and Helen Waddell has reminded us that they used it magnificently for their different purposes.

'Where shall we look for standard English but to the words of the standard man?' Let us worry, if we must worry, about the return of the Dark Ages, or the state of our health. The language is in rude health, so long as we can go on using it, abusing it, complaining about it, and changing it in so many rich and varied ways.

From
Words Fail Me

What's in a Catch Phrase?

But what, exactly, is a catch phrase? The standard dictionaries, even the best of them, are singularly inadequate and vague, perhaps because it is easier to define one, not directly but by saying what it is *not* and by offering a few cunningly diversified examples. I sympathize with the lexicographers, for it's extraordinarily difficult to define a catch phrase satisfactorily.

One definition is 'a phrase designed to catch the public fancy' – for instance, a political or an advertising slogan. But I exclude such phrases, unless, as occasionally happens, they achieve a much wider application and a change in significance. As I see it, a catch phrase is roughly – very roughly indeed – a unit of conversation; a phrase originating as a smart or forcible or ironic repartee or comment and becoming an emotional counter with the affective element gradually diminishing. A catch phrase has something in common with a proverbial saying but only rarely anything in common with a fully qualified proverb; a few proverbial sayings began as catch phrases, and a few catch phrases as proverbial sayings. A very famous quotation, provided it be brief, will sometimes lose its quality of quotation and be applied in contexts and senses remote from those of the original. Occasionally a catch phrase becomes a cliché or, if the sense or the application drastically changes, a cliché becomes a catch phrase. Only in a historical dictionary will these nuances and transitions emerge at all clearly. But, in the main, 'once a catch phrase always – until, that is, it disappears – a catch phrase'.

From a general consideration of such phrases, three characteristics show up, one being how idiomatic and pithy most of them are; another, how very English, how Anglo-Saxon, the best of them are – they eschew 'fine language' with its Greek and Latin polysyllables; and how very much longer-lived than most people, including the majority of scholars, suppose (or seem to suppose) they are, although, of course, many catch phrases are comparatively short-lived. Only a very few can be classed as ephemeral.

The third feature being the most easily demonstrable, I

select three phrases, which are necessarily British, not American: *black's your eye*; *I'll have your guts for garters*; and *hay is for horses*. *Black's your eye* is included in the best dictionaries of proverbs and proverbial sayings. Obviously it isn't fully and properly a proverb, but that it may, either originally or at some later stage of its long history, have been or become a proverbial saying, I shouldn't care to deny; on the other hand, it was certainly, at some period and perhaps always, a catch phrase. Dating from the fifteenth century, or perhaps the fourteenth, it is well attested up to the year 1828, as the late Professor F. P. Wilson's admirable third edition (1970) of *The Oxford Dictionary of English Proverbs* makes clear. The quotations in that and other dictionaries suggest that until some time in the eighteenth century *to say black is your eye* was genuinely a proverbial saying, and that *black's your eye* derives from it and is, no less genuinely, a true catch phrase. The general sense of the saying is 'to imply an adverse criticism of someone' and that of the catch phrase is one of contemptuous defiance or accusation. The phrase is now, I think yet would not swear, obsolete; I do, however, remember its being used as late as the 1920s.

I'll have your guts for garters has probably been current, especially among Cockneys, since the late seventeenth century, for in Robert Greene's *James the Fourth* (c. 1591), at III, ii, occurs the threat, 'I'll make garters of thy guts, thou villain', and an early seventeenth-century parish register records what must be the original form: *I'll have your guts for garter points*, where a *point* is 'a tagged lace or cord' (*OED*) for fastening or attaching one part of clothing to another. The sense ranges from dire to comically ironic threat, and the phrase is now seldom used by those who do not belong to the linguistically privileged world of Cockneys.

A third example of longevity among catch phrases is afforded by *hay is for horses*. In Swift's wonderful recording of educated colloquialism, *Polite Conversation*, published in 1738 but commenced some thirty years earlier, a footman calls to a visitor, '*Hey*, Miss' and witty Miss retorts, '*Hay is for horses*'. The reproof – one of the domestic catch phrases (compare '*she*' *is a cat's mother*) – is still current, although perhaps slightly obsolescent. In the present century, the variant '*ay is for 'orses* – where '*ay* has been prompted by *eh* (in place of exclamatory *hey*) – is very frequent; for instance, it forms the first letter of the Comic Phonetic Alphabet, which, if you remember, continues as '*B* is for honey, *C* is for fish . . .'

Interesting historically, yet still more interesting for other reasons, is *does your mother know you're out?* – dated by Sir Gurney 'Quotations' Benham at *c.* 1840. This predominantly British catch phrase seems to have crossed the Atlantic at tremendous speed, for it occurs, 1840, in one of Thomas Chandler Haliburton's 'Sam Slick' books, *The Attaché*, where the brash young salesman, in New York for the first time, goes to the theatre and is invited behind the scenes; a saucy girl of the chorus line, spotting him for the 'hick' he is, asks him, 'Does your mother know you're out?' Theories about the origin vary, but at least it's almost certainly *not* obstetric. Although undoubtedly obsolescent, it is not, especially among those over sixty, obsolete.

A few further, not too carefully selected, catch phrases will provide enough material for everyone to hit upon a definition satisfactory to himself. *I couldn't care less* became popular in, if I remember correctly, 1940. Its most significant feature is its semantic origin, in that catch phrase of the 1930s, *I couldn't agree more*, for it exemplifies a tendency of such phrases to fall into, and therefore, to follow, a pattern.

Catch phrases of agreement are expectably numerous. One may note the enthusiastic *I'll say it is!*; the synonyms, *you can say that again* or *you can say that twice*, the latter adopted from America but the former perhaps suggested by the much earlier English *say it again!*; the derivative elaboration, *you can say that in spades*, which, because of its specialism and comparative artificiality, was already, in Britain at least, obsolescent by 1970, even though it was adopted only *c.* 1945; and *that makes two of us*, predominantly and originally British, dating from *c.* 1940 and addressed to someone who has just expressed either complete ignorance or considerable bewilderment.

The irony detectable in several of the preceding phrases recurs in, for instance, *that'll be the day*, where *that* is heavily emphasized. It was coined, I believe, late in 1918, and it had, at first, the variant *that'll be the bloody day*; it arose as a soldiers' exclamation and may have been satirical of *der Tag*, the day Germany would conquer Britain or, more generally, that on which Germany would attain her dream place in the sun. The mild and humorous doubt it expresses is no less civilized than endearing.

From these somewhat haphazard comments the intelligent could – and the amiable will – deduce or, at worst, admit that catch phrases, in the mass, may reflect a people's thought-ways and speech-ways and, in many particular examples, possess sociological and historical, as well as linguistic, value.

From
In His Own Words

Erica Jong
Fanny

Fear of Flying by the American writer Erica Jong was, according to its publisher, one of the ten bestselling novels of the 1970s: a highly provocative and energetic feminist novel set in the present. In Fanny, *however, she attempted something very different, a novel in the style of Fielding and set in 18th-century England. In this passage from half-way through the book, the heroine has just spent her first night in Mother Coxtart's notorious brothel.*

I fear that the World hath altogether a diff'rent Notion of my History from reading Mr. John Cleland's scandalous Book, *Memoirs of a Woman of Pleasure*, for which he stole my History, e'en my Christian Name; but being a Man, and a Man of very Eccentrick Understanding and Questionable Parts at that, he could not but sentimentalize my History, giving me an humble unlearnt Country Childhood (with Parents conveniently carried off by the Pox) and claiming that I met Mother Coxtart (whom he calls Brown – thus confusing her with another venerable Abbess of the Day) at a Registry Office where I had supposedly gone to seek a Place as a Chambermaid.

The dastardly Mr. Cleland, seeking nothing but to repay

his num'rous Debts by writing an Inflaming Book, and under-standing almost nothing of the Thoughts and Sensations of the Fair Sex, fashion'd from my Life a nauseously sugar'd Tale (as studded with Inflaming Scenes as a Plum Pudding with brandied Fruits) about a poor Country Girl who comes to the City, quite inadvertently becomes a Whore, but nonetheless is faithful at Heart (if not at some lower Organ) to her belovèd Charles, and becomes an honest Woman at the Last, con-cluding her Days in "the Bosom of Virtue" (as Mr. Cleland quaintly styles it).

That the Book was written by a credulous Man, not a canny Woman, may easily be seen by the excessive Attention Mr. Cleland pays to the Description of the Masculine Organ, for which he hath more Terms than Lancelot Robinson hath Names for the corresponding female one! Only a Man (and an indiff'rently-endow'd one at that) would dwell so inter-minably upon the Size and Endurance of sundry Peewees, Pillicocks, and Pricks – for a Woman hath better Things to do with her Reason and her Wit.

Be that as it may, I will soon have Occasion to tell you how I met Mr. Cleland and how the Blackguard came to steal my History. Suffice it for the present to say that not one Whit of his "Memoirs" is true, save the Christian Name of the Heroine, the bare Fact of her having been driven to a Life of Whoredom for a Time, and certain Features (tho' scarcely all) of the physical Description of his "Fanny."

Her Hair he describes as "glossy Auburn" – which, I suppose, is not too far off the Mark (tho' my Hair was e'er more red than brown). But "black Eyes" I ne'er had, nor was my Chin either cleft or pitted as he alleges, nor was I e'er in love with any Person named Charles!

All the most Curious and Compelling Facts of my Life – my Travels with the Merry Men, my Introduction to the Craft of the Witches, my Studious and Learnèd Childhood at Lymeworth, my Love of Latin and English Authors, my Perplexing Meditations on Philosophy – he saw fit to ignore (for a Man can ne'er understand that a Woman may be a sometime Whore and yet love Latin!), and he made me out instead a perfect Ninny.

By Jove! I resent his pallid Portrait by which the World *thinks* it knows me. Innocent of London's Wicked Ways, I may indeed have been when first he met me, but surely I was no simp'ring Idiot!

Alas, Belinda, most Men can only see us either as the Embodiment of Virtue or the Embodiment of Vice; either as

Bluestockings or Unlearnt, Painted Whores; either as Trollops or as Spinsters; as Wives or Wantons; as Good Widows or Bad Witches. But try to tell 'em, as I have, that a Woman is made of Sweets and Bitters, that she is both Reason and Rump, both Wit and Wantonness – and you will butt your Head against a stone Wall! They'll have it one Way or the other! Be clever, if you must, and forfeit Reputation for Beauty and Sensuality, as well as all Pleasures of the Flesh. Or have your Pleasures and your Loves – and in their Minds you'll always be a Witless Whore!

(By the by, 'tis not quite so in France, where Women of Beauty and of Brains are not unknown, and oft' the greatest Courtesans have been renown'd for Learning as well as Liquorishness. But here in Merry England, where the Men, I fear, are all a little queer, 'twill never wash!)

But on with my Tale.

I found myself, then, a Prisoner in Mother Coxtart's West End Brothel, a Prisoner of my Poverty, her watchful Eye (and the Eyes of the Girls and the Butler as well). Of Druscilla, Kate and the beauteous Evelina, you have already had a Taste; there were seven other Girls as well – altho' four of 'em were off in Buckinghamshire at a Private Revel and I was not to make their Acquaintance until later. Three more I met the following Day: Molly, Roxana, and Nell. Molly was very plump and blond, with a turn'd-up Nose and red Cheaks like a Milkmaid. Roxana was pale and dark and seem'd fore'er coughing in her Handkerchief. Nell was scrawny and plain, but as she was reputed to know devilish Tricks in Bed, she was much sought after nonetheless.

The first Morning I awoke in Bed beside Evelina. She was languid and lovely, and with her honey-colour'd Skin, she put one in mind, as I have said, of Tropick Isles; I made bold to strike up an Acquaintance by enquiring of her Birthplace.

"Martinique, Sweetheart," she replies, rolling o'er sleepily in Bed, "and I near caught me Death in London many a Time. The Weather here is *fierce*." She shiver'd as if to better make her Point. "What o' yer own pretty Self, Sweetheart?"

"Wiltshire."

"An' where's that?"

"'Tis a County to the West of here, methinks, but this being the first Time I am in London, and my Way here having been so curious and indirect, I cannot rightly say...."

"Oh," says Evelina, quite bor'd with my Geography, and plainly not wishing to hear more of my Travels.

"What brings you here across the Seas?" I ask.

"A Man, *bien sûr*," says she. "A wretchèd Englishman that promis'd me a fine Career upon the Stage, a Coach an' Six, an' all me Heart's Desires. He left me quick enough."

"And what of your Career upon the Stage?"

"Poo," says she, "the Managers hire their Mistresses first, an' the Roles fer Colour'd Wenches is few enough. A Touch o' the Tar Brush makes a merry Mistress, but a starvin' Player. Most Girls play once or twice, hopin' to snare some Duke fer their Keeper an' leave the Stage. 'Tis no Life fer a Lady."

"And what of this Life?"

"'Tis not so bad once ye learn to outwit the Old Bitch.

She's a sly one. She'll try to take yer Money fer yer Clothes an' Food before she'll let ye see a Penny. Ye must watch her like a Hawk. She keeps a little Book wherein she *says* she balances yer Keep 'gainst yer Take. Hah! Wait fer her to pay ye and ye'll starve in Hell! The Trick is to get paid *direct* – or have yer Swains put Clothin' on yer Back and Jewels 'round yer Neck. Then ye can fence 'em for some Cash. Some Girls got Swains who give 'em South Sea Stock, or Bank o' England Notes, or East India Bonds. That's good, but fer me own Part I have a Swain who says he'll set me up. I'll soon be out o' here an' into Keepin', God help me."

I listen'd intently to all this good Advice, wond'ring if Evelina truly had a loyal Swain or if she was merely dreaming.

——Clive James——
Fanny Dissected

Not long ago there was a popular novelist called Jeffrey Farnol, who is now entirely forgotten – which, when you think about it, is as long ago as you can get. Farnol wrote period novels in a narrative style full of e'ens, dosts, 'tises, and 'twases. Men wearing slashed doublets said things like 'Gadzooks!' in order to indicate that the action was taking place in days of yore. Farnol was manifestly shaky on the subject of when yore actually was, but he had a certain naïve energy and his books were too short to bore you. His masterpiece *The Jade of Destiny*, starring a lethal swordsman called Dinwiddie, can still be consumed in a single evening by anyone who has nothing better to do.

Erica Jong knows a lot more than Farnol ever did about our literary heritage and its social background. Her new book, which purports to be the true story, told in the first person, of the girl John Cleland made famous as Fanny Hill, draws on an extensive knowledge of eighteenth-century England. This is definitely meant to be a high-class caper. Nevertheless Jeffrey Farnol would recognize a fellow practitioner. There is something Gadzooks about the whole enterprise. On top of that it is intolerably long. Where Farnol's Dinwiddie, after skewering the heavies, would have made his bow and split, Jong's Fanny hangs around for hours.

Jong's Fanny, it turns out, would have been a writer if circumstances had not dictated otherwise. Circumstances are to be congratulated. Left to herself, Jong's Fanny would have covered more paper than Ruskin. There is something self-generating about her style.

> I wrote Tragedies in Verse and Noble Epicks, Romances in the French Style and Maxims modell'd upon La Rochefoucauld's. I wrote Satyres and Sonnets, Odes and Pastorals, Eclogues and Epistles. But nothing satisfied my most exalted Standards (which had been bred upon the Classicks), and at length I committed all my Efforts to the Fire. I wrote and burnt and wrote and burnt! I would pen a Pastoral thro'out three sleepless Nights only to commit it to the Flames! And yet were my Words not wasted, for ev'ry budding Poet, I discover'd, must spend a thousand Words for ev'ry one he saves, and Words are hardly wasted if, thro' one's Profligacy with 'em, one learns true Wit and true Expression of it.

Five hundred pages of that add up to a lot of apostrophes, i'faith. But the fault lies not with the 'tises and 'twases. A historical novel can survive any amount of inept decoration if it has some architecture underneath. Take, for example, Merejkovsky's *The Romance of Leonardo da Vinci*, in the learned but stylistically frolicsome translation by Bernard

Guilbert Guerney.

> 'Nay, nay, God forfend, – whatever art thou saying, Lucrezia! Come out to meet her? Thou knowest not what a woman this is! Oh, Lord, 'tis a fearful thing to think of the possible outcome of all this! Why, she is pregnant! . . . But do thou hide me – hide me! . . .'
> 'Really, I know not where. . . .'
> ' 'Tis all one, wherever thou wilt, – but with all speed!'

As transmitted to us by the industrious Guerney, Merejkovsky's Leonardo is every bit as noisy as Jong's Fanny. But *The Romance of Leonardo da Vinci* is a good novel in the ordinary sense and as a historical novel ranks among the greatest ever written. The characters and the action help you to penetrate history – they light up the past. Jong's Fanny makes the past darker. By the end of the book you know less about the eighteenth century than you did when you started.

Jong deserves some credit for trying to bring back yesterday, but what she is really doing, inadvertently, is helping to make you feel even worse about today. She uses pornography to preach a feminist message. This is a peculiarly modern confusion of motives. At least Cleland had the grace to leave out the philosophizing, although it should be remembered that those few general remarks which he put in were more pertinent in every way than anything which his successor has to offer. Here is Cleland's Fanny at a critical moment.

> And now! now I felt to the heart of me! I felt the prodigious keen edge with which love, presiding over this act, points the pleasure: love! that may be styled the Attic salt of enjoyment; and indeed, without it, the joy, great as it is, is still a vulgar one, whether in a king or a beggar; for it is, undoubtedly, love alone that refines, ennobles and exalts it.

Admittedly Cleland's prose has been somewhat neatened up for modern publication, but you can still see that even in its original state it must have been a less strained instrument than that wielded by Jong's Fanny. Cleland has other points of superiority too. For one thing, his pornographic scenes are actually quite effective. Indeed they are too effective, since pornography exceeds requirements if it makes you want to know the girl. Cleland's *Fanny Hill* might not strike women as a book written from the woman's viewpoint, but it can easily strike men that way. The book's concern is with women's pleasure, not men's. Cleland's Fanny does a powerfully affecting job of evoking what a woman's pleasure is like, or at any rate what a man who likes women would like to think a woman's pleasure is like. She leaves a man sorry for not having met her.

For Jong's Fanny, whose full name is Fanny Hackabout-Jones ('Fannikins to lovers besotted with her charms'), the same cannot be said. She is a bore from page one. Even in moments of alleged transport she has one eye on her literary prospects. You just know that she will one day write *Fear of Flying*. One of her early encounters is with Alexander Pope. Erica – Fanny, sorry – tries to interest Pope in her verses, but he is interested only in her breasts. Pope is but the first of several famous men who make themselves ridiculous by pursuing Jong's Fanny. (Swift involves her in a threesome with a horse.) All they see, you see, is Fannikins's cunnikin. Passion blinds them to her attainments as a philosopher.

And yet, clearly, 'twas not the Best of all Possible Worlds for Women – unless, as Mr. Pope had argu'd, there was a hidden Justice behind this Veil of seeming Injustice. . . . Fie on't! 'Twas not possible that God should approve such goings-on! A Pox on the Third Earl of Shaftesbury and his damnable Optimism!

Running away from home, Jong's Fanny falls in with a coven of witches. The witches, you will not be surprised to learn, are prototype feminists. They are given names like Isobel and Joan in order to allay your suspicions that they are really called Germaine and Kate.

'Fanny, my Dear,' says Isobel, 'let me tell you my Opinion concerning Witchcraft and then Joan can tell you hers. 'Tis my Belief that in Ancient Times, in the Pagan Albion of Old, Women were not as they are now, subservient to Men in ev'ry Respect. . . .'
'E'en the very word "Witch,"' Joan interrupted,

'derives from our Ancestors' Word "Wicca," meaning only "Wise Woman."'

Isobel lookt cross. 'Are you quite finish'd, Joan?' says she. 'Will you hold your Tongue now and let me speak?'

An oppressive male chauvinist society makes sure that these pioneer women's liberationists are appropriately raped and tortured, but meanwhile Jong's Fanny has become installed in a London brothel, where she shows an unusual talent for the trade. Colly Cibber's son ties her to the bed ('Now I am truly trapp'd in my own Snares, my Arms and Legs spread wide upon the Bed so I can make no Resistance, my Ankles and Wrists chafing 'gainst the Silver Cords.') Then he enters her. ('. . . Theo's Privy Member makes its Presence felt near my not quite unsullied Altar of Love.') Then he does something I can't quite figure out. ('He sinks upon me with all his Weight and wraps his bandy Legs 'round my own. . . .') How bandy can a man be?

Jong seems to take it for granted that a woman's lust can be aroused against her will, if only her assailant presses the right buttons – a very male chauvinist assumption, one would have thought. Cleland's Fanny was more discriminating. But then, Cleland's Fanny knew her own feelings. Jong makes Cleland one of her Fanny's literary lovers. Jong's Cleland is interested in role swapping and has a propensity for climbing into drag. Thus Jong lays the ghost of Cleland's commendable success in fleshing out a feminine character. She says that *he* had a feminine character. Perhaps so, but what he mainly had was imagination.

Jong's Fanny is meant to be an edifying joke, but the joke is not funny and the edification is not instructive, although it is frequently revealing. Setting out to show up Cleland, Jong unintentionally declares herself his inferior. As to the pornography, Cleland knew when to stop: his Fanny always concedes, while describing the moment of ecstasy, that beyond a certain point words fail her. Words fail Jong's Fanny at all times, but she never stops pouring them out. Finally the sheer disproportion of the enterprise is the hardest thing to forgive.

I quite liked *Fear of Flying*: there was the promise of humor in it, if not the actuality. But in this book, which sets out to be light, comic, and picaresque, everything is undone by an utter inability to compress, allude, or elide. Is Peter de Vries to be the last author in America of short serious books that make you laugh? Joseph Heller's *Good as Gold* is at least twice as long as it should be. By the time you get down to Erica there seems to be no awareness at all of the mark to aim at. If Max Beerbohm couldn't sustain *Zuleika Dobson*, how did Erica expect to keep Fanny going for triple the distance on a tenth the talent? I'faith, 'tis a Puzzle beyond my Comprehension.

From
The New York Review of Books

Peter De Vries
Columbine

It is Columbine, standing beside my bed with a nutritive goodie, a bowl of custard no less, let in by my mother who then retires deferentially, closing the door soundlessly behind her as she slips away like an Oriental servant, or pretending to have slipped away, because she is listening outside with her head cocked for every word, like an Oriental servant. She is herself shaken by continuing rumors that she is a Turk. Could they be not entirely unfounded . . . ?

Colly is now four years older than when first frightened by cosmic monstrosity, perceptibly rounding, not quite so tuning-forkish yet vibrant to wind and wave. Some of her verses attest it. The oval face tapers delicately to a firm chin, one that a good bone structure tells the speculating youth that at forty it will be unwattled. The eyes are chocolate pastilles. This is good. But why does she part her auburn hair from the middle outward and downward, like those New England spinsters who in portrait oils come down to us so resembling spaniels?

'What's the matter with you, Uncle Punk?'

One had played Puck in a high-school production of *A Midsummer Night's Dream*, well enough for the nickname to have stuck for a while. Its corruption by louts and dolts made one grit one's teeth. With the courtesy 'uncle' of Columbine's, hung over from the days when the difference in our ages might have accommodated a note of sportive respect, the combination was something dismal to a degree.

'What's psyching you out?'

What could I tell her that she didn't already know? The sun would burn out in AD 47,000,000,000, by which time the rest of the solar system and we with it would be uncountable millennia down the Dispose-All. Such things no longer bothered Colly, who was through her crisis and in the bloom of happiness that would, according to Russell, in some version again be mine as well, once I had crawled on my epistemological belly through this hideous cave each of us must traverse before gaining the garden of chastened acceptance awaiting us on the other side. Each of us, unless totally bovine, has got to eat some despair. It is written. We must sooner or later be trundled into surgery for what her brother and my good friend Ambrose called an illusionectomy. It's either that or the lobotomy performed by some religion or other. So ran Ambrose's remorseless options.

'You really look like hell. I mean what's got you spooked out?'

Why, the inexcusable distance from Betelgeuse to Potlatch, Idaho. What else?

She was absorbing the slang of the day with great speed, with whatever that might imply in the way of burgeoning suitability for oneself; so that like Proust's narrator reaching out from *his* bed to gather Albertine in on the strength of the same evidence – the use of a few reassuring expressions in rapid succession – I impulsively put my hand out to take hers when, bending over me, she murmured, 'Hang tough, Unc Punk.' There were to be literary echoes of quite another kind as well.

Twitching back from my touch, she went to the door and jerked it open with an abruptness that sent my possibly Ottoman mother scuttling, fetched a spoon from the kitchen downstairs, returned, then sat sidesaddle on the bed and force-fed me the custard, like Leonard Woolf getting a little something into Virginia, once again prostrated by the approaching publication date of a new book, with its attendant terror of what reviewers would say of it, and of her. It made her literally ill. Later our sweetling fixed me some hot tea, the cup again cackling when I lifted it from the saucer. I could smell the soap in which she had just bathed. 'You're twenty and she's fourteen, for God's sake,' I said to myself, closing my eyes as again I inhaled her fragrance. 'Do you want to go to prison?' Made librarian, liked by the warden, up for parole . . .

'Remember the night you showed me the – what were those meteorites again?'

'The Orionids.'

'How scared I was? It might be fun to look for some more of those fireworks through your telescope.' I groaned something in the negative. Colly pinched my great toe through the covers. 'Ambrose thinks he can help you. He had the schmerks himself once. Got unbalanced reading too much philosophy. I didn't realize, you know, men, um, can go through a mental crisis like that. I thought it had to be loss of *religious* faith sent you bonkers.'

'Then you do know what this is all about.'

'I wanted to hear it from you. Anyway, remember what Shakespeare said.'

'What was that?'

'I dunno.' She laughed. 'Isn't there something in Shakespeare for every occasion? Well, you read too much. You and Ambrose both.'

'You're very sweet, Colly,' I said, ashamed of the foxfire in my loins again. Parole denied, demoted to punch press operator, shunned by the other prisoners . . .

'Thanks. Well, hang in there, Punk. I know you can get yourself nailed together.'

A milestone in our personal relations almost slipped by unnoticed. She had dropped the Uncle foolishness. I didn't realize it until she was gone.

From
Consenting Adults

Martin Amis
Mary

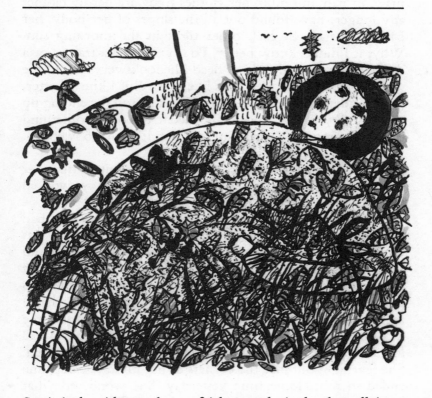

Statistical evidence shows fairly conclusively that all 'amnesiacs' are at least partially aware of what they're missing out on. They know that they do not know. They remember that they do not remember, which is a start. But that doesn't apply to *her*, *oh* no.

Of course, the initial stage is always the most difficult in a case like this. I'm pleased, actually. No, I am. We've got phase one over with, and she has survived quite creditably. Between ourselves, this isn't my style at all really. The choice wasn't truly mine, although I naturally exercise a degree of control. It had to be like this. As I said earlier, she *asked* for it. . . . So what have we here?

A rising stretch of London parkland, a silver birch tree crooked over a shiny hollow, a girl in the recent dew. The time is 7.29 a.m., the temperature 51° Fahrenheit. Over her body the wind-dried leaves click their tongues – and no wonder. What in hell has happened to the girl? Her face is made of hair and mud, her clothes (they are hardly clothes any longer) have found out all the slopes of her body, her bare thighs clutch each other tight in the morning sun. Why, if I didn't know better, I'd say she was a tramp, or a ditched whore, or drunk, or dead (she looks very near to the state of nature: I've seen girls like that). But I know better, and, besides, people usually have good reason for ending up the way they do. Whatever happened to this one? Something did. Let's move in closer. Let's find out. It's time to wake up.

Her eyes opened and she saw the sky. For quite a time her thoughts insisted on being simultaneous. They worked themselves out like this.

At first she didn't know where she was or how she had got there. She assumed that that was what memory was doing to her, subtracting day after day so that she would always have to start from the beginning, and never get ahead. Then she remembered the day before and (this was probably an earlier thought, the second thought perhaps) the day before reminded her of the idea of memory and the fact that she had lost hers. And she had lost it, she had still lost it, and she still didn't know what exactly this entailed. She sent light out into the corners of her mind . . . but time ended in mist, some time yesterday. She wondered what happened when you lost it, your memory. Where did it go, and was it lost for good or were you meant to be able to find it again? Well, here I still am, she thought finally; at least I haven't died or anything like that. Something about sleep worried her, but she let it pass. And even she could tell it was a beautiful day.

She sat up, testing her wet senses, and blinking at the light that had made the long journey back again while she had slept. Small but influential creatures were screaming at her from above. She looked up – and realized she could name things. It was simple, just a trick of the mind's eye. She knew the name for the birds; she could subdivide them too, to some extent (sparrows, a hooded crow staring at her humourlessly); she could even loosely connect them with memories of the day before: the jumpy, thin-shouldered, frowning, supplicant dogs, a long cat flexing its claws on the glass of a shop window. She wasn't sure how things worked or what they had to do with each other, how alive they all were, or where she fitted in among them. But she could name things, and she was pleased. Perhaps everything was simpler than she thought.

As soon as she stood up she saw them. In the middle distance over the damp green land there was a wasted, scattered area against a line of forgotten buildings. Other people were there, some standing, some still lying flummoxed on the floor, some sitting in a close huddle. For a moment she felt the squeeze of fear and a reflex urged her to hide again; but she was too pleased and too weary, and she had an inkling that nothing mattered anyway, her own thoughts or life itself. She started to move towards them. How bad at walking she was. They seemed to be people of the fifth and second kinds, which was encouraging in its way.

As she limped into the slow range of their sight, one of them turned and seemed to eye her coolly, without surprise. Even at this distance their faces gave off a glow of distemper, suggesting rapid changeability beneath the skin. She was getting nearer. They did not turn to confront her although some knew she was coming.

'Mary had a little lamb,' one of them was saying in a mechanical voice not directed at her, '– its face was white as snow . . .'

She came nearer. They could harm her now if they liked. But nothing had happened yet, and it occurred to her exhaustedly that she could probably walk among them as she pleased (for what it was worth), that indeed she was condemned to move among the living without exciting any notice at all.

Then one of them turned and said, 'Come on, who are you?'

'Mary,' she lied quickly.

'I'm Modo. That's Rosie.'

'Neville,' another said.

'Hopdance,' said the fourth.

'Come on then, come in the warmth.'

With nonchalance, with relief, they included her among

themselves. She sat on their square grill, beneath which a vast subterranean machine thrashed itself rhythmically for their heat.

'Here, wet your whistle, Mary. Keep the cold out,' said Neville, handing her a shiny brown bottle. She tasted its spit and fizz before Rosie claimed it.

Neville went on, to no one in particular, 'Twenty-two years of age, I was one of the top six travellers for Littlewoods. My own car, the lot. They wanted to do a, an article on me in the papers. But I said – no, I don't want no publicity.'

'No, you don't want no publicity,' agreed Rosie sternly.

'You can keep your publicity, mate. That's what I told them.'

'Publicity . . . ? Hah!' said Hopdance, then shook his head, as if that settled publicity's fate once and for all.

She resolved to be on the lookout for publicity. It was obviously a very bad thing if it was to be so vigilantly shunned even here . . . She peered at them through their hot breath. Their skin was numb and luminous, but all their eyes were ice. I'm one of them, she thought, and perhaps I always

have been. And as she looked from face to face, sensing the varieties of damage which each wore, she guessed that there were probably only two kinds of people. There were only two kinds of people: it was just that all kinds of things could happen to them.

Correct: but only as far as it goes. (I generally find I've got some explaining to do, particularly during the early stages.) These people are tramps, after all.

You know the kind of people I mean. The reason they are tramps is that they have no money. The reason they have no money is that they won't sell anything, which is what nearly everyone else does. You sell something, don't you, I'm sure? I know I do. Why don't they? Tramps just don't want to sell what other people sell – they just don't want to sell their time.

Selling time, time sold: that's the business we're all in. We sell our time, but they keep theirs, but they don't get any money, but they think about money all the time. It's an odd way of going about things, being a tramp. Tramps like it, though. Being a tramp is increasingly popular, statistics show. There are more and more tramps doing without money all the time.

I'm obliged to deal with these sort of people fairly frequently. In a sense it's inevitable in my line of work. I'd far rather not, of course: they're always wasting my time. I'd avoid them if I were you. You're much better off that way.

From
Other People: A Mystery Story

John Seymour
Dropping In

The science of 'self-sufficiency' has recently been propounded and championed by John Seymour in a series of books, several of which have been enormously popular. In Getting it Together *he provides a step-by-step guide to dropping out of the rat race and setting up your own self-sufficient smallholding.*

Well, here we are, stuck on our muddy holding miles out in the countryside, we've got our food producing together, we've found a way to earn some filthy money, we have a roof over our heads and some stock and equipment. We also have, if I am not mistaken, quite a large overdraft at the bank.

But there has to be more to life than simply producing your own food and eating it and paying off your overdraft.

Of course, there's procreation. Whatever else the new settlers are doing, they certainly seem to be doing plenty of that. And it can be argued that if a woman or a man lives honestly, pays for what she or he gets, rears up some fine, healthy children and hands the torch of what she or he knows on to them, then she or he is serving the life force. Such people may not have contributed to the progress of life towards the Divine, but at least they have kept open the option that such a development might happen in the future.

When you retire to the country and spend at least part of your life in simple and manual pursuits, you find yourself far better able to take stock of the way civilisation has gone in the great world beyond the boundary of your holding. Your holding itself becomes your real world, therefore you look at the other, lesser world beyond your fences with a dispassionate eye and can understand it better than you could when you were immersed in it yourself.

If I am not very mistaken you come to understand that that world out there is a very sad and sick world indeed. There you are, in your little kingdom, striving with all your strength to husband and nurture the life force – and out there you see vast human forces doing all that they can to destroy it. You see the napalm bombing of the Brazilian forests carried out to achieve financial profits for a few wicked men; the murder of the last of the world's great fish stocks to provide fish-meal for the feeding of battery hens and broiler chicks; the slaughter of the noble whale to provide perfume for silly women and food for their pet dogs; the covering of the green surface of the earth with tarmac and concrete; the corruption of the world's peasants – the only people who have been leading lives which nurture and do not damage the life of the earth. You see the insatiable agribusinessmen striving to destroy every form of life on vast acreages in order to favour their one profit-making crop; you see apparently honest and sane scientists following lines of research that they *know* will probably lead to the destruction of all life; you see nuclear engineers and physicists who know perfectly well, deep down in some well-suppressed part of their minds, that what they are doing will maim and destroy future generations and yet they do it for salary and pension – they do it to pay their childrens' school fees at expensive schools knowing full well that their grandchildren and great-grandchildren will have to pay the price in mutilation and misery; you see the 'civilised' nations engaging in an unseemly scramble to sell increasingly vicious weapons to the foolish leaders of the so-called 'Third World'.

The list goes on and is apparently endless. And you come to realise that post-industrial man has gone mad. Materialism; humanism (the worship of mankind) – these religions, for black religions they are, have led men down a dark and desperate path. Our leaders tell us we must have nuclear power because without it we will have to freeze in the dark. In other words we may, if we do not have it, have to put up with a little less warmth, a little less comfort, a little less 'growth'. Our governments are all committed to 'growth'. What is this 'growth'. Is it the growth of the human spirit, the growth of the true moral and spiritual stature of mankind? It is not. It is the growth of the proliferation of rubbish, and to proliferate the rubbish it is necessary to rape our mother, the earth.

Therefore we *drop-ins* – we who drop into a saner and less exploitive kind of life – have a terrifying responsibility. We must be content with nothing less than with building a new civilisation – a new world order. It is when men are crammed into huge conurbations that they become sick and dangerous to the rest of the biosphere. The tiny handful that are left on the deserted acres outside are driven into raping the land to provide ever more food for the parasitic wens (the word wen means a cancer). Man becomes a destructive parasite on the earth. In all the truly golden ages of mankind towns and cities have been of a humane size – flowerings, as it were, of rural cultures. Townsmen have had their roots in the family acres not far away. It is when people are cut off from these roots and survive rootless in the great brick, tarmac and concrete jungles that they lose their way.

The life force knows what to do with the species that have become purely destructive and have lost their purpose for her aims. It may be that the species that used to be called *Homo sapiens*, and that has now become *Homo destructens*, is due for the chop anyway. If so, so be it. Other forms will arise which will carry on the purposes of the life force. But, as humans, it is right that we should resist this end.

So the return to our birthright is more than just selfish and practical: it is religious. This is the only word we have to describe it, whether we believe in a God or not. In pure urban materialism mankind has gone up a blind alley – an alley that will end up by destroying him if he persists in trying to follow its course. There is no way of telling how many other species of life he will take with him to destruction. In the long run it probably does not matter. If all life were destroyed on this planet tomorrow more life would evolve, unless something happened to the earth. Time stretches far enough for there to be a thousand more attempts by the life force to evolve life on this planet, nurture it, and have it, finally, destroy itself yet again through selfishness and greed. After a thousand attempts perhaps one will succeed.

But this consideration should not affect us in the least. We have only one duty (and only one true pleasure, which lies in the performance of this duty), and that is to work to further the purposes of the life force. It may not always be easy to see in which way the performance of this duty lies. Often we may find ourselves perplexed. Pure reason – reason alone – is never enough to show us the right way. Reason must be reinforced and informed by something else, too. I have read that we have two halves to our cerebrum: a left side and a right side. The left side has been developed to unprecedented heights; the right side completely ignored. It is the neglect of the right side that has made us mad, that has made us blind and insensitive and aware only of our own selfish needs – the selfish needs of man alone. It is this that has led us into the most dangerous heresy yet held – the heresy that our species is something apart from nature. If God did indeed give man 'dominion over the beasts of the field and the birds of the air', as is written in the Bible, he did not mean us to use this dominion unreasonably and unlawfully. All right, we who belong to small areas of the earth's surface have dominion over the animals and plants on them, at least up to a certain point. We are, to that extent, kings of our kingdoms. But the good king rules *for the sake of his subjects*. He is their servant. We must learn these two rules: *it is the land which owns the husbandman, not the husbandman who owns the land; and the king is the servant of his subjects.*

Man is part of nature just as a robin is. If man tries to 'conquer nature' he will destroy himself because it is something of which he is a part.

It is probably possible to persuade intelligent people that the above statements are true by reason alone. Reason alone will lead people to realise that it will not be possible to store radioactive material safely for a hundred thousand years (while adding to the store all the time); reason alone will tell anybody that it cannot be right to keep dousing our planet with hellish chemicals that poison life, and that any agent that harms one form of life will harm another. But, alas, reason alone will not cause us to act in the right manner and forego these things.

We who return to our birthright, the land, are in a position that is rapidly becoming rare on this planet in that we have time and space to cultivate that part of our brain that has been suppressed by materialism. We can cultivate our power of feeling and being as well as our power of knowing and reasoning. As we hoe our turnips the reasoning part of our minds takes a rest and we can allow our being to be truly aware of the fields around us, and the woods, and the marshes and the hills, and the life in these things, and to feel that we are part of this life, not a special part but just a part, and that our reason has been given to us so that we may play our part well and honestly to further the purposes of the life force.

Books, words, reasoning – these things can never develop this consciousness in us. Hoeing turnips, lovingly nurturing plants and animals (aye, and as lovingly killing and eating them occasionally – it's all part of the role of the true husband-man: the lion husbands the wild zebra and the bison husbands the prairie grass), watching and *feeling* the turn of the seasons, *feeling* the life-and-death-and-life-and-death that goes on all around us, for ever and ever, and that we are part of it. These activities and non-activities can reawaken our hearts and spirits and enable us to see the universe with the inner eye. You think that the five senses of which you are mentally aware tell you the truth, nothing but the truth, and the whole truth? Do not believe it. Certain limited aspects of the truth, yes, but the whole truth – no! And until a large section of mankind becomes capable of perceiving the whole truth again and not just the less important aspects of it, we have every reason to despair of the hopes for the future of life on this planet. And we will not become capable just as long as we live insulated from the rest of nature by glass and concrete, plastic and tarmac, and our own insatiable materialistic greed.

So let us come back to our birthright: let us repair the ruined smallholdings and cottages, and build new ones, and bring such pressure to bear on our 'masters' – on the great know-all government – as will cause the release of the empty acres for the good purposes of nature and of mankind.

I do not advocate that we should all be self-sufficient small-holders. But let us practise our various skills and trades and professions not cut off entirely from the rest of nature, but affected by her throughout our lives. Even suffer the cold and the heat and the wet and the drought? Yes! The blind and insensitive men who keep birds and animals in Belsen houses tell us that these creatures are happy because 'they are always at optimum temperature'. They know not what they are talking about. All forms of life that exist on this planet, including hens, were *evolved* (or *created*, if that is your theology) to withstand heat and cold, wet and drought. We were, too. I would rather be crippled with rheumatism in my old age and know that I had really lived in the real world as a human being was meant to live than be cossetted all my life with air conditioning in overheated office or factory buildings and never know what it is to suffer – and to glory in – 'the heat o' the sun and the furious winter's rages'.

Judaean theology tells us that God put Adam and Eve into the Garden of Eden to 'dress it and keep it'. Just imagine what this world could be like if the whole of humankind did just that – if people spread out over the land again, and each one strove with all his might and main to turn his little bit of it (at least the little bit *that he belonged to*) into a small part of Paradise.

Imagine a land in which the towns and cities were the true flowerings of a fruitful and happy countryside, in which the countryside was husbanded as it should be husbanded – by men and women and not with huge machines and poisonous chemicals – in small plots, each bearing the imprint of some individual or small group of individuals – with gardens and orchards and arable land and pasture and woodland and wilderness all mixed in happy, fruitful confusion – with the homes of husbandmen forming a natural part of the landscape – with happy, free children laughing and playing, working with their elders, and learning real things in a real way, not cooped up for the best part of their childhood in dreary classrooms having their minds mutilated and maimed by pedagogues.

Why are our present conurbations (I cannot bring myself to call them by that beautiful word *city*), our existing *wens*, so hideously ugly? – because they were built for ignoble ends. Every building in them was built for one reason only – to make a rich man richer. The humble cottages of peasants, the village churches, the great cathedrals, the majestic barns, the fine, timber-framed villages of the honest weavers, the splendid sailing ships – all these things were built, even though perhaps the builders didn't know it, for the glory of God.

You cannot have a noble artifact if it is created for an ignoble end.

I prophesy that in a thousand years' time, if humans still roam this earth, some of them will visit, occasionally, the ruins of London and New York and Birmingham and Tokyo, and stand and stare and wonder, and say: 'Is it possible that there were men and women who could actually put up with this?'

From
Getting it Together

Henry David Thoreau
Self-Sufficiency

Near the end of March 1845 I borrowed an axe and went down to the woods by Walden Pond, nearest to where I intended to build my house, and began to cut down some tall arrowy white pines, still in their youth, for timber. It is difficult to begin without borrowing, but perhaps it is the most generous course thus to permit your fellow-men to have an interest in your enterprise. The owner of the axe, as he released his hold on it, said that it was the apple of his eye; but I returned it sharper than I received it. It was a pleasant hillside where I worked, covered with pine woods, through which I looked out on the pond, and a small open field in the woods where pines and hickories were springing up. The ice in the pond was not yet dissolved, though there were some open spaces, and it was all dark-coloured and saturated with water. There were some slight flurries of snow during the day that I worked there; but for the most part when I came out on to the railroad, on my way home, its yellow sand heap stretched away gleaming in the hazy atmosphere, and the rails shone in the spring sun, and I heard the lark and peewee and other birds already come to commence another year with us. They were pleasant spring days, in which the winter of man's discontent was thawing as well as the earth, and the life that had lain torpid began to stretch itself. One day, when my axe had come off and I had cut a green hickory for a wedge, driving it with a stone, and had placed the whole to soak in a pond hole in order to swell the wood, I saw a striped snake run into the water, and he lay on the bottom, apparently without inconvenience, as long as I staid there, or more than a quarter-of-an-hour; perhaps because he had not yet fairly come out of the torpid state. It appeared to me that for a like reason men remain in their present low and primitive condition; but if they should feel the influence of the spring of springs arousing them, they would of necessity rise to a higher and more ethereal life. I had previously seen the snakes in frosty mornings in my path with portions of their bodies still numb and inflexible, waiting for the sun to thaw them. On the 1st of April it rained and melted the ice, and in the early part of the day, which was very foggy, I heard a stray goose groping about over the pond and cackling as if lost, or like the spirit of the fog.

So I went on for some days cutting and hewing timber, and also studs and rafters, all with my narrow axe, not having many communicable or scholar-like thoughts, singing to myself, –

'Men say they know many things;
But lo! they have taken wings, –
The arts and sciences,
And a thousand appliances;
The wind that blows
Is all that anybody knows.'

I hewed the main timbers six inches square, most of the studs on two sides only, and the rafters and floor timbers on one side, leaving the rest of the bark on, so that they were just as straight and much stronger than sawed ones. Each stick was carefully mortised or tenoned by its stump, for I had borrowed other tools by this time. My days in the woods were not very long ones; yet I usually carried my dinner of bread and butter, and read the newspaper in which it was wrapped, at noon, sitting amid the green pine boughs which I had cut off, and to my bread was imparted some of their fragrance, for my hands were covered with a thick coat of pitch. Before I had done I was more the friend than the foe of the pine tree, though I had cut down some of them, having become better acquainted with it. Sometimes a rambler in the wood was attracted by the sound of my axe, and we chatted pleasantly over the chips which I made.

By the middle of April, for I made no haste in my work, but rather made the most of it, my house was framed and ready for the raising. I had already bought the shanty of James Collins, an Irishman who worked on the Fitchburg Railroad, for boards. James Collins' shanty was considered an uncommonly fine one. When I called to see it he was not at home. I walked about the outside, at first unobserved from within, the window was so deep and high. It was of small dimensions, with a peaked cottage roof, and not much else to be seen, the dirt being raised five feet all round as if it were a compost heap. The roof was the soundest part, though a good deal warped and made brittle by the sun. Doorsill there was none, but a perennial passage for the hens under the door board. Mrs. C. came to the door and asked me to view it from the inside. The hens were driven in by my approach. It was dark, and had a dirt floor for the most part, dank, clammy, and aguish, only here a board and there a board which would not bear removal. She lighted a lamp to show me the inside of the roof and the walls, and also that the board floor extended under the bed, warning me not to step into the cellar, a sort of dust-hole two feet deep. In her own words, they were 'good boards overhead, good boards all around, and a good window,' – of two whole squares originally, only the cat had passed out that way lately. There was a stove, a bed, and a place to sit, an infant in the house where it was born, a silk parasol, gilt-framed looking-glass, and a patent new coffee-mill nailed to an oak sapling, all told. The bargain was soon concluded, for James had in the meanwhile returned. I to pay four dollars and twenty-five cents to-night, he to vacate at five to-morrow morning, selling to nobody else meanwhile: I to take possession at six. It were well, he said, to be there early, and anticipate certain indistinct but wholly unjust claims on the score of ground-rent and fuel. This he assured me was the only encumbrance. At six I passed him and his family on the road. One large bundle held their all, – bed, coffee-mill, looking-glass, hens, – all but the cat; she took to the woods and became a wild cat, and, as I learned afterward, trod in a trap set for woodchucks, and so became a dead cat at last.

I took down this dwelling the same morning, drawing the nails, and removed it to the pond-side by small cartloads, spreading the boards on the grass there to bleach and warp back again in the sun. One early thrush gave me a note or two as I drove along the woodland path. I was informed treacherously by a young Patrick that neighbour Seeley, an Irishman, in the intervals of the carting, transferred the still tolerable, straight, and drivable nails, staples, and spikes to his pocket, and then stood when I came back to pass the time of day, and look freshly up, unconcerned, with spring thoughts, at the devastation; there being a dearth of work, as he said. He was there to represent spectatordom, and help make this seemingly insignificant event one with the removal of the gods of Troy.

I dug my cellar in the side of a hill sloping to the south, where a woodchuck had formerly dug his burrow, down through sumach and blackberry roots, and the lowest stain of vegetation, six feet square by seven deep, to a fine sand where potatoes would not freeze in any winter. The sides were left shelving, and not stoned; but the sun having never shone on them, the sand still keeps its place. It was but two hours' work. I took particular pleasure in this breaking of ground, for in almost all latitudes men dig into the earth for an equable temperature. Under the most splendid house in the city is still to be found the cellar where they store their roots as of old, and long after the superstructure has disappeared posterity remark its dent in the earth. The house is still but a sort of porch at the entrance of a burrow.

At length, at the beginning of May, with the help of some of my acquaintances, rather to improve so good an occasion for neighbourliness than from any necessity, I set up the frame of my house. No man was ever more honoured in the character of his raisers than I. They are destined, I trust, to assist at the raising of loftier structures one day. I began to occupy my house on the 4th of July, as soon as it was boarded and roofed, for the boards were carefully feather-edged and lapped, so that it was perfectly impervious to rain, but before boarding I laid the foundation of a chimney at one end, bringing two cartloads of stones up the hill from the pond in my arms. I built the chimney after my hoeing in the fall, before a fire became necessary for warmth, doing my cooking in the meanwhile out of doors on the ground, early in the morning; which mode I still think is in some respects more convenient and agreeable than the usual one. When it stormed before my bread was baked, I fixed a few boards over the fire, and sat under them to watch my loaf, and passed some pleasant hours in that way. In those days, when my hands were much employed, I read but little, but the least scraps of paper which lay on the ground, my holder, or tablecloth, afforded me as much entertainment; in fact, answered the same purpose as the *Iliad*.

It would be worth the while to build still more deliberately than I did, considering, for instance, what foundation a door, a window, a cellar, a garret, have in the nature of man, and perchance never raising any superstructure until we found a better reason for it than our temporal necessities even. There is some of the same fitness in a man's building his own house that there is in a bird's building its own nest. Who knows but if men constructed their dwellings with their own hands, and provided food for themselves and families simply and honestly enough, the poetic faculty would be universally developed, as birds universally sing when they are so engaged? But alas! we do like cow-birds and cuckoos, which lay their eggs in nests which other birds have built, and cheer no traveller with their chattering and unmusical notes. Shall we forever resign the pleasure of construction to the carpenter? What does architecture amount to in the experience of the mass of men? I never in all my walks came across a man engaged in so simple and natural an occupation as building his house. We belong to the community. It is not the tailor alone who is the ninth part of a man: it is as much the preacher, and the merchant, and the farmer. Where is this division of labour to end? and what object does it finally serve? No doubt another *may* also think for me; but it is not therefore desirable that he should do so to the exclusion of my thinking for myself.

True, there are architects so-called in this country, and I have heard of one at least possessed with the idea of making architectural ornaments have a core of truth, a necessity, and hence a beauty, as if it were a revelation to him. All very well perhaps from his point of view, but only a little better than the common dilettantism. A sentimental reformer in architecture, he began at the cornice, not at the foundation. It was only how to put a core of truth within the ornaments, that every sugar plum in fact might have an almond or caraway seed in it, – though I hold that almonds are most wholesome without the sugar, and not how the inhabitant, the indweller, might build truly within and without, and let the ornaments take care of themselves. What reasonable man ever supposed that ornaments were something outward and in the skin merely, – that the tortoise got his spotted shell, or the shell-fish its mother-of-pearl tints, by such a contract as the inhabitants of Broadway their Trinity Church? But a man has no more to do with the style of architecture of his house than a tortoise with that of its shell: nor need the soldier be so idle as to try to paint the precise *colour* of his virtue on his standard. The enemy will find it out. He may turn pale when the trial comes. This man seemed to me to lean over the cornice, and timidly whisper his half truth to the rude occupants who really knew it better than he. What of architectural beauty I now see, I know has gradually grown from within outward, out of the necessities and character of the indweller, who is the only builder, – out of some unconscious truthfulness, and nobleness, without ever a thought for the appearance; and whatever additional beauty of this kind is destined to be produced will be preceded by a like unconscious beauty of life. The most interesting dwellings in this country, as the painter knows, are the most unpretending, humble log huts and cottages of the poor commonly; it is the life of the inhabitants whose shells they are, and not any peculiarity in these surfaces merely, which makes them *picturesque*; and equally interesting will be the citizen's suburban box, when his life shall be as simple and as agreeable to the imagination, and there is as little straining after effect in the style of his dwelling. A great proportion of architectural ornaments are literally hollow, and a September gale would strip them off, like borrowed plumes, without injury to the substantials. They can do without *architecture* who have no olives nor wines in the cellar. What if an equal ado were made about the ornaments of style in literature, and the architects of our Bibles spent as much time about their cornices as the architects of our churches do? So are made the *belles-lettres* and the *beaux-arts* and their professors. Much it concerns a man, forsooth, how a few sticks are slanted over him or under him, and what colours are daubed upon his box. It would signify somewhat, if, in any earnest sense, *he* slanted them and daubed it; but the spirit having departed out of the tenant, it is of a piece with constructing his own coffin, – the architecture of the grave and 'carpenter' is but another name for 'coffin-maker.' One man says, in his despair or indifference to life, 'Take up a handful of the earth at your feet, and paint your house that colour.' Is he thinking of his last and narrow house? Toss up a copper for it as well. What an abundance of leisure he must have! Why do you take up a handful of dirt? Better paint your house your own complexion; let it turn pale or blush for you. An enterprise to improve the style of cottage architecture! When you have got my ornaments ready I will wear them.

Before winter I built a chimney, and shingled the sides of my house, which were already impervious to rain, with imperfect and sappy shingles made of the first slice of the log, whose edges I was obliged to straighten with a plane.

I have thus a tight shingled and plastered house, ten feet wide by fifteen long, eight-feet posts, with a garret and a closet, a large window on each side, two trapdoors, one door at the end, and a brick fire-place opposite. The exact cost of my house, paying the usual price for such materials as I used, but not counting the work, all of which was done by myself, was as follows: and I give the details because very few are able to tell exactly what their houses cost, and fewer still, if any, the separate cost of the various materials which compose them:

Boards	$8 03½	Mostly shanty boards.
Refuse shingles for roof and sides	4 00	
Laths	1 25	
Two second-hand windows with glass	2 43	
One thousand old bricks . .	4 00	
Two casks of lime	2 40	That was high.
Hair	0 31	More than I needed.
Mantle-tree iron	0 15	
Nails	3 90	
Hinges and screws	0 14	
Latch	0 10	
Chalk	0 01	
Transportation	1 40	{ I carried a good part on my back.
In all	$28 12½	

These are all the materials excepting the timber, stones, and sand, which I claimed by squatter's right. I have also a small wood-shed adjoining, made chiefly of the stuff which was left after building the house.

From
Walden

Maureen and Bridget Boland
Defending the Old Wives' Garden

Step on it

A member of the panel of the BBC's admirable Gardeners' Question Time programme, speaking of identifying small creatures in the garden, said that as a lad he was told: 'If it moves slowly enough, step on it; if it doesn't, leave it – it'll probably kill something else.'

Never spray against Greenfly

There is a giant conspiracy between the insecticide manufacturers and writers on gardening to encourage the public to spend fortunes and waste hours spraying their roses against aphids. A single clove of garlic planted beside each rose is guaranteed by the present writers (who have not been bought by the lobby – though perhaps only because they have never been approached) absolutely to keep greenfly from the plant. The roots will take up from the soil a substance from the garlic inimical to greenfly, and if in early spring a few hatch out from eggs of parents careless of their offspring's welfare they will neither lay nor survive themselves. Whatever it is that the rose takes up from the garlic does not affect its own scent, and so long as the garlic is not allowed to flower there will be no odour of garlic in the garden. Try it for one year with one group of roses in one bed protected by garlic, spraying all the others in the garden as much as you need, and you will never waste money or time again. All members of the onion family, including chives, are partially effective, but garlic is the only completely efficient answer, the systemic insecticide to end all others. In very dry weather, water the garlic so that the excretions from its roots will be sure to be taken up by the thirsty rose.

Woolly Aphis and Whitefly

Nasturtiums are said to be your answer to aphids on fruit trees, growing the long trailing kind wound up the trunks; and also against whitefly in the greenhouse. If the latter is true it must be because of exhalation rather than of emanation from the roots, since most greenhouse plants are grown in pots and the Old Wives do not suggest growing a nasturtium in every one.

Ants

Our ancestors were more anti-ant than we are, blaming them for much of the damage done by aphids. 'If,' writes an old herbalist, 'you stamp lupins (which are to be had at the Apothecaries) and therewith rub round the bottom or lower part of any tree, no ants or pismires will go up and touch the same tree.' [I started to look up 'pismire' in the dictionary, to provide a scholarly footnote, but decided that I would sooner retain my own fantasy image of a fabulous monster like those in a mediaeval bestiary, all the more terrible for being only an eighth of an inch long. Then, a sense of academic duty prevailing, I did look it up; and all it said was 'ant'. B.B]

Caterpillars

Robert Ball, a Member of the Royal Society, wrote at length to the gardener Richard Bradley in 1718 about how all noxious pests, notably caterpillars, were borne in great clouds on the east wind, originating in Tartary. Windbreaks of trees, high hedges and wattle fences should therefore be placed to protect the whole garden or particular plants from that side, for no caterpillars would be found to the west of them.

Earwigs

The same Mr Bradley advised hanging 'Hoggs-hoofs, the Bowls of Tobacco-Pipes and Lobster-claws on the tops of sticks' among plants 'and killing the vermin that lodge in them every morning'.

Slugs

Richard Bradley 'learned from a curious gentleman in Hertfordshire' of the efficacy of wrapping the trunk of a fruit tree with two or three strands of horsehair 'so full of stubs and straggling Points of the Hair that neither a slug nor a snail can pass over them without wounding themselves to Death'. For wall-grown trees he recommended nailing the horsehair rope to the wall completely outlining the tree; for espaliers, winding one strand round the bottom of the stem and one round the bottom of each stake. For cauliflowers a rope should be laid all round the bed.

A shortage of horsehair ropes in this degenerate age need not induce despair: an admirable trap may be made with a little beer in a jam jar laid on its side.

Deer

In a woodland district, the only sure way to keep deer out of a garden is to build a wall nine feet high all round it, or a solid wooden paling whose upkeep would cost more in the long run than the outlay on a wall. The rugosa rose Alba will grow to seven feet high and make in time a dense, impenetrable hedge; but if deer can jump nine feet high what is their long jump record? One remembers the stag in *The Lady of the Lake*: 'With one brave bound the copse he cleared'. Anyway, rugosas will not grow well under trees, and our garden in places blends into the surrounding woods; to erect a paling in these sections would be a sin. After we had lived here a short while we realised that we could never sacrifice the sight of the deer, at sunrise and at dusk, passing through the garden and pausing to drink at stream or pond; but all the young shoots of our roses were nibbled off. We planted enormous tree-climbing varieties like Himalayan musk and Kiftsgate which will grow to thirty or forty feet, and protected their lower stems with chicken wire while they were young, and such huge shrub roses as Nevada, whose lower, outside shoots alone suffered. We read that sprinkling lion manure would terrify the deer, and could well believe it; but then keeping the lions to provide the manure would terrify us (though we also read that lion skins would make another useful by-product, for wrapping clothes in them would infallibly keep out moths).

Then an Old Wife provided a much easier solution. Tie an old piece of thick cloth such as flannel on the end of a bamboo cane and dunk it in creosote, and stick it in the ground like a little flag near each rose, or at each corner of a bed. The deer will not risk coming near the strong smell, which will prevent them scenting the approach of danger. After a day or so the smell will not be apparent to humans unless they actually sniff the cloth. The flags should be re-dipped at intervals during the summer if there is heavy rain. The scent of violets will (in humans, too) have the effect of temporarily paralysing the olfactory nerve after a few moments, but their flowering season is not long enough to serve instead of creosote to protect your roses.

Birds

Alarmed at the expense of wire netting for our fruit cage, we used nylon netting. The squirrels sat on the crossbars gnawing neat holes, through which so many birds entered that we soon seemed to be keeping an aviary rather than a fruit cage. We reverted to the Old Wives' practice of winding threads of black cotton about among the fruit; the birds have difficulty judging the distance of such threads against the sky and fear entangling their wings if they have to take off in a hurry. It is, at any rate, a deterrent. Nylon thread will not snap when branches are blown about in the wind, or when (undeterred) birds do blunder into it.

One Old Wife has proved that primulas and yellow crocus, elsewhere ruined by birds, are left untouched growing beside a lavender hedge. We propose to grow lavender among our soft fruit, at any rate along the back of a strawberry bed; it will do no harm to try it, but we shall watch the growth and flavour of the berries compared with others grown elsewhere, for strawberries are kittle cattle and may dislike the proximity of so strong a herb.

Moles

Small lumps of acetylene fuel put down the runs are effective, the damp in the soil activating them; but they should be stored in a really air-tight container. We had kept some in a damp shed in a too loosely-covered jar; it was greyish instead of black when we used it, and we found a new hill the next day in the place where we had just removed the old one, with the fuel, now white, cheerfully crumbled among the freshly turned earth of the new run.

Gerard, the sixteenth-century herbalist, advises the placing of garlic in the mouth of a mole's run, 'and you shall see him run out, astonied'. We did, and we waited, and we didn't. Perhaps we did not wait long enough.

The growing of caper spurge in the garden is also recommended as a deterrent; we grow caper spurge, and it may deter some, but living on the edge of woodland we have so many moles that unless the whole garden was full of nothing but caper spurge it is unlikely that it would deter them all.

But if molehills you have, use the beautifully crumbled soil, mixed with sand, for potting.

Cats

An Old Wife, troubled with neighbours' cats that rolled on her catmint and lay sunning themselves on her favourite alpines, wrote to a national newspaper that she had discovered a cure: lay a length of the inner tube of a bicycle tyre on the lawn, and the cats will think it a snake and give the garden a wide berth.

Wild Cats

If you are troubled with these, it is said that they 'will flee from the smoke of rue and bitter almonds'.

From
Old Wives' Lore for Gardeners

Francis Bacon
Of Gardens

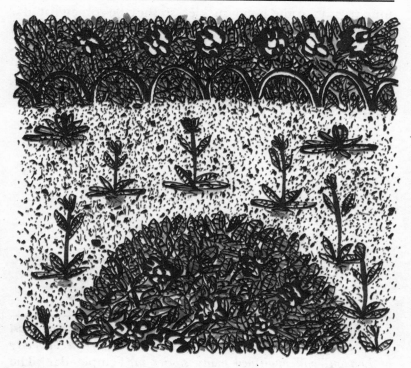

And because the breath of flowers is far sweeter in the air (where it comes and goes, like the warbling of music) than in the hand, therefore nothing is more fit for that delight, than to know what be the flowers and plants that do best perfume the air. Roses, damask and red, are fast flowers of their smells; so that you may walk by a whole row of them, and find nothing of their sweetness; yea, though it be in a morning's dew. Bays, likewise, yield no smell as they grow; rosemary little, nor sweet marjoram; that which, above all others, yields the sweetest smell in the air is the violet, specially the white double violet, which comes twice a year, about the middle of April, and about Bartholomew-tide. Next to that is the musk-rose; then the strawberry leaves dying with a most excellent cordial smell; then the flowers of the vines – it is a little dust, like the dust of a bent, which grown upon the cluster in the first coming forth. Then sweet briar; then wall-flowers, which are very delightful to set under a parlour or lower chamber window; then pinks and gilliflowers, specially the matted pink, and clove gilliflower; then the flowers of the lime tree; then the honeysuckles, so they be somewhat afar off. Of bean flowers I speak not, because they are field flowers; but those which perfume the air most delightfully, not passed by as the rest, but being trodden upon and crushed are three – that is burnet, wild thyme, and water mints; therefore you are to set whole alleys of them, to have the pleasure, when you walk or tread.

Charlotte Mew
The Farmer's Bride

Charlotte Mew (1869–1928) was an eccentric writer of short stories and poetry. She lived almost her entire life in genteel poverty in London, and published many stories in Temple Bar, The Egoist *and other journals. Among those who recognised her individual genius and her 'queer original' voice was Thomas Hardy, who copied out her poem 'Fin de Fête' on the back of a British Museum Reading Room slip which was found on his desk after his death. Two months later Charlotte Mew committed suicide at the age of 58.*

Three Summers since I chose a maid,
Too young maybe – but more's to do
At harvest-time than bide and woo.
    When us was wed she turned afraid
Of love and me and all things human;
Like the shut of a winter's day
Her smile went out, and 'twadn't a woman –

More like a little frightened fay.
    One night, in the Fall, she runned away.

'Out 'mong the sheep, her be,' they said,
'Should properly have been abed;
But sure enough she wadn't there
Lying awake with her wide brown stare.
So over seven-acre field and up-along across the down
  We chased her, flying like a hare
Before our lanterns. To Church-Town
    All in a shiver and a scare
We caught her, fetched her home at last
    And turned the key upon her, fast.

She does the work about the house
As well as most, but like a mouse:
    Happy enough to chat and play
    With birds and rabbits and such as they,
    So long as men-folk keep away.
'Not near, not near!' her eyes beseech
When one of us comes within reach.
    The women say that beasts in stall
    Look round like children at her call.
    I've hardly heard her speak at all.

Shy as a leveret, swift as he,
Straight and slight as a young larch tree,
Sweet as the first wild violets, she,
To her wild self. But what to me?

The short days shorten and the oaks are brown,
    The blue smoke rises to the low grey sky,
One leaf in the still air falls slowly down,
    A magpie's spotted feathers lie
On the black earth spread white with rime,
The berries redden up to Christmas-time.
    What's Christmas-time without there be
    Some other in the house than we!

She sleeps up in the attic there
　Alone, poor maid. 'Tis but a stair
Betwixt us. Oh! my God! the down,
　The soft young down of her, the brown,
The brown of her – her eyes, her hair, her hair!

Thomas Hardy
At Castle Boterel

As I drive to the junction of lane and highway,
　And the drizzle bedrenches the waggonette,
I look behind at the fading byway,
　　And see on its slope, now glistening wet,
　　　Distinctly yet

Myself and a girlish form benighted
　In dry March weather. We climb the road
Beside a chaise. We had just alighted
　　To ease the sturdy pony's load
　　　When he sighed and slowed.

What we did as we climbed, and what we talked of
   Matters not much, nor to what it led, –
Something that life will not be balked of
   Without rude reason till hope is dead,
     And feeling fled.

It filled but a minute. But was there ever
   A time of such quality, since or before,
In that hill's story? To one mind never,
   Though it has been climbed, foot-swift, foot-sore,
     By thousands more.

Primaeval rocks form the road's steep border,
   And much have they faced there, first and last,
Of the transitory in Earth's long order;
   But what they record in colour and cast
     Is – that we two passed.

And to me, though Time's unflinching rigour,
   In mindless rote, has ruled from sight
The substance now, one phantom figure
   Remains on the slope, as when that night
     Saw us alight.

I look and see it there, shrinking, shrinking,
  I look back at it amid the rain
For the very last time; for my sand is sinking,
  And I shall traverse old love's domain
    Never again.

March 1913.

——John Fowles——
Green Chaos

I remember a strange event, in that suburban road in Essex where I was born. One of the elderly residents went slightly mad on the death of his wife; he drew his curtains and turned his back on the outside world. There was at first considerable sympathy for the poor man, until it was realized that the outside world included his own garden. No grass was cut, no beds weeded, no trees pruned; the place ran riot with dandelion, ragwort, nettles, fireweed, heaven knows what else. Such a flagrant invitation to the abominable fifth column deeply shocked my father and his neighbours; and all their sympathy promptly shifted to this Quisling's immediate neighbours, now under constant paratroop invasion from the seeded composites and willow-herbs. I passed this derelict horror one cold winter day and to my joy saw one of Britain's rarest and most beautiful birds, a waxwing, happily feeding among a massive crop of berries on a tree there. But that was only a tiny poetic revenge.

Most of us remain firmly medieval, self-distancing and distanced from what we can neither own nor fully control, and from what we cannot see or understand. Just as the vast bulk of science fiction has decreed that anything that visits us from outer space must (in defiance of all probability) come

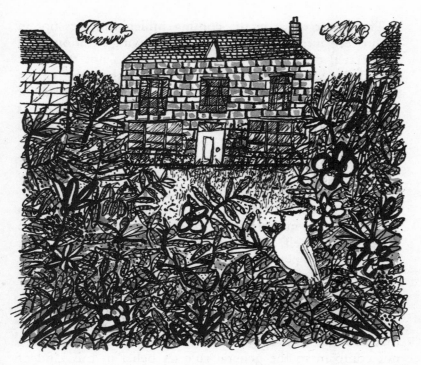

with evil intent, so do we still assess most of nature, or at least where it comes close to us. Some deep refusal to accept the implications of Voltaire's famous sarcasm about the wicked-ness of animals in defending themselves when attacked still haunts the common unconscious; what is not clearly for mankind must be against it. We cannot swallow the sheer indifference, the ultrahumanity, of so much of nature. We may deplore the deforestation of the Amazon basin, the pollution of our seas and rivers, the extermination of the whale family and countless other crimes committed against the wild by contemporary man. But like nature itself, most of these things take place outside our direct knowledge and experience, and we seem incapable of supposing that responsi-bility for them (or lack of responsibility) might begin much closer to home, and in our own species' frightened past quite as much as in its helpless present – above all in our eternal association of ignorance with fear. I do not know how else one accounts for the popularity of such recent and loathsome manifestations of a purely medieval mentality as the film *Jaws*, and all its unhappy spawn.

The threat to us in the coming millennium lies not in nature seen as rogue shark, but in our growing emotional and intellectual detachment from it – and I do not think the remedy lies solely in the success or failure of the conservation movement. It lies as much in our admitting the debit side of the scientific revolution, and especially the changes it has effected in our modes of perceiving and of experiencing the world as individuals.

Science is centrally, almost metaphysically, obsessed by general truths, by classifications that stop at the species, by functional laws whose worth is valued by their universality; by statistics, where a Bach or a Leonardo is no more than a quotum, a hole in a computer tape. The scientist has even to generalize himself, to subtract all personal feeling from the conduct of experiment and observation and from the enunciation of its results. He may study individuals, but only to help establish more widely applicable laws and facts. Science has little time for minor exceptions. But all nature, like all humanity, is made of minor exceptions, of entities that in some way, however scientifically disregardable, do not conform to the general rule. A belief in this kind of exception is as central to art as a belief in the utility of generalization is to science; indeed one might almost call art that branch of science which present science is prevented, by its own constricting tenets and philosophies (that old *hortus conclusus* again), from reaching.

I see little hope of any recognition of this until we accept three things about nature. One is that knowing it fully is an art as well as a science. The second is that the heart of this art lies in our own personal nature and its relationship to other nature; never in nature as a collection of 'things' outside us. The last is that this kind of knowledge, or relationship, is not reproducible by any other means – by painting, by photography, by words, by science itself. They may encourage, foster and help induce the art of the relationship; but they cannot reproduce it, any more than a painting can reproduce a symphony, or the reverse. Ultimately they can only serve as an inferior substitute, especially if we use them, as some people use sexual relationships, merely to flatter and justify ourselves.

There is a deeper wickedness still in Voltaire's unregenerate animal. It won't be owned, or more precisely, it will not be disanimated, unsouled, by the manner in which we try to own it. When it is owned, it disappears. Perhaps nowhere is our human mania for possessing, our delusion that what is owned cannot have a soul of its own, more harmful to us. This disanimation justified all the horrors of the African slave trade. If the black man is so stupid that he can be enslaved, he cannot have the soul of a white man, he must be mere animal. We have yet to cross the threshold of emancipating mere animals; but we should not forget what began the emancipation of the slaves in Britain and America. It was not science or scientific reason, but religious conscience and fellow-feeling.

Unlike white sharks, trees do not even possess the ability to defend themselves when attacked; what arms they sometimes have, like thorns, are static; and their size and immobility means they cannot hide. They are the most defenceless of creation in regard to man, universally placed by him below the level of animate feeling, and so the most prone to destruction. Their main evolutionary defence, as with many social animals, birds and fishes, lies in their innumerability, that is, in their capacity to reproduce – in which, for trees, longevity plays a major part. Perhaps it is this passive, patient nature of their system of self-preservation that has allowed man, despite his ancient fears of what they may harbour in terms of other creatures and the supernatural, to forgive them in one aspect, to see something that is also protective, maternal, even womb-like in their silent depths.

All through history trees have provided sanctuary and refuge for both the justly and the unjustly persecuted and hunted. In the wood I know best there is a dell, among beeches, at the foot of a chalk cliff. Not a person a month goes there now, since it is well away from any path. But three centuries ago it was crowded every Sunday, for it is where the Independants came, from miles around along the border of Devon and Dorset, to hold their forbidden services. There are freedoms in woods that our ancestors perhaps realized more fully than we do. I used this wood, and even this one particular dell, in *The French Lieutenant's Woman*, for scenes that it seemed to me, in a story of self-liberation, could have no other setting.

This is the main reason I see trees, the wood, as the best analogue of prose fiction. All novels are also, in some way, exercises in attaining freedom – even when, at an extreme, they deny the possibility of its existence. Some such process of retreat from the normal world – however much the theme and surface is to be of the normal world – is inherent in any act of artistic creation, let alone that specific kind of writing that deals in imaginary situations and characters. And a part of that retreat must always be into a 'wild', or ordinarily repressed and socially hidden, self: into a place always a complexity beyond daily reality, never fully comprehensible or explicable, always more potential than realized; yet where no one will ever penetrate as far as we have. It is our passage, our mystery alone, however miserable the account that is brought out for the world to see or hear or read at second-hand.

The artist's experience here is only a special – unusually prolonged and self-conscious – case of the universal individual one. The return to the green chaos, the deep forest and refuge of the unconscious is a nightly phenomenon, and one that psychiatrists – and torturers – tell us is essential to the human mind. Without it, it disintegrates and goes mad. If I cherish trees beyond all personal (and perhaps rather peculiar) need and liking of them, it is because of this, their natural correspondence with the greener, more mysterious processes of mind – and because they also seem to me the best, most revealing messengers to us from all nature, the nearest its heart.

No religion is the only religion, no church the true church; and natural religion, rooted in love of nature, is no exception. But in all the long-cultivated and economically exploited lands of the world our woodlands are the last fragments of comparatively unadulterated nature, and so the most accessible outward correlatives and providers of the relationship, the feeling, the knowledge that we are in danger of losing: the last green churches and chapels outside the walled civilization and culture we have made with our tools. And this is however far we may have fled, or evolved away from knowledge of, attachment to, interest in the wild, or use of its imagery to describe our more hidden selves and mental quirks.

To see woods and forests merely scientifically, economically, topographically or aesthetically – not to understand that their greatest utility lies not in the facts derivable

from them, or in their timber and fruit, or their landscape charm, or their utility as subject-matter for the artist – proves the gathering speed with which we are retreating into outer space from all other life on this planet.

Of course there are scientists who are aware of this profoundest and most dangerous of all our alienations, and warn us of it; or who see hopes in a rational remedy, in more education and knowledge, in committee and legislation. I wish them well in all of that, but I am a pessimist; what science and 'reason' caused, they cannot alone cure. As long as nature is seen as in some way outside us, frontiered and foreign, *separate*, it is lost both to us and in us. The two natures, private and public, human and non-human, cannot be divorced; any more than nature, or life itself, can ever be truly understood vicariously, solely through other people's eyes and knowledge. Neither art nor science, however great, however profound, can ultimately help.

I pray my pessimism is exaggerated, and we shall recover from this folly of resenting the fact that we are to all practical intents and purposes caged on our planet; of pretending that our life on it is a temporary inconvenience in a place we have outgrown, a boarding-house we shall soon be leaving, for whose other inhabitants and whose contents we need have neither respect nor concern. Scientists speak of biological processes recreated in the laboratory as being done *in vitro*; in glass, not in nature. The evolution of human mentality has put us all *in vitro* now, behind the glass wall of our own ingenuity.

There is a spiritual corollary to the way we are currently deforesting and denaturing our planet. In the end what we must most defoliate and deprive is ourselves. We might as soon start collecting up the world's poetry, every line and every copy, to burn it in a final pyre; and think we should lead richer and happier lives thereafter.

From
The Tree

Two Love-Letters

The first of these letters, from a country boy to his girl, was picked up on the beach at Sidmouth in 1887 by William de Morgan. The other was written about forty years ago by a girl in a hospital ward in London, on the day before her death. They were reproduced together in Iris Origo's remarkable anthology The Vagabond Path.

Dear Marey, dear Marey, I hant got no partcler news to tell ye at present but my sister that marryd have got such a nice littel babey, and I wish how as that we had got such a little dear too. Dearest Mary, I shall not be happy until then. Dearest Mary pure and holy meek and loly lovely Rose of Sharon. Sometimes I do begin to despare as I am afraid our knot will never be tied, but my Master have promised I how as that when I git ye he will put ye in the Dairy yard to feed the Piggs and give ye atin pense a week. . . . I be coming over tomorrow to buy the ring and you must come to the stashun to meet me and bring a pese of string with you the size of your fingar. . . . Father is going to give us a bedstead and Granny a 5 lb note to buy such as washing stand fire irons mousetrap and Sope, and we must wayte till we can to buy carpeting and glass, crockery-ware and chiny. . . . And Father is going to get us a Rooseter for our Weding Brakefast. Dearest Mary pure and holey meek and loly lovely Rose of Sharon. So no more at present from your future husband William Taylor.

Dear Alf, I seen you last night in my dream. O my dear I cried waking up. What a silly girl you been and got! The pain is bad this morning but I laugh at the sollum looks of the sisters and the sawbones. I can see they think I am booked but they dont know what has befallen between you and me. How could I die and leave my dear. I spill my medecine this morning thinking of my dear. Hoping this finds you well no more now yours truly Liz.

Eleanor Farjeon
A Letter
from Charles Dickens

'I'm going back to England!'

The announcement from Ben Farjeon to his friends came like a bombshell. For a visit did he mean?

'No, for good! I'm going back to England to write. I've had a letter from Charles Dickens! He says I can write! I'm going back.'

'What nonsense, Farjeon! You can write as well here as there.'

No, he must go to England.

But the paper?

He would give it up.

But his career?

His career was in England. Dickens said he could write!

Think twice, Ben! Here in Dunedin you've everything before you! Friends, fame, success, property, fortune – all on the way. Stay in Dunedin, and you can't *help* prospering. Go to England, where nobody knows you, and you must begin all over again.

What did that matter? What did fame, success, and fortune

matter? Charles Dickens had acknowledged his Christmas story! Charles Dickens had found his dedication 'acceptable.' He might become a contributor to *All the Year Round*! He would throw up everything, and go back to England. Farjeon, you're a fool! But how often had that been said to him before; and when had it stopped him, on the spur of his moment?

It took a certain time to settle things. He couldn't leave the paper all at once; his property and affairs must be put in order. There were presentations, silver ink-stands, silver snuff-boxes, a gold card-case with his initials in diamonds; there were leave-takings, and, I dare say, heart-breakings; and B. L. Farjeon, barely thirty, returned to England, having compressed into little more than a dozen years a lifetime of experience – and of 'copy.'

The 'Dickens Letter' was a legend of our childhood. We knew how Papa's home-coming had happened. But curiously enough, the letter itself we never saw. It wasn't in Mama's wonderful autograph album, begun in America when she was Maggie Jefferson. The Charles Dillon I O U was there – why not the 'Dickens Letter'? We never asked; I suppose we took it for granted that the letter was lost.

But after Papa's death it came to light. Among his multitude of papers we found the little oblong envelope, engraved C. D. on the flap, with a sixpenny stamp on the front, the London W.C. postmark, My 29 66, the 'Private' in blue ink in the top corner, and the signature 'Charles Dickens' at the bottom:

> B. L. Farjeon Esquire
> *Times Office*
> *Dunedin*
> *Otago*
> *New Zealand.*

The Dickens letter at last!
Mother and Harry and I read it together –
> *Gad's Hill Place,*
> *Higham by Rochester, Kent*
> *Tuesday TwentyNinth May, 1866*

Dear Sir

      I am concerned to find that I have by an accident

left your letter of last January's date unanswered.

Your dedication, as an interesting and acceptable mark of remembrance from the other side of the world, gave me great pleasure. And I read the little book with much satisfaction.

But I am bound to lay before you the consideration that I cannot on such evidence (especially when you describe yourself as having written "hurriedly"), form any reasonably reliable opinion of your power of writing an acceptable colonial story for All The Year Round. As to my reproducing this story, such a proceeding is as wide of the design and course of that journal as anything can possibly be.

If you write and offer for All The Year Round, any original communication, I will read it myself, very heartily desiring to accept it, if I can deem it suitable to those pages. Do not, I beg, suppose that I intend to discourage you when I say no more. I simply mean to be honest with you and to discharge a duty that I owe to you and to myself.

Accept my thanks And believe me Dear Sir

Faithfully yours
Charles Dickens

There was a moment's pause. Then,

'I don't call that so *very* encouraging,' said Mother.

And suddenly we all began to laugh. How like Father! To throw up everything impetuously, everything he had done and made and become, to rush away from where he was to somewhere else, and begin all over again in a heat of excitement, because Charles Dickens had written him – this letter! This very kind and very moderate letter. Oh, how like Father!

From
A Nursery in the Nineties

Evelyn Waugh
Two Letters to a Daughter

To Margaret Waugh

Combe Florey House

3 June [1957]

Darling Meg

A sad and saddening letter from you. I am sorry you are in hot water. You do not have to tell me that you have not done anything really wicked. I know my pig. I am absolutely confident that you will never never be dishonourable, impure or cruel. That is all that matters.

I think it is a weakness of girls' schools that they have no adequate punishments. When a boy is naughty he is beaten and that is the end of it. All this admonition makes for resentment and the part of your letter that I don't like at all is when you say the nuns 'hate' you. That is rubbish. And when you run down girls who behave better than you. That is mean. Chuck it, Meg.

It is only three weeks since Mother Bridget was writing warmly of your 'great efforts' to reconcile yourself to school. If you have lapsed in the meantime it is only a naughty mood. Don't whine about it.

As to your leaving early – we can discuss that next holidays. I was miserable at Lancing and kept asking my father to take me away. I am very glad now that he did not. The same with Bron. The whole of our life is a test & preparation for heaven – most of it irksome. So each part of our life is an irksome test & preparation for something better. I think you would greatly enjoy Oxford and get the best out of it. But you can't get there without much boring labour and discipline.

Don't get into your silly head the idea that anyone hates you or is unfair to you. You are loved far beyond your deserts, especially by your

Papa

Combe Florey House

7 June [1957]

Darling Meg

I send you all my love for your birthday. I hope it is a very happy day despite the savage persecution of Mother Bridget.

You have certainly made a resourceful & implacable enemy in that holy lady. She has written to both Colonel Batchelor and Mrs Critchley-Salmonson strong denunciations of your moral character and behaviour. I have sent these documents to my solicitors and hope you will soon appear in the courts suing her for libel. Damages will be so heavy that no doubt the school will have to close down.

She has done more than that. She has written to the committee of the St James's Club warning them not to admit you to luncheon on 23rd. I have had a letter from the Chairman asking whether it is true that you steal the silver when asked to luncheon. She also told them that you are invariably drunk & disorderly. I call that a bit thick.

But her most cruel move has been to circularize all the London fishmongers warning them under pain of mortal sin not to have any white-bait during your visit to London. The poor men are so frightened of her that they have forbidden the fishermen to catch any for the next fortnight.

Her powers are infinite. She has agents everywhere. I fear you have got yourself into an appalling predicament.

I have just received a letter from Lady Diana who writes: 'Since learning from Mother Bridget of Margaret's terrible wickedness I wish you to destroy the photograph of her and me which was taken last year. I do not want there to be any evidence of my ever having met the odious girl.'

All this malevolent campaign must, I am afraid, rather over-cloud your birthday. Nevertheless I hope you have some pleasure in eating the cakes which, I know, the other girls will refuse to share with you.

Sweet Meg, don't be a donkey. Everyone loves you – particularly I – me? which I wonder is grammatical.

Your loving
Papa

From
The Letters of Evelyn Waugh

Andrew Motion
The Letter

This poem was the winner of the 1980 Observer poetry prize. Andrew Motion was born in 1952, and has published a collection of poems and a critical study of Edward Thomas.

If I remember right, his first letter.
Found where? My side-plate, perhaps,
or propped on our heavy brown tea-pot?
One thing is clear – my brother leaning
across to ask *Who is he?* half angry
as always that summer before enlistment.

Then alone in the sunlit yard, mother
unlocking a door to call *Up so early?*
– waving her yellow duster good-bye
in a small sinking cloud. The gate creaks
shut and there in the lane I am running
uphill, vanishing where the woodland starts.

The Ashground. A solid contour swept
through ripening wheat, and a fringe
of stippled green shading the furrow.
Now I am hardly breathing, gripping
the thin paper and reading *Write to me.*
Write to me please. I miss you. My angel.

Almost shocked, but repeating him line
by line, and watching the words jitter
under the pale spidery shadow of leaves.
How else did I leave the plane unheard
so long? But suddenly there it was –
a Messerschmitt low at the wood's edge.

What I see today is the window open,
the pilot's unguarded face somehow
closer than possible. Goggles pushed up,
a stripe of ginger moustache, and his eyes
fixed on my own while I stand
with the letter held out, my frock blowing,

before I am lost in cover again,
heading for home. He must have banked
at once, climbing steeply until his jump

and watching our simple village below –
the Downs swelling and flattening, speckled
with farms and bushy chalk-pits. By lunch

they found where he lay, the parachute
tight in its pack, and both hands spread
as if they could break the fall. I still
imagine him there exactly. His face pressed
close to the sweet-smelling grass. His legs
splayed wide in a candid unshamable V.

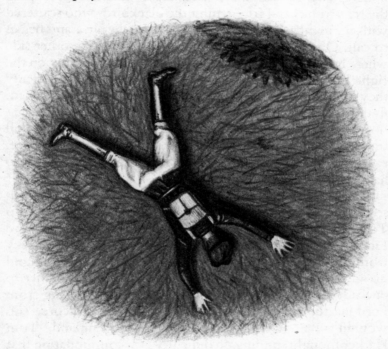

Isabel Colegate
Tom Harker

Tom had watched the shooting party going home, as the
afternoon ended and a faint mist began to rise from the
ground. He had climbed over the park wall into the beech
wood, his collie scrambling over behind him, and had waited
beside one of the trees, looking over the park towards the
copse where the guns traditionally took their last stand on the

second day of a three day shoot. Three of them were well within his view, the others beyond the trees of the copse. He remained unobtrusive because such was his habit; but had he been seen it was not likely that anyone would have objected – a big shoot in which well-known sportsmen were taking part often attracted spectators, and he was in a position where there could have been no fear of his interfering with the sport.

He heard the beaters in the wood as they came through the undergrowth, occasionally whistling or calling out, tapping the tree-trunks and frightening the blackbirds who scattered with alarm calls through the bushes. Then the pheasants began to call. One or two must have flown out on the other side where he could not see them – 'Over!' he heard 'Over on the right!' – then shots, then a few more shots, and then suddenly they all seemed to break, hundreds of pheasants it seemed, flying out over the guns (beautifully presented, as usual, Tom noted, in grudging recognition of Glass's expertise), and all the guns seemed to be firing at once. He could see his three, each with two loaders, one to receive the empty gun, one to hand it back re-loaded, while the shooter himself never moved his gaze from the oncoming birds. A few birds seemed to be getting away over the man furthest away from Tom, but the two nearest him – they were Lord Hartlip and Lionel Stephens – were shooting with a speed and accuracy from which as a fellow sportsman he was unable to withhold his admiration. A smaller bird made a sudden appearance to one side of the wood, flying very fast. An easy swing from Lord Hartlip and it fell, a woodcock to add to his score. You wouldn't see better sport anywhere in England, Tom Harker thought, finding no difficulty in accommodating that notion in his mind along with his views about the strangle-hold of the rich on the life-blood of the working man. The fusillade of shots coming to an end, he heard Glass's voice calling loudly 'All out, Sir Randolph,' and watched the men who had been shooting relax, strolling towards each other, hands in their pockets or lighting cigarettes, having handed their guns to their loaders to be carried home, while the dogs, encouraged by their handlers, hurried about their work of retrieving the fallen birds, and the game cart, drawn by the old cart-horse whose job this had been for nearly twenty years, drew near to receive its final burden of the day. The beaters in their distinguishing, long cream-coloured smocks emerged from the wood. He saw Glass talking to a group of them – giving them their instructions for tomorrow probably – while Sir Randolph walked over to join them, his odd, wide-brimmed old hat marking him out from the others. What a long time they took to disperse, Tom thought. Didn't they want to get home to their tea? There were even one or two ladies with them, who having joined the party for lunch had stood with the guns afterwards and, unlike the rest of the wives, daughters or whatever they might be, had stuck it out until the end, perhaps because it was such a warm afternoon. After the early morning mist, the sun had shone all day – back at the house it had been a great day for flapping dusters at the insects – and Minnie had said at lunch, 'Really the autumn colours are better than ever this year,' and Sir Randolph had said, 'You say that every year,' looking at her plump slightly flushed face (she was wearing her new tweeds and was a good deal too hot) with that rather ironical, rather penetrating look which not everyone knew betokened affection. Minnie was a foolish woman in many ways and not everyone knew that in her husband's eyes her foolishness constituted a great part of her charm.

The ladies were walking up and down in front of the rows of dead birds, nearly all of which had by now been picked up and laid beside the road where they could be counted and admired. Groups of men, those who had been shooting as well as the beaters and gamekeepers, gathered and dispersed in front of the sacrifice thus displayed. Tom, who needed to know the coast was clear before pursuing his own affairs, shifted from one foot to another, waiting for them to get a move on.

Slowly the shooting brake, drawn by two black horses, was led forward from the shelter of the copse. It was a big black equipage, funereal in aspect – indeed Sir Randolph's mother, who had died in 1898, being herself ten years younger than the century, had been carried in her coffin to the church-yard by its means – with a raised seat in front and room for six people to sit facing each other behind. The ladies climbed in. There was more delay while politenesses were exchanged about which gentlemen should accompany them. At last, a full complement of passengers being found, they moved off

down the drive towards the house, whose chimneys could be seen among the surrounding ornamental trees half a mile or so away.

The game waggon was then quickly loaded, and with its iron upper structure festooned with pairs of birds, hares swinging more heavily behind, it was laboriously turned and set off in the opposite direction towards Home Farm, followed by the smaller cart which carried spare cartridges and was drawn by a stout chestnut cob whose alternative employment was to pull the milk float. These were farm horses and were not stabled at the house. They passed quite close to where Tom was standing, the sound of their heavy feet clear in the still evening, the last light of which touched the polished brass of their headplates and on their heavy collars.

The four or five remaining members of the house party were now walking quite briskly back towards the house, the

loaders and dog-handlers following them and about to turn
off the main drive towards the back part of the house, the
kennels and gun rooms, while the rest of the beaters and
gamekeepers dispersed in the general direction of the village.
Tom waited until they were nearly all out of sight, and until
the gold of the late afternoon had been succeeded by the soft
pinkish-grey of the early dusk before he moved. The mist
was now rising much more noticeably from the ground, still
low but thickening, beginning to spread a layer of damp haze
which in the morning would linger on the lower ground like
spilt milk, while the sky above it became the pale clear blue
of another late October day. Tom moved quietly round the
outskirts of the park, keeping to the trees, until the ground
began to slope down towards the thick belt of woodland
which bordered the river. Here, at a gate which opened onto
one of the wide grassy rides which at intervals had been cut
through the wood towards the river and which tomorrow
should see the most spectacular of the pheasant shooting, he
stopped and fumbled in the capacious pockets of his long
jacket. Here, while the men who had been busy all day were
going home and Glass's normally unremitting supervision of
his domain would be temporarily relaxed, was the place,
with the bitch's help, to net a rabbit.

From
The Shooting Party

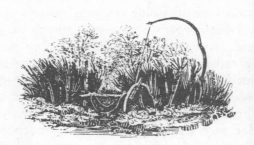

Iris Murdoch
In the Sea

Gertrude pulled off her coat. They were both dressed for cool weather, but the April sun was now suddenly warm, even hot. Tall Anne was wearing now, for out of doors, the blue and white check woollen dress which she had bought at the village shop in what seemed a remote previous existence. (She wore the dark blue tweed dress for evenings.) Round her neck she wore a long mauve Indian scarf which Gertrude had given her. She had refused to let Gertrude 'dress her'. She wore black knee-length woollen stockings with the stout convent walking shoes. Her hair had been growing, but she had decided to keep it cut fairly short. Gertrude liked it like that too. She recalled the big golden mane of Anne's student days, but this silver-blonde fur was now more precious. Walking, a little sun had browned Anne's thin face, but only lightly, pallidly. Her rather narrow blue-green eyes were, as Gertrude put it, shaded or hazed over, still puzzled by the world. Gertrude was wearing, under her coat, a brown almost summery light jersey dress, sprigged with yellow-brown flowers. Her face had changed a little, become perhaps permanently strained and older. So very much crying had worn it a little, as if it had been touched, like the stones, by a lightly pressing finger. Her bright clear brown eyes stared more from deeper sockets, her fine mouth drooped more, lengthened by two faint descending lines. Her hair, which she had only lately started to wash regularly again, was its old self however, knowing not of grief, profoundly and variously brown, longish, now wind-tangled flying upon the collar of her brown-sprigged dress. She had become slimmer, she was shorter than Anne but she walked as fast.

Sun had now taken charge of the whole landscape. Over the emerald turf of the headland an invisible lark was crazily singing.

'Oh – the sun – it's the first time – '

'Yes.'

'Oh Anne, look at the sea, it's all blue now, and flashing, like signals – '

'Yes. Almost ready for swimming.'

'You were a demon driver. You were a demon swimmer too.'

'I thought I'd never swim again.'

'What about a swim now, would you?'

'Are you daring me! Or do you think I'd funk it, like driving Manfred's car?'

'It's much too cold, of course, I was joking.'

'It's not all that cold. I think now you mention it I'll go in.'

'You mean now? Anne, don't be silly – it's *icy* cold! You aren't serious – '

'I am,' said Anne. 'It's a wonderful idea. If you want to see me swim, I'll swim!'

'I don't! Oh please, *please.*'

Anne had already kicked off her shoes and was pulling off her socks. The flat grey stones were smooth and chill under her bare feet. She undid the Indian scarf and the belt of her dress.

'Anne, don't be *crazy*, look at those waves – I wasn't daring you, we aren't nineteen!'

Anne was now in a sudden wild frenzy to get into the sea. A strange piercing sensation like sexual desire had sent a spear through her entrails. She dragged her half-unbuttoned dress violently over her head. A moment later, dressed only in the little golden cross upon its chain which hung close about her neck, she advanced into the running creamy foam. She went on quickly, stumbling a little upon the shifting stones, until the white water was above her knees.

'Anne – Anne – *stop* – '

The sea was intensely and beyond expectation cold. Wild mad exhilaration licked her naked body. The beach descended steeply, a wave met her breast-high and broke over her head. Gasping then yelping with the cold she lost her footing, then leapt into the following wave and was swimming, kicking, lifted up by the strong incoming rollers, her eyes blinking away the spray, seeing the blue-green white-flecked crests of the advancing waves and the brilliant light of the blue sky beyond. She cried out now in wild joy, feeling her limbs becoming warm in the fierce water as she swam out strongly from the shore and gave herself confidently to the huge movement of the sea.

Anne had been an athletic girl, a golfer, a swimmer, a tennis player. Physical strength and physical prowess had been taken for granted in her life, part of a calm sense of superiority which had never faltered until it had run to its destined fulfilment in an ecstatic submission to God. She was strong Anne Cavidge. She felt this now as she turned on her back and kicked the rhythm of the waves into a matted foam round about her. Enough now. She dolphin-leapt into the fast elegant crawl which she had not forgotten, any more than she had forgotten walking, and headed toward the land. The sea was indeed very cold.

As she now swam back she felt, like an unexpected blow, a sudden lassitude. What had happened to the strength in which a moment ago she had been exulting? Her arms no longer moved effortlessly, they were puny and aching, and her naked body was coated with a profound cold. The nuns had prided themselves on keeping fit. Garden walks were not enough. Anne had followed a regime of exercises. Perhaps it had become less strict as the years went by. The vigour of youth was gone. What's the matter with me, she thought. I'm weak, of course I haven't forgotten how to swim, but I'm weak, my limbs are strengthless. Anne gasped, swallowed salt water. She continued to swim toward the land, but now with a terrible exhausted slowness. Over the flecked jumping wave-crests she could see the figure of Gertrude upon the shore very far away, and beyond her the grey cube of the cottage. Perhaps there was a current taking her out to sea! It could not be just her own weakness which made the land seem to recede? She tried harder, spurred now by fear. Was she going

to drown now, stupidly, *wickedly*, before Gertrude's eyes?
Yesterday she had climbed the cliff to impress Gertrude. It had
really been quite difficult.

Gertrude could see Anne swimming hard to get back
against some force which seemed to be preventing her.
Gertrude could see too the malignant violence of the breaking
waves as they smashed down on to the stones. It was easier to
leap out against those waves than to swim in with them. The
sea seemed to have become greater and fiercer in the short
interval since Anne had rushed into it. I dared her, thought
Gertrude, it is my fault. Now, just when I have found her, she
is going to die in front of me, to drown helplessly and disappear. Gertrude could scarcely swim. She had always feared
the sea. She called 'Anne! Anne!' wringing her hands.

Anne, now nearer to the shore, had also begun to understand the strength of the waves, their great size and how
violently they broke. Their deafening noise, which she did
not apprehend as sound, but as some deadly terrifying
vibration, was overwhelming. She looked behind her. The

sun must be clouded as the high backs of the incoming rollers were now almost black. Her courage failed, and she began to swim to and fro parallel to the shore, unable to decide to attempt the ordeal of return. She felt in her body, mingled with the chaotic roaring of the broken water, the tremendous force of the oncoming waves, now sweeping her shorewards, so that she had to resist their power in order to stay where she was. She tried to swim out to sea again. She must not become conscious of the cold. She was the helpless plaything of great mechanical forces which could kill her in seconds. She tried to *think*.

The problem was this, that when she came in, carried by a wave into the area of the breakers, she would not have sufficient strength to scramble out quickly enough or stand up firmly enough not to be knocked down by the next wave which would then pass over her and draw her back in the undertow. She had not noticed in her former exultation, but she could see and feel now, how steeply the beach shelved, so that where the waves were actually breaking she might scarcely be able to touch the bottom. She could also now discern, amid that unbridled complex of forces, the terrifying clatter of the grey stones as the receding waves drew them down and back into the sea.

Oh my God, oh my God, help me, thought Anne. She thought, I have got to chance it, and now. Already in her weakness she was scarcely swimming but simply fighting with the sea, losing her breath and gasping and swallowing water in the attempt to keep her head up. She did the only intelligent thing open to her. She turned again to look at the huge black-backed waves that were coming in behind her, and chose one which was a little smaller than the others to carry her, now swimming furiously, right in toward the beach. She saw, close to her now, the slope of dark shifting stones and the spread of the creaming raging foam. As the wave with which she was travelling began to break she ceased swimming and tried to touch bottom. The foaming white water rushed past her and over her, then her feet touched, deep down the shifting sloping race of the stones, drawn by the force of the water which was already beginning to flow back. She could see, half-turned, the high just-curling crest of the next wave. She attempted to leap so as to keep her head above it, but it was impossible. She could not gain footing, the water was too deep and too fast as it retreated beneath the incoming roller which now leaned over Anne like a translucent black-green wall. She lost her balance, her strength was gone. The wave crashed down over her engulfing her completely. Her head was below the water, her breathless mouth was open.

Gertrude, paralysed with terror, had seen and understood her friend's dilemma. She too had estimated the mechanical forces of the waves, the point of breaking, the slope of stones, the sucking speed of the undertow, the impossibility of standing erect. She saw exactly what Anne was trying to do, and how difficult it was. She saw her friend's body, helpless, struggling, naked as the damned consigned to hell, about to perish utterly; and at the moment when Anne's head disappeared from view under the crushing curling descent of the second wave, Gertrude entered the water.

Anne, as she saw the vast size of the wave above her, and as she lost her footing and descended into a dim cave of swirling foam, and as the sea entered her mouth which had opened to gasp for breath, thought, I am drowned, this is the end Oh forgive me, forgive me. The next thing she knew was daylight and the sight of a human arm, and the brown material of Gertrude's dress, darkened by the water. Anne's feet were again upon the stones and she had taken another breath. She breathed, she took two stumbling agonising steps, gripping the arm, the brown material. The two women fell and the foam raced about them. Then they rose again and Gertrude pulled Anne into the shallows and then up beyond the water on to the land.

They sat down on the stones, Anne choking, gasping, spitting, then breathing more quietly.

Gertrude said, 'Are you all right?'

'Yes. Are you?'

'Yes.'

'Thanks for rescuing me.'

'I thought you were a goner.'

'Me too. I'm very sorry.'

'You really are a prize idiot.'

'Yes. Yes. Yes.'

'Look, put my coat on. Can you walk?'

Anne put on Gertrude's coat and picked up her own clothes. Arm in arm, shuddering with cold, they climbed up on to the grass below the cottage. Then suddenly they stopped, holding on to each other and laughing, laughing their old laugh, but with a touch of hysteria.

'All the same,' said Gertrude, 'you looked rather lovely dressed in your cross.'

From
Nuns and Soldiers

Herman Melville
Loomings

Call me Ishmael. Some years ago – never mind how long precisely – having little or no money in my purse, and nothing particular to interest me on shore, I thought I would sail about a little and see the watery part of the world. It is a way I have of driving off the spleen, and regulating the circulation. Whenever I find myself growing grim about the mouth; whenever it is a damp, drizzly November in my soul; whenever I find myself involuntarily pausing before coffin warehouses, and bringing up the rear of every funeral I meet; and especially whenever my hypos get such an upper hand of me, that it requires a strong moral principle to prevent me from deliberately stepping into the street, and methodically knocking people's hats off – then, I account it high time to get to sea as soon as I can. This is my substitute for pistol and ball. With a philosophical flourish Cato throws himself upon his sword; I quietly take to the ship. There is nothing surprising in this. If they but knew it, almost all men in their degree, some time or other, cherish very nearly the same feelings towards the ocean with me.

There now is your insular city of the Manhattoes, belted round by wharves as Indian isles by coral reefs – commerce surrounds it with her surf. Right and left, the streets take you waterward. Its extreme down-town is the battery, where that noble mole is washed by waves, and cooled by breezes, which a few hours previous were out of sight of land. Look at the crowds of water-gazers there.

Circumambulate the city of a dreamy Sabbath afternoon. Go from Corlears Hook to Coenties Slip, and from thence, by Whitehall, northward. What do you see? – Posted like silent sentinels all around the town, stand thousands upon thousands of mortal men fixed in ocean reveries. Some leaning against the spiles; some seated upon the pier-heads; some looking over the bulwarks of ships from China; some high aloft in the rigging, as if striving to get a still better seaward peep. But these are all landsmen; of week days pent up in lath and plaster – tied to counters, nailed to benches, clinched to desks. How then is this? Are the green fields gone? What do they here?

But look! here come more crowds, pacing straight for the water, and seemingly bound for a dive. Strange! Nothing will content them but the extremest limit of the land; loitering under the shady lee of yonder warehouses will not suffice. No. They must get just as nigh the water as they possibly can without falling in. And there they stand – miles of them – leagues. Inlanders all, they come from lanes and alleys, streets and avenues – north, east, south, and west. Yet here they all unite. Tell me, does the magnetic virtue of the needles of the compasses of all those ships attract them thither?

Once more. Say, you are in the country; in some high land of lakes. Take almost any path you please, and ten to one it carries you down in a dale, and leaves you there by a pool in the stream. There is magic in it. Let the most absent-minded of men be plunged in his deepest reveries – stand that man on his legs, set his feet a-going, and he will infallibly lead you to water, if water there be in all that region. Should you ever be athirst in the great American desert, try this experiment, if your caravan happen to be supplied with a metaphysical professor. Yes, as every one knows, meditation and water are wedded for ever.

But here is an artist. He desires to paint you the dreamiest, shadiest, quietest, most enchanting bit of romantic landscape in all the valley of the Saco. What is the chief element he employs? There stand his trees, each with a hollow trunk, as if a hermit and a crucifix were within; and here sleeps his meadow, and there sleep his cattle; and up from yonder cottage goes a sleepy smoke. Deep into distant woodlands winds a mazy way, reaching to overlapping spurs of mountains bathed in their hill-side blue. But though the picture lies thus tranced, and though this pine-tree shakes down its sighs like leaves upon this shepherd's head, yet all were vain, unless the shepherd's eye were fixed upon the magic stream before him. Go visit the Prairies in June, when for scores on scores of miles you wade knee-deep among Tiger-lilies – what is the one charm wanting? – Water – there is not a drop of water there! Were Niagara but a cataract of sand, would you travel your thousand miles to see it? Why did the poor poet of Tennessee, upon suddenly receiving two handfuls of silver, deliberate whether to buy him a coat, which he sadly needed, or invest his money in a pedestrian trip to Rockaway Beach? Why is almost every robust healthy boy with a robust healthy soul in him, at some time or other crazy to go to sea? Why upon your first voyage as a passenger, did you yourself feel such a mystical vibration, when first told that you and your ship were now out of sight of land? Why did the old Persians hold the sea holy? Why did the Greeks give it a separate deity, and own brother of Jove? Surely all this is not without meaning. And still deeper the meaning of that story of Narcissus, who because he could not grasp the tormenting, mild image he saw in the fountain, plunged into it and was drowned. But that same image, we ourselves see in all rivers and oceans. It is the image of the ungraspable phantom of life; and this is the key to it all.

Now, when I say that I am in the habit of going to sea whenever I begin to grow hazy about the eyes, and begin to be over conscious of my lungs, I do not mean to have it inferred that I ever go to sea as a passenger. For to go as a passenger you must needs have a purse, and a purse is but a rag unless you have something in it. Besides, passengers get seasick – grow quarrelsome – don't sleep of nights – do not enjoy themselves much, as a general thing; – no, I never go as a passenger; nor, though I am something of a salt, do I ever go to sea as a Commodore, or a Captain, or a Cook. I abandon the glory and distinction of such offices to those who like them. For my part, I abominate all honourable respectable toils, trials, and tribulations of every kind whatsoever. It is quite as much as I can do to take care of myself, without taking care of ships, barques, brigs, schooners, and what not. And as for going as cook, – though I confess there is considerable glory in that, a cook being a sort of officer on ship-board – yet, somehow, I never fancied broiling fowls; – though once broiled, judiciously buttered, and judgmatically salted and peppered, there is no one who will speak more respectfully, not to say reverentially, of a broiled fowl than I will. It is out of the idolatrous dotings of the old Egyptians upon broiled ibis and roasted river horse, that you see the mummies of those creatures in their huge bake-houses the pyramids.

No, when I go to sea, I go as a simple sailor, right before the mast, plumb down into the forecastle, aloft there to the royal mast-head. True, they rather order me about some, and make me jump from spar to spar, like a grasshopper in a May meadow. And at first, this sort of thing is unpleasant enough. It touches one's sense of honour, particularly if you come of an old established family in the land, the Van Rensselaers, or Randolphs, or Hardicanutes. And more than all, if just previous to putting your hand into the tarpot, you have been

Herman Melville

lording it as a country schoolmaster, making the tallest boys stand in awe of you. The transition is a keen one, I assure you, from a schoolmaster to a sailor, and requires a strong decoction of Seneca and the Stoics to enable you to grin and bear it. But even this wears off in time.

What of it, if some old hunks of a sea-captain orders me to get a broom and sweep down the decks? What does that indignity amount to, weighed, I mean, in the scales of the New Testament? Do you think the archangel Gabriel thinks anything the less of me, because I promptly and respectfully obey that old hunks in that particular instance? Who ain't a slave? Tell me that. Well, then, however the old sea-captains may order me about – however they may thump and punch me about, I have the satisfaction of knowing that it is all right; that everybody else is one way or other served in much the same way – either in a physical or metaphysical point of view, that is; and so the universal thump is passed round, and all hands should rub each other's shoulder-blades, and be content.

Again, I always go to sea as a sailor, because they make a point of paying me for my trouble, whereas they never pay passengers a single penny that I ever heard of. On the contrary, passengers themselves must pay. And there is all the difference in the world between paying and being paid. The act of paying is perhaps the most uncomfortable infliction that the two orchard thieves entailed upon us. But *being paid*, – what will compare with it? The urbane activity with which a man receives money is really marvellous, considering that we so earnestly believe money to be the root of all earthly ills, and that on no account can a moneyed man enter heaven. Ah! how cheerfully we consign ourselves to perdition!

Finally, I always go to sea as a sailor, because of the wholesome exercise and pure air of the forecastle deck. For as in this world, head winds are far more prevalent than winds from astern (that is, if you never violate the Pythagorean maxim), so for the most part the Commodore on the quarter-deck gets his atmosphere at second hand from the sailors on the forecastle. He thinks he breathes it first; but not so. In much the same way do the commonalty lead their leaders in many other things, at the same time that the leaders little suspect it. But wherefore it was that after having repeatedly smelt the sea as a merchant sailor, I should now take it into my head to go on a whaling voyage; this the invisible police offcer of the Fates, who has the constant surveillance of me, and secretly dogs me, and influences me in some unaccountable way – he can better answer than any one else. And doubtless, my going on this whaling voyage, formed part of the grand programme of Providence that was drawn up a long time ago. It came in as a sort of brief interlude and solo between more extensive performances. I take it that this part of the bill must have run something like this:

'*Grand Contested Election for the Presidency of the United States.*
'WHALING VOYAGE BY ONE ISHMAEL.
'BLOODY BATTLE IN AFGHANISTAN.'

Though I cannot tell why it was exactly that those stage managers, the Fates, put me down for this shabby part of a whaling voyage, when others were set down for magnificent parts in high tragedies, and short and easy parts in genteel comedies, and jolly parts in farces – though I cannot tell why this was exactly; yet, now that I recall all the circumstances, I think I can see a little into the springs and motives which being cunningly presented to me under various disguises, induced me to set about performing the part I did, besides cajoling me into the delusion that it was a choice resulting from my own unbiased freewill and discriminating judgment.

Chief among these motives was the overwhelming idea of the great whale himself. Such a portentous and mysterious monster roused all my curiosity. Then the wild and distant seas where he rolled his island bulk; the undeliverable, nameless perils of the whale; these, with all the attending marvels of a thousand Patagonian sights and sounds, helped to sway me to my wish. With other men, perhaps, such things would not have been inducements; but as for me, I am tormented with an everlasting itch for things remote. I love to sail forbidden seas, and land on barbarous coasts. Not ignoring what is good, I am quick to perceive a horror, and could still be social with it – would they let me – since it is but well to be on friendly terms with all the inmates of the place one lodges in.

By reason of these things, then, the whaling voyage was welcome; the great flood-gates of the wonder-world swung open, and in the wild conceits that swayed me to my purpose, two and two there floated into my inmost soul, endless processions of the whale, and, mid most of them all, one grand hooded phantom, like a snow hill in the air.

From
Moby Dick

Alan Coren
Moby Junk

This article was inspired by a piece in The Times *under the headline 'Dolphins fear cry of glass fibre whale', which reported: 'The prototype of a mechanical killer whale, designed to frighten dolphin away from Japan's fishing waters, appears to deceive the ocean's most intelligent mammal, when recorded cries of the whale are transmitted from within the equipment.'*

Call me Ishmael. I think it's a really terrific name, I practise it in front of the mirror a lot, it has, you know, *resonance*.

My publisher came up with it just before I sailed on the *Pequod*, he is a very now person, he is right in there where tomorrow publishing is putting it together.

It isn't Ishmael Anything, or Anything Ishmael, it's a whole new marketing concept, just the one name, like Capucine, Gucci, Regine, all that. It was bound to happen on the book scene sometime, my publisher says, and sometime just blew in.

The book was his idea, too. We met at Jacky's a few months

back, and he'd seen this spread I did for *Cosmo* about how you can judge people's libido from how thin their watches are, and he said: 'The next big thing is whales. Did you hear where they're going, what is it, extinct, and everybody who is anybody is out of their skulls with worry, Liz Taylor, Princess Michael, Twiggy, you wouldn't *believe* how much Big People are into whales, I see quartermillion hardback, *minimum*! Do a book, about 10 × 8, something substantial, double page pix. So what am I talking about? I am talking about *Jaws* with *heart*, that's what I'm talking about!'

I met Queequeg at the Spouter-Inn. I really dig Nantucket, it's full of very creative persons, top agency men, tax geniuses, ex-Watergate guys who are putting all their stash into decor consultancy, everyone has these weekend places up there; they all hang it out at the Spouter-Inn, it has these wonderful polystyrene beams, terrific repro barometers everywhere, a roaring Flamo Fumefree Adjustaflicker fire, and a whole load of marvellous *kitscherei* – Mickey Mouse ice cubes in plastic pineapples, cryogenic swizzle sticks with little male chauvinist pigs on the end, genuine Gottlieb pin-tables, you really have to see it. Anyhow, I was sitting in the Chappaquiddick Room (they've done it up as a submerged Chevy Impala; one wall is nothing but fog-lights with live guppies in them) when I saw this huge, I mean *huge*, coloured guy, covered in tattoos. I had eighteen shots of him in the Pentax before I even went across to ask if he'd like his Campari freshened.
    'Call me Ishmael,' I said.
    'Terrific,' he replied. 'Call me Queequeg.'
    'Queequeg who?'
    'Just Queequeg.'
    I reeled!
    'You have to be kidding!' I cried. 'You're an author, too?'
    He shook his head.
    'I whale,' he said.
    I relaxed.
    'An alto player,' I said, 'I should have guessed. With all the rhythm you people have – you know, sometimes I feel maybe slavery wasn't such a bad thing, it taught you pain, it made you *respond*. Tell me, do you know *Melancholy Baby*?'
    He looked at me kind of funny; then he reached behind

him and brought out this enormous pole with a terrible barb on one end.

'Jesus!' I cried. 'You play *that*?'

Next morning, when he came to give back my copy of *Giovanni's Room*, he said:

'Look, man, how'd you like to sail on the *Pequod*?'

'The *Pequod*! It's exactly what I've been looking for! But could you swing it?'

'No sweat, man,' said Queequeg. 'We're low on scribes this trip. Lensmen, sound crews, environment freaks, you name it, they're busting out of every goddam hatch; but no scribes. It's killing the Captain. He's very, you know, yesterday; he's really into verbal communication. Let's go and see him.'

'Terrific!' I cried, grasping his hand. And noticing, as I did so, that his tattoos seemed to have vanished.

'Transfers,' explained Queequeg, when I enquired. 'Where's your head at, man? Everybody's into acrylic water-solubles now. It's where being a matelot is. Listen, if I'm gonna go sticking needles into my goddam arm, it sure as hell ain't gonna be ink I'm shooting!'

And here the huge harpoonist laughed his thunderous laugh.

I have to admit my first sight of the *Pequod* was disappointing.

'It has a funnel, for God's sake!' I said to Queequeg. 'It has, like, rigging.'

'Yeah,' said Queequeg. 'That's Ahab, all right.'

'I was hoping for a pool,' I said. 'Do you carry Scalectrix?'

Queequeg shook his enormous head.

'Fridays we fix a sauna up aft,' he said. 'We tap the boiler. But it's pretty, you know, ad hoc.'

We started up the gangplank, towards a squat, swarthy figure standing at the top.

'Who's he?' I whispered.

'Starbuck,' replied Queequeg. 'First mate.'

'*Who* Starbuck?' I enquired anxiously. 'Jack? Warren? Burt?'

'Just Starbuck.'

My heart sank. Maybe I didn't have such a hot publisher,

after all.

'Watch him,' muttered Queequeg, 'he's a God-freak. Very heavy.' He raised his voice as we reached the top. 'Morning, Starbuck. This is Ishmael. He's sailing with us.'

'Really?' cried Starbuck, a blaze starting in his piggy eyes. 'How'd you like to go to Guyana?' He shoved a clipboard under my nose. 'If I get fifty-one per cent of the crew to sign, we'll send a deposition to the Captain.' He shoved a pen into my hand. 'It's this really terrific cult, very fundamentalist, you'll love it, they have girls, liquor, the food is out of this world, sucking pig, armadillo on the half-shell, roast – '

'BELAY THERE, STARBUCK!'

Gulls rose, shrieking, at the voice! It rolled across Nantucket Bay like thunder! It froze the blood in my very veins! My head whipped up, in time to see its owner, peg-leg swinging, hurtle along the deck towards us, snatch the clipboard from Starbuck's hand, and send it winging on a spinning arc into the sea.

'THOU SHALT HAVE ONE GOD ONLY!' roared the Captain. His terrible eye rolled upward, and his terrible finger followed. 'I know Him, and He knows me!' His free hand gathered around Starbuck's throat. 'None of your trashy plastic faiths, Mister Mate, none of your Johnny-come-lately evangelistic rubbish, none of – '

'Okay, okay,' here Starbuck, wriggling, spread concessionary hands, 'how about Bali, it's hardly out of our way, there's this Unitarian consciousness-raising group, they believe up to four per cent of the Old Testament, Captain, and if you only saw how some of them dames is built, you'd – '

The Captain flung him aside, and turned his great head to me.

'You must be Captain Ahab,' I said pleasantly. 'I'm sorry, I didn't catch your first name.'

'Just Ahab,' he growled.

'Oh.'

'I'll not be doing,' he bellowed, 'with any of your cheap trashy, TV-dinner-on-your-lap names, with your Kevins and your Craigs, your Melvyns and your Russells, your Jonathans and – '

'I really like your leg,' I said, frantic to stem his rage. 'It's very chic.'

In the long silence, I could hear the creak of something shippy.

'Ah,' said Ahab, at last, and quietly. 'Chic, is it? Trendy, perhaps? *In*?'

'Well,' I said, 'perhaps not *in*, exactly, I mean what is *really* in is prosthetic tibia-plus-whole-foot units in space alloys, just one more wonderful Apollo spin-off, they're so good you can actually wear wedges without tottering, and – '

The breath left my body as Ahab's thick forearm pressed me against the mast.

'*This* peg,' he growled, his face a millimetre from mine, 'was hand-carved from a sperm-whale's jaw by *craftsmen*! She is a custom leg, a bespoke leg, she is none of your tatty Moon rubbish! That tin trash may do very well for your inter-galactic pansy scum with their natty silver suits, I ain't saying it don't, but is it a leg for a seafaring man with a heart full of boiling blood?'

I shook my head vigorously.

'Absolutely not!' I cried. 'No, no, no, that leg is *you*!'

He dropped me, and spun away.

'Cast off for'ard!' roared Captain Ahab. 'Cast off aft!'

I didn't talk to him for the next eight days as the *Pequod* ploughed north to whale-water, but I saw him standing motionless on the bridge, his terrible eye glittering over the doings below as *Vogue* models posed that year's sable anoraks against the davits, and the documentary Arriflexes whirred, and the crew sang shanties into the microphones of a dozen different record labels, and bearded politicians in faded denims told bearded journalists in faded denims of the desperate need to find synthetic substitutes for ambergris.

But on the ninth morning, bored with pounding my IBM, I took the liberty of mounting the bridge.

'I was wondering, Captain,' I said, 'whether you would care for a hand of kaluki? You looked so, I don't know, *solitary*.'

The grey face, with its livid scar, turned slowly from its motionless scanning of the sea.

'Kaluki, is it?' he muttered. 'Or canasta, perhaps? Back-gammon, bridge, Cluedo? Scrabble, cribbage, gobs, Up Jenkins, eh, Mister Ishmael, while the cauldrons of hell bubble?'

I sighed.

'I sometimes wonder,' I said, waving a hand towards the activity below, 'how you stand us all.'

Ahab spat fluently.

'I stand 'ee,' he said, 'on account of ye finance the Quest. I put up with the rubbish and the squawking and the posing and the mincing and the natter because it pays the bill. It keeps the *Pequod* afloat. It'll settle the account of Moby Dick!'

'Moby Dick?' I exclaimed. 'Could that be the great white whale who took your leg off at the knee, since when your whole life and being has been committed to his pursuit and destruction, with all the symbolic overtones that that entails?'

'Aye,' said Ahab. 'That's 'im.' He turned his head towards the sea again. 'They wants to be chartered accountants, they wants to live in detached freehold premises, they wants Porsches for the golf clubs and Volvos for the wife, they wants double ovens and video-cassette recorders and solar panels for the swimming pool, they wants Colour Supplements and three weeks on the Costa Smeralda and a Filipino couple in a flat over the garage, they wants quartz-digital this and silicon-chip that and a waferthin pocket calculator ye can slip into your flipper to enable 'ee to compute tax-benefits while snorkelling off Grand Bahama – but what is all that to the *real* Quest, eh?'

I cleared my throat.

'I take it,' I said, 'that as far as Saving The Whale is concerned, your wholehearted support cannot fully be – '

'THAR SHE BLOWS!'

Our two heads swivelled simultaneously upward, to where Queequeg hung pointing from the crow's nest. Ahab flicked out his telescope, smacked it against his eye, and staggered.

''Tis him!' he screamed. ''Tis him!'

And it was.

So we crammed on steam, and we crammed on sail, and we crammed on lenses and type-ribbons and microphones and tape-recorders, and we hugged ourselves with excitement for a day and a night, as we tracked the great white whale in its ultimate sprint, with sweating Queequeg crouched in the prow, harpoon in hand (for the Captain would have no truck with pansy guns and newfangled trash); but when the great white whale paused, at last, exhausted, it was Ahab himself who stumped to the bow, and snatched the spear from Queequeg's hand, and Ahab himself, with a terrible cry, who hurled it down to the glistening flanks.

And, therefore, Ahab himself whose foot was caught in the spilling line, and Ahab himself who was plucked from the prow, and Ahab himself who was lashed to his quarry with the kind of irony you normally get only in hand-tooled uniform editions, and Ahab himself who was dragged to the bottom with the ruined whale.

Leaving us on the bobbing *Pequod* with the earnest prayer that his dying ears had never picked up the unmistakable clunk of busted clockwork.

From
Tissues for Men

———————Jan Morris———————
The Venetians in Corfu

The Venetians may have been wary of the Corfiotes, but they loved Corfu. So delectably set there, so benign of climate and beguiling of silhouette, not too far from home, not too close for discomfort, it provided a perfect setting for the colonial enterprise, for a merchant setting himself up as a country gentleman, or a servant of state ready to retire from his labours. It was almost like another island in their own lagoon: and indeed when in 1753 the Sardinas family of Corfu were elevated to the nobility for their services in battle, they were simultaneously elected to the pages of another Golden List, that of their native island of Mazzorbo, an almost indistinguishable settlement some five miles north of Venice.

Corfu Town remains recognizably Venetian. Because the Republic held it continuously for four hundred years it has an air of civilized constancy and well-being unique among Greek towns. It is hemmed in still between the two fortresses, and its much-loved Esplanade, arcaded by the French in later years, provided with bandstands and gravel cricket pitches by the British, is nothing more than the open field of fire decreed by the engineers of the Old Fort. Tall, jumbled and hung with washing are the houses of Corfu, aggrandized sometimes by the shadowy outline of a *palazzo*, long since declined to flats or tenements, and crowned here and there with authentically Venetian campaniles, from whose belfries on Sunday mornings properly cracked and fruity bells ring out across the water.

Here are the shady flagged streets of Venice, the arcaded shops, the alleys of ample vegetables and sweet-smelling breads, the skulking market rats, the ingratiating grocers, the nodding black-shawled women, the strolling bravos, the glimpses of sacred pictures through the glazed inner doors of crooked churches. The Venetians brought to Corfu, besides their forts and war-galleys, their coffee-houses, their concerts, their operas and their taste for cultivated dalliance: by the eighteenth century it was the duty of the Venetian naval commander not only to supervise the upkeep and disposition of his ships, but also to arrange for the annual visit of the Commedia dell' Arte players.

'All the bad habits of the Corfiotes', a British administrator was to write, 'come from the Venetians.' He was thinking, no doubt, partly of their somewhat languid temperaments, and certainly there is something very Italianate about the leisurely evening stroll of the Corfiotes up and down the Liston, the paved promenade beside the Esplanade, fast-talking ladies arm in arm, lines of students linked across the pavement, solemn men in Homburg hats, paper under their arm, gravely discussing events in Athens up and down, up and down beneath the trees. The custom was introduced to Corfu by the Venetians, who made it the privilege of the Corfiote nobility and actually named the promenade the Liston after the Lista d'Oro. (And if, by the way, you want to consult that catalogue, where better than the library of the Reading Club, which is housed in a delectable small Venetian *palazzo* overlooking the bay, and is rich enough in leather, prints, smells of wood and furniture polish, hospitable librarians and savants sunk in ancient narratives, to make the most dedicated scholar of Venetiana, fresh from the libraries of San Marco itself, feel comfortably at home?)

In the country too, for all those Turkish incursions, there are signs of Venice still. Not only did the Venetians build, at the very end of their stay, the island's first proper roads, but by offering subsidies they clothed all Corfu with the olive tree, whose dark green foliage and now wrinkled trunks set the very tone of the countryside today and seem as immemorial as the rocks themselves. Some of these magical trees are said to be survivors of the original plantings six hundred years ago, and if you want to get a true idea of Venice's aesthetic impact upon the island, try walking up one of the wooded hills that overlook Corfu Town from the south: for there, looking down over the blue waters that the galleys once patrolled, one can see the red roofs and white walls of the Venetian presence, the bell-towers and the castles, framed between the leaves of the most ineradicable legacy of them all, the olive, which once and for all plucked this island from its Balkan hinterland and made it part of the Mediterranean idea.

Corfu is another Venetian possession where you may see

Venetian country houses – not medievally castellated like the Naxos tower-houses, but serene and modestly bucolic, couched in almond trees and gladioli, with wistaria winding its way up the garden cypresses, and anemones sprouting in the shade. At Kothokini, for example, in the rolling country south of Corfu Town, there is a house of the Sardinas family, those counts of Corfu and Mazzorbo. It is not a very big house and has rather a ship-like air to it, even to a flagpole; but it is unmistakably squirely in manner, having a private chapel in its cobbled yard, a big barn, and a little hamlet clustered respectfully around its walls – the Sardinas had the right to give sanctuary to fugitives from the law, and prospered for over several centuries from the fees they charged, not to mention their monopoly of the Corfu salt-pans.

It is a lovely place. Sardinas still own it, and it has kept its style intact. Its low-ceilinged rooms are shabby but gentlemanly, stuffed with quaint curios, and there are family crests about the place, and old portraits, and pedigrees on parchments. It is like Longhi's Venice transplanted. On a hot afternoon it seems to dream there: as the loud Greek music thumps away from the village radios over the wall, and you sit in the rambly garden with your host beneath the pergola, so there drifts over you the sense of privileged seclusion that must have seduced the Sardinas in the first place.

They were, so to speak, exotics in this simple setting. The holiest Venetian shrine of Corfu is the little church of the

Blessed Virgin at Kassiopi, on the north coast. Its site has always been sacred to seafarers. The Romans built a temple there, and for many centuries sailors made a point of stopping there on their voyages to and from the east – Nero offered oblations at Kassiopi on his way to compete as a lute-player in the Isthmian Games at Corinth. A very early Christian church succeeded the temple, and when it was destroyed by the Turks in 1537 the Venetians replaced it with one of their own.

This became exceedingly holy too. Later in the century a young man was unjustly condemned for theft and blinded by order of the Venetian judges. Fraught with pain and despair he wandered sightless around the island until he reached Kassiopi, and there spent the night within the church. He was awakened by gentle hands pressed upon his eyes, and when he opened them he saw the Virgin Mary standing kindly over him. The vision faded, his sight remained, and the news was taken at once to the Bailie, who recognized the event as a miracle and hastened to Kassiopi to make amends. A Mass is celebrated still, every 8 May, to commemorate the day.

But beside the door of the church the Venetians erected a marble plaque rather truer to their memory, I think, than the tale of the blinded boy. It was placed there when the church was rebuilt in 1538, and recorded that, the building having been destroyed by 'cruel Turkish pirates', it was reconstructed by three pious Venetians: Niccolò Suriano, Proveditor of the Fleet, Filippo Pasqualigo, Commander of the Adriatic Sea, and Pietro Francisco Malipiero, Commander of the Triremes.

Sometimes in the interior of Corfu, in some shaded clearing among the olives, you may notice a tented encampment pitched higgledy-piggledy beneath the trees; and when you stop the car to take a closer look, like jackals out of the wood the gypsies will fall upon you, carrying their babies in their arms – whining, crying, pushing their skinny fingers through the windows, beating on the windscreen, swarming wildly all around, and eventually pursuing you out of sight, as you proceed shakily on your way, with hideous but fortunately unintelligible curses.

Blame the Venetians. The gypsies were encouraged to come to Corfu because of their skill in horse-breeding, and probably nowhere else in Europe did they acquire such standing. Gypsies thrived elsewhere in the Venetian Empire – at Nauplia they were given particular rights of tenure, at Methoni, as we saw for ourselves, they prospered in pigs. Nowhere else, though, were they so institutionalized as they were in Corfu, where every grade of society was somehow fitted into the imperial structure.

There they constituted a feudal fief of their own, under a baron appointed by the Venetians – 'an office of not a little gain', so a Corfiote historian assures us, 'and of very great honour'. Very great power too, for the gypsy baron had almost complete authority over his feudatories. They were his private army. They were his corps of servants. He could punish them how he liked, short of killing them. In 1502 we hear of a Corfiote sea captain receiving the fief as a reward for running the blockade of Methoni, which had just fallen to the Turks; later it went to one of the island's most eminent scholars, for his services during the Turkish invasion of 1537. Every May Day the gypsies came to town to do honour to their lord. Drums beating, fifes squealing, they marched through the streets carrying his feudal banner above them, and setting up a maypole outside his house, sang a peculiar ditty in his praise, and handed over their feudal dues.

In return for all this the gypsies had valuable rights of their own. They could not be conscripted for the galleys, or made to do forced labour for the Republic. They formed their own military unit, under a gypsy commander, and throughout the four centuries of Venetian rule, thanks to these ancient privileges, their horse-copers' skills and no doubt their evasive woodland ways, they flourished exceedingly. No wonder they have reverted to the predatory now.

A different destiny awaited the Jews of Corfu, whose ghetto still stands in the shadow of the New Fort, in the tangle of narrow streets behind the bus station. It is difficult to identify because since the Nazi occupation of Corfu in World War II it has shrunk from a large and cultured community to a few shops and houses and a solitary synagogue. Almost all its inhabitants were shipped away to slave camps or gas chambers. In the Venetian heyday, though, the Corfu ghetto was the richest and most influential in the empire, and held a peculiar fascination for the Venetians because Judas Iscariot

was popularly supposed to have been a Corfiote – a lineal descendant was commonly pointed out to the more gullible travellers, as one of the island's sights.

The Venetians could never escape Jewry. In all their chief possessions and trading posts they found clusters of Jews, clannish and disputatious, at once disconcerting and indispensable. Jews were the intermediaries and interpreters of their commerce – the Jews of Turkey in the sixteenth century nearly all spoke four or five languages, and sometimes ten or twelve. The Republic was always ambivalent towards them. Perhaps the Venetians felt a little too close to Jewry for their own comfort, for there has always been, in my own view, something Hebrew in the bearing, the enterprise, the style, the separateness and even the look of the Venetians. Much Jewish blood, I do not doubt, went into Venetian veins in the course of their centuries of intercourse with the Levant, and the oriental strain that everyone noted in things Venetian was often less Muslim or Byzantine than Jewish.

At home in Venice the Jews were powerful, but rigidly circumscribed. Shylock could finance his argosies to the east, but the chances were that he was obliged to return at dark to the Jewish quarter of the city, the first of all the ghettos – originally on the island of Giudecca, which took its name from the Jews, then in the north-western corner of the city, on the site of a disused iron-foundry (a *getto* is a metal-casting). It was the Venetians who invented the idea of a special costume to mark out the Jews – first it was a yellow hat, then a red – and the Jews were harshly taxed, deprived of all civic rights, and once, in 1572, expelled from the Republic altogether.

Not for long, though, because Venice could not do without them. They controlled much of the city's trade, in spices, woollens, sugar and silks, and they were irreplaceable on Rialto, the central money market. They were respected, too, as people of learning and finesse, and consulted for their scholarship as for their way with money. The rules that governed them were often waived or winked at, and in the daytime they were to be seen on the streets of the city looking anything but persecuted – their ladies, it was said in the sixteenth century, 'gorgeous in their apparel, jewels, chains of gold and rings . . . having marvellous long trains like princesses that are borne up by waiting women.'

As at home, so in the colonies: the Jews were generally safe under Venetian rule, if they were seldom easy. The Venetians, being independent sorts of Christians, did not often regard the Jews with the savage fanaticism common in Europe then, but at the same time Jews played a prominent part in the demonology of their empire. Jewish women were blamed for the immorality (and hence disloyalty) of the Cretan cities – in the sixteenth century a Gentile caught there in sexual intercourse with a Jewess could get ten years in the galleys, while the Jewess could be burned. It was a Jewish axeman who had murdered Erizzo, after the fall of Euboea in 1470, and a Jewish executioner who had flayed Bragadino in 1571. It was the Jew, Joseph Nasi, who was generally supposed to have instigated the Turkish attack on Cyprus: certainly he was for many years a formidable commercial rival to the

Venetians, with his network of associates all over the east, his agents from the Levant to western Europe and his access to the Sultan's ear. Another Jew, actually born a Venetian subject, signed on behalf of the Sultan the treaty that gave Cyprus to the Turks; indeed it was partly the association of Jews with the humiliating loss of Cyprus, and with the slow whittling away of Venetian power in the east, that led to the expulsion order of 1572.

But the Jews were never expelled from Corfu. Like the gypsies, they were special there. They had been on the island since the end of the twelfth century, when a Greek-speaking Hebrew colony was established and a synagogue was built – the first example of Greek demotic prose is said to have been a translation of the book of Jonah made by its rabbis. When in 1386 the Corfiote deputation went to Venice to ask for the protection of the Republic, two of the six delegates were Jews; under the Venetians the community grew and flourished and became vital to the workings of the colony. A second synagogue was built. The ghetto, though walled and gated, became the richest quarter of town. The Jews adopted the language of their rulers and were principal bankers and traders of the island. Without them its financial system would have collapsed; it was not Venetian benevolence, but plain self-interest, that exempted the Jews of Corfu from the banishment.

Even here their status was anomalous. Rich and influential though they were, they were forbidden to own land, they were obliged to wear the star of David on their clothing and they were liable always to be enlisted for the more degrading tasks of state, like manning the galleys, or performing that familiar chore of medieval Jewry, executing people. The Greeks were not discouraged from their ancient prejudices against them, and every Easter Saturday, as a substitute for actually stoning them, made a point of dropping old crockery noisily out of their windows, preferably upon passing members of the community.

Still they multiplied and were useful. They fought bravely in the Turkish siege of 1715: the Venetian mercenary commander, the German Count Johann von der Schulenburg, was so impressed that he suggested to the Signory the settling of more Jews in the island, if only for their military aptitude.

By the end of Venetian rule in Corfu the Jews were said to have constituted more than a quarter of the whole population, making the island the nearest thing to Zion that existed. Nobody mourned the fall of Venice more than the Jews of Corfu, and with reason, for never again, under any successor government, did they achieve such power and prosperity, and in the end the worst of all the empires, arriving similarly out of the north, took them away and killed them. To the end their vernacular remained the Venetian dialect of Italian.

A few have come back since, and one of the synagogues is alive again. Next door to it the president of the community has a television shop, and a few other Jews keep shops and run businesses in the neighbourhood. They do not seem very happy. They still hear the clatter of the crockery on Easter Saturday. They show you their Auschwitz tattoos and conduct you round the synagogue with a trace of sad resentment.

From
The Venetian Empire

─────Peter Tinniswood─────
Our Own Dear Queen

It is a fact not generally known that in her youth Queen Victoria had the makings of a cricketer of considerable stature.

Indeed it is the opinion of many historians of 'the summer game' that but for the cares of state and the burdens of excessive childbearing, she could well have reached Test Match standard.

Contemporary records reveal that the young Victoria was

endowed with an excess of the cricketing virtues – the athletic grace of a Frank Woolley, the snow white teeth of a Learie Constantine, the combative pugnacity of a Freddie Trueman, the dark, hairy legs of a W. G. Grace.

There are many experts who firmly believe that after her death Queen Victoria achieved reincarnation in the form of Mr George Duckworth of Lancashire and England.

While the resemblance, facially and vocally, cannot be denied, I myself tend to the view that, if reincarnation did take place, it came in the shape of Mr B. D. 'Bomber' Wells of Gloucestershire and Nottinghamshire.

His broad beam and the slow waddle to the wicket before delivery of the ball always seemed to me to have a regal quality that was not to be explained by Altham's coaching manual, but bore all the hallmarks of a person well-used to the state opening of colonial parliaments and the rigours of nineteenth-century confinement and pregnancy.

Dear 'Bomber' Wells!

How different the history of our beloved country and indeed the wide world beyond might have been, had he succeeded to the throne in 1837 – though I am bound to say I have slight doubts about his ability to cope with the demands of Prince Albert of Saxe-Coburg-Gotha.

This odious German princeling has in my view cast a dark, malign shadow over this country, which to this very day has still to be lifted.

How else to explain the benighted summer of 1980 with its long and dreary succession of rain-affected county cricket matches, its dripping sight screens, its sodden squares and its elevation to the prime ministership of a woman with the manners of an ink monitor and the charm of a power-mad swimming baths attendant?

How else indeed?

I believe passionately that most of the great calamaties of this century can legitimately be placed at the feet of this nauseous German princeling – the loss of Empire, the decline of pride and patriotism, the enfeebling of manly courage and vigour, the demise of the leg spinner, the retirement from the *Daily Telegraph* of Mr E. W. Swanton, father and grand-father respectively of that celebrated Hollywood film star, Miss Gloria Swanton.

Do I exaggerate? Do I overstate my case?

I think not.

Consider this.

Had this country been ruled in its pomp and in its prime by a monarch who had played Test Match cricket, opened the innings for her country at Headingley, been struck in the ribs by Spofforth at the Oval, smashed in the teeth by Gregory at Old Trafford, bitten on the buttocks by the groundsman's ferrets at Trent Bridge, is it conceivable that Britain should be in its present desperate plight with women newsreaders on the moving television screens and threatened centre page pin-ups of Brian Johnston in Wisden's Almanack?

Nothing will dissuade me from the opinion that had Queen Victoria been allowed to develop her cricketing ability to its fullest potential, this dear country of ours would still be 'mistress of the seas', 'mother of the free' and holders in perpetua of the Corbillon Cup.

And what relevance has Prince Albert to this?

The answer is simple.

He it was who forbad his wife, his youthful, fresh and innocent bride, from wielding the willow, donning the pads and weaving her subtle spells with the crimson rambler.

Let us consider the facts calmly and objectively.

The historical canon relates that Queen Victoria first met her putative consort at Windsor on October 10th, 1839.

This is not, in fact, the case.

In an appendix omitted in somewhat mysterious circumstances from Heygarth's *Scores and Biographies* there is a reference to a cricket match held in June 1838 at Crabbe Park, in which Queen Victoria, playing for William Blunt's Eleven, took seven wickets for seven runs and struck three successive sixes off the redoubtable F. W. Lillywhite.

She scored an undefeated 87 in 25 minutes, the ferocity of her hitting being only matched many years later by Mr G. L. Jessop, and the fluency of her stroke play having no equal until the arrival of 'the silken-shirted Hindu' Mr K. S. Ranjitsinjhi, whose descendants incidentally now run a most agreeable Tandoori chicken restaurant on the outskirts of Keating New Town.

Unknown to our so-called academic historians with their limp bow ties and discoloured waistcoats, Prince Albert was in the close vicinity of the cricket ground engaged in business of a quite different nature.

He was on an unofficial visit to this country examining and evaluating the latest developments in animal husbandry and land management.

It was while he was in a neighbouring field inspecting a novel and amusing device for the instant decapitation of poachers that he was struck a violent blow behind the left temple by a ball smitten out of the ground over deep square leg by Queen Victoria.

He was knocked unconscious.

On regaining his senses he inquired as to the nature of the blow which had caused an irregular egg-shaped protruberance to appear on his close-cropped, bullet-shaped cranial extremity.

'Lord save us, sir,' said the farmer. ''Tis the Queen what done it. It must be her batting. The stumper is standing up at the wicket.'

There and then Albert resolved to marry the young Victoria, daughter of Edward, Duke of Kent, niece of Leopold, first King of the Belgians, and devoted drinking companion of Mr Fuller Pilch.

Why did he make this decision?

I believe that at the very moment the leather-bound sphere struck his temple there were released in him all those primeval stirrings of violence, bestiality and brutality inherent in the soul of every Hun who ever lived.

A woman who could inflict pain!

A woman who could knock unconscious a man in the prime of his life!

She must be his.

Nothing less could satisfy the loathesome yearnings of his black Teutonic heart.

The marriage took place on February 10th, 1840.

The Encyclopaedia Britannica states that the Queen was 'dressed entirely in articles of British manufacture'.

This was indeed the case.

For under her dress of purest Macclesfield silk she wore Gunn and Moore cricket pads, Daymart thermal string vest and Gray-Nicolls abdominal protector made of stout Sheffield steel and covered with the tartan of the Gordon Highlanders.

Later that evening in the bridal chamber as the young Queen commenced to disrobe the Prince was enchanted by what, to his untutored eye, was the novelty of this garb.

The sensuous slap of cricket pads against chaste and pristine flesh as his new bride practised her off drive, the tumble of silken hair over smooth young shoulders as she removed her I Zingari cricket cap, the faint, exotic whiff of Sloane's Liniment as she wheeled over her arm in that distinctive 'square on' delivery style aroused in him strange, exciting and not unwelcome feelings of desire in the nether regions of his popping crease.

It was with a happy and pumping heart that he retired to his nuptial bed.

Imagine his chagrin when his young bride insisted on taking a net before joining him in the conjugal container.

It is my belief that the humiliations he suffered that honeymoon night contributed more than anything else to his subsequent gravity of mien, his humourless, his grinding rigid code of morals and his ceaseless and finally successful efforts to stop the young Queen's cricketing activities.

Picture the scene that honeymoon night.

The young bride crouches at the wicket.

The young groom, clad in night shirt and velvet smoking hat, trots stiffly to the wicket.

And in his first three deliveries bowls two long hops and a daisy cutter.

Could any man suffer greater humiliation on his wedding night?

Could anything be more designed to strengthen his will to turn his ebullient, feckless and vivacious young spouse into the authoritarian, dour and austere woman, whose devotion to the duties of state and childbearing was awesome in its comprehensiveness?

Nine children!

No wonder she had such trouble with her run up.

But let us consider the reasons for this prodigality of progeny in greater detail.

Was it really the full and riotous flowering of the maternal instinct?

Was it, in fact, something more than the altruistic desire to provide spouses for a whole legion of European kings, archdukes and landgraves, whose descendants to this very day are to be seen bathing topless without togs on the beaches of southern France and providing their endorsements to the boards of loathsome companies engaged in the manufacture of microwave ovens and digital toenail clippers?

I think so.

Let the dark facts speak for themselves.

It is historically indisputable that after her marriage Queen Victoria refused steadfastly to abandon her cricketing proclivities.

Despite all her husband's despotic discipline she was frequently to be seen opening the batting incognito for Quidnuncs and the Free Foresters, carousing in the back parlour of 'The Bat and Ball' at Hambledon and pulling the heavy roller with 'the best of them' at 'The White Hart Hotel' in Bromley.

In vain did Prince Albert remonstrate with her.

In vain did he appeal to her sense of responsibility and duty.

There was only one thing for him to do.

Involve her in a constant succession of pregnancies.

This he did, secure in the knowledge that no man in the history of 'the summer game' had ever played Test cricket successfully after the third month of pregnancy.

His plan was propitious.

By the time of his death Queen Victoria's cricketing activities had entirely ceased and her beloved Gray-Nicolls abdominal protector lay rusting in an obscure and dark corner of the royal mews and her prized Geoffrey Boycott autograph cricket bat was relegated to ceremonial duties at the Tower of London.

When I now think of our dear Queen's long reign, I do not think of a monarch who saw vast tracts of the atlas shaded pink and the creation of an Empire on which the sun never set.

No, I think of and mourn the passing of a lady who, had her immense talents and inclinations been allowed to run their natural course, could have been the finest all-round cricketer of her generation and, when age took its inevitable toll, could have developed into an umpire of the most outstanding calibre.

Who is to say, in fact, that she has not already achieved eminence in the personage of Mr Bill Alley?

From
Tales from a Long Room

Benny Green
Eccentric Cricketers

W.G. GRACE.

Although there is no question that the patron saint of eccentricity resides somewhere in the Grace family, it is not easy to decide on whose shoulders the mantle falls, on Edward Mills the Coroner, or William Gilbert the Doctor. Which of these two astonishing originals embodies the more succulent absurdities, E.M., whose irascible romanticism was reflected not only in his persistent pulling of balls outside the off-stump to the leg boundary but also in his pursuit of barrackers in the crowd, or W.G., who contradicted the classical orthodoxy of his own batting technique with his slyly comic bending of the rules?

The secret of both brothers was a simplicity of approach amounting to pure genius, a slapstick pragmatism harking back to the Georgians. In this regard it is much to the point that their maternal grandfather George Pocock, whose favourite mode of transport was kite carriage, was the sometime organist at Portland Wesleyan Church at Kingsdown near Bristol, and that, after a skirmish between organists and deacons, he left for ever, taking the organ with him; years later E.M., as a schoolboy at Long Ashton, was given out lbw by a dubious decision and applied the family precedent by walking off the field with the stumps under his arm.

The same cavalier attitude to both the spirit and the letter of the law persisted throughout E.M.'s long career, and with typical Gracean gusto he not only refused to conceal his chicanery but actually revelled in it, whether as player or as administrator. F. A. Leeston-Smith, playing for Weston-super-Mare against Thornbury, once hit E.M. for 4 successive sixes, an event which the Coroner later recalled as follows:

F. L. Cole made one off my first ball, Leston-Smith six off my second, six off third, six off fourth, six off fifth, when the umpire said, 'I'm afraid it is over, Doctor'. I said, 'Shut up. I am going to have another, and off this one he was stumped'.

It was hardly likely that such a man, when appointed to the secretaryship of a county club, would bother with the conventional proprieties; the minutes of a Gloucestershire session of 1873 read as follows:

Committee meeting held at the White Lion Hotel, Bristol, on Thursday, November 25 at 3 o'clock. Present: E. M. Grace and that's all.

Naturally the alliance of the Coroner and the Doctor was many-faceted; in 1882 the Australian G. J. Bonnor, asked how he had been dismissed in a match at Clifton, replied, 'I was talked out by the fielders'. Bonnor, however, was no pillar of orthodoxy himself, being rumoured to have come out to bat for Non-Smokers against Smokers with a large cigar clamped between his teeth. As for W.G., his place as the champion of sporting perversity is too secure to require further documentation, but it is worth saying that he remains the only published author of the 19th century who believed that no good could come of reading books, that he once raided the Lord's pavilion and kidnapped William Midwinter for a match at the Oval, that among his sporting accomplishments was the ability to empty a magnum of champagne and then balance the bottle on his head, and that A. J. Webbe remembered at his mother's home in Eaton Square, 'W.G. marching round the drawing room after dinner bearing the coal scuttle on his head for a helmet, with the poker carried as a sword'.

Eccentrics generally may be sub-divided into the Expert-technical, the Inept-Aspiring, and the Dotty-Idolatrous. In the first category falls Charles Burgess Fry, who, on being no-balled for throwing, tied his bowling arm in a splint, buttoned down his shirt sleeve and was only frustrated in his plan to reduce the umpires to absurdity through the refusal of his captain, W. L. Murdoch, to put the plan into operation. Later Fry, the only opening batsman ever to be offered the throne of Albania, summed up his own technique by saying that he had only one shot but could make it go to 9 different parts of the field. Eccentricity of subtly differing kind must be attributed to the aforesaid Midwinter, who not only indulged in wilful dissimulation himself, but induced the administrators of two hemispheres to indulge in it also, which explains how he found himself playing for Australia against England in 1876, for England against Australia in 1881, and for Australia against England in 1882. Midwinter, the first inter-continental cricketer, is famous for a miraculous metamorphosis achieved in his travels, having embarked for Australia in 1880 as 'W. Midwinter' and returned the following April as 'W. Midwinter; Gent'. This elevation, however, pales before the bewildering social fluctuations of Grace's cousin, W. R. Gilbert, who was listed by *Wisden* as an amateur until 1886, as a professional 1887–1923 ; as an amateur again in 1924; as a professional again posthumously from 1925–34; as an amateur again 1934–40; and subsequently as nothing at all.

Intermittent idiosyncracy must be ascribed to Robert Peel, the Yorkshire bowler who could on occasion drink himself into a condition more or less indistinguishable from eccentricity, who was described in one *Wisden* match report as 'having to go away' and who was eventually ushered out of first-class game by Lord Hawke, for a nameless misdemeanour often said to have been his running in the wrong way and bowling at the pavilion in the mistaken belief that it was a batsman. On a less secular level there was the curious case of the Leicestershire batsman Albert Knight, who was in the habit of placing a request for extra-terrestrial assistance from the Almighty before facing his first delivery, a tactic of such manifest unfairness that the Lancashire bowler Walter Brearley was moved to complain to the MCC.

There was George Gunn, one of the most brilliant of batsmen, whose great century for England against Australia at Sydney in 1908 was marred, he always said, by the congenital inability of the cornetist in the orchestra on the ground to play in tune. His successor at Trent Bridge, Charlie Harris, often expressed the sterner tendencies of a more utilitarian age by remarking to the fielders as he walked in to bat, 'Good morning fellow-workers'.

One must also nod at the great hitter C. I. Thornton, who was once seen at Sittingbourne dressed in a borrowed night-shirt stalking wild duck; of more relevance was his wonderful plan to play an innings 'ball by ball in the manner of certain well-known batsmen'. Sadly he was out first ball 'when leaving the ball alone in the customary manner of a certain defensive player'. Hesketh Pritchard forsook a successful career by going to Patagonia in the mistaken conviction that when he arrived there he would find a Giant Sloth; Billy Buttress of Cambridgeshire, a gifted ventriloquist, enjoyed sitting in railway carriages causing other passengers to search their luggage for non-existent mad cats and dogs; Charles Newhall of the Philadelphians always went in to bat carrying a lemon, which he placed by stumps so that he might suck it for inspiration before each stroke; T. C. O'Brien spent part of the 1891 season appearing, for no discernible reason, as one J. E. Johnston; the Hon Lionel Tennyson, said to have beguiled the longeurs of a Gentlemen v Players match by laying odds of 10–1 that his grandfather had written 'Hiawatha', was never clear in his mind, as Hampshire captain, if he had hired his valet as wicket-keeper or his wicket-keeper as valet.

Although E. H. D. Sewell was a good player, it is as an honorary member of the Inept-Aspiring group that he has endeared himself to posterity. Sewell, who was once no-balled for delivering with both feet off the ground, said it was the first time in his life that he had been mistaken for an acrobat. He published several books; these tended to be discursive. One volume included a team of bearded players, the menu for a banquet, a plea for the smashing of more pavilion windows, a rewriting of Kipling's verse, a discussion of dress waistcoats, and a photograph of himself wearing a gas mask. One wonders what he would have made of Lord Frederick Beauclerk, who batted in a beaver hat.

When on overseas tours the slow bowler Julius Caesar

always cried when required to sleep alone. This problem never worried the Yorkshireman Ted Wainwright, who always took his bat to bed with him; an interesting variation on this theme was provided by the New York millionaire Hesketh K. Nayler, who treated his own impotency with homeopathic doses of fat ladies with no clothes on playing cricket with balloons; sadly his case never came to the attention of Dr Freud. Further sexual innuendo is provided by the Duke of Dorset, who in 1754 sacked his mistress, the ravishing Bacelli, for running him out. Even worse running between wickets was committed by John Boot of Newark, who in 1737 died in a collision with his batting partner.

Harry Bagshaw (Derbyshire) was buried in 1927, in accordance with his instructions, dressed in his umpire's coat holding a cricket ball. Walter Cave (Surrey) invented the idea of candleholders on pianos. T. A. Fison (Highgate School) once scored as follows: '264 Retired to catch train for Continent', while G. E. Hemingway, having hit the ball into a bed of nettles, ran 250 while the fieldsmen debated who should retrieve it. Charles Absolom, a famous London club cricketer, took 100 wickets in a season when he was 80 years old. G. J. V. Weigall (Cambridge and Kent) described the omission of Frank Woolley from the England side as 'the worst crime since the Crucifixion', refused to eat veal-and-ham pie during a match, and once, on arriving at a village ground to be told there was no clock, complained, 'No clock, sir? The clock is more important than a lavatory.'

Finally there are the Dotty-Idolatrous, whose passion for the game is equalled only by their inability to excel at it. These include the dramatist Sir James Barrie, who claimed to be a slow bowler so slow that if he produced a delivery of which he disapproved, he could run down the pitch and fetch it back; he once described a perfect wicket as being 'a little on the creamy side'. The poet J. C. Squire would put himself on to bowl at one end, saying 'At the other end the glint of the sun on the stumps would put me off'. Sir Julien Cahn batted in inflatable pads, and is said to have bowled 'not so much up and down as to and fro'. No summary of cricketing eccentricity would be complete without reference to Lord Justice Norman Birkett, who as a small boy said his prayers every night by asking the Deity to look after the entire Surrey XI, which he named, man by man, ending with 'and God bless leg-byes'; also to an Epsom stockbroker called Arthur Courcy, who was so stirred by the climactic moments of the England v Australia 1882 Test match at the Oval that he bit through the handle of his brother-in-law's umbrella; last of all to the poet Robert Graves, who has recorded as follows a lull in the fighting on the Western Front:

24 June, 1915. Vermelles. This afternoon we had a cricket match, officers v sergeants, in an enclosure between some houses out of observation from the enemy. Our front line is three-quarters of a mile away. I made top score, 24; the bat was a bit of rafter, the ball a piece of rag tied with string; and the wicket a parrot cage with the clean, dry corpse of a parrot inside. Machine-gun fire broke up the match.

From
Barclays World of Cricket

Mrs Leslie Stephen
Crumbs in Bed

Virginia Woolf's mother, Julia Stephen, wrote a pamphlet entitled Notes from Sick Rooms *and published it privately in London in 1883. It has recently been reissued.*

Among the number of small evils which haunt illness, the greatest, in the misery which it can cause, though the smallest in size, is crumbs. The origin of most things has been decided on, but the origin of crumbs in bed has never excited sufficient attention among the scientific world, though it is a problem which has tormented many a weary sufferer. I will forbear to give my own explanation, which would be neither scientific nor orthodox, and will merely beg that their evil existence may be recognised and, as far as human nature allows, guarded against. The torment of crumbs should be stamped out of the sick bed as if it were the Colorado beetle in a potato field. Anyone who has been ill will at once take her precautions, feeble though they will prove. She will have a napkin under her chin, stretch her neck out of bed, eat in the most uncomfortable way, and watch that no crumbs get into the folds of her nightdress or jacket. When she lies back in bed, in the vain hope that she may have baffled the enemy, he is before her: a sharp crumb is buried in her back, and grains of sand seem sticking to her toes. If the patient is able to get up and have her bed made, when she returns to it she will find the crumbs are waiting for her. The housemaid will protest that the sheets were shaken, and the nurse that she swept out the crumbs, but there they are, and there they will remain unless the nurse determines to conquer them. To do this she must first believe in them, and there are few assertions that are met with such incredulity as the one – I have crumbs in my bed. After every meal the nurse should put her hand into the bed and feel for the crumbs. When the bed is made, the nurse and housemaid must not content themselves with shaking or sweeping. The tiny crumbs stick in the sheets, and the nurse must patiently take each crumb out; if there are many very small ones, she must even wet her fingers, and get the crumbs to stick to them. The patient's night-clothes must be searched;

crumbs lurk in each tiny fold or frill. They go up the sleeve of the night-gown, and if the patient is in bed when the search is going on, her arms should hang out of bed, so that the crumbs which are certain to be there may be induced to fall down. When crumbs are banished – that is to say, temporarily, for with each meal they return, and for this the nurse must make up her mind – she must see that there are no rucks in the bed-sheets. A very good way of avoiding these is to pin the lower sheet firmly down on the mattress with nursery pins, first stretching the sheet smoothly and straightly over the mattress. Many people are not aware of the importance of putting on a sheet *straight*, but if it is not, it will certainly drag, and if pinned it will probably tear. The blankets should be put on lightly, one by one, not two or three at a time. There is an appreciable difference in the way in which coverings are laid upon people. Each covering should be laid on straight and smooth; no pulling straight should be done afterwards. If the patient is in bed when her bed is made, the lower sheet should be half rolled up and laid on the edge; the patient should then be lifted over the roll on to the fresh sheet, half of which has been spread over half of the bed. The old sheet can easily be pulled away, and when the new one is unrolled it can at once be tucked in and pinned if required. The upper sheet is rolled or folded breadth-ways and laid under the blankets, beginning at the feet; it is then quickly drawn up and the old one removed, the blankets not being disturbed. All blankets and quilts should be so arranged as not to drag and not to slip; any extra covering which is required only over the feet should not drag down to be pulled off by each movement of the patient, or by a careless passer by; it should be supported on a good footboard to the bed. If there is not a good footboard, it is well to improvise one by putting a plain deal board at the end of the bed between the mattress and the bars, as the legs of a towel-horse or a chair are very liable to be kicked by passers by, and the bed gets shaken, a thing much to be avoided.

If an eider-down quilt is wanted, it should be pinned with American safety pins on to the top covering.

A sick bed is apt to become close and unpleasant, but the nurse may refresh it without chilling the patient if she raises the top sheet, with the coverings resting on it, three or four times, thus fanning the bed and causing the patient no fatigue or chill. An invalid can air her own bed in this way if she can raise her knees; she need then only lift the outer edge of the sheet up with her hand and raise one knee up and down; but this of course requires some strength, and the bed will be more effectually aired by some one standing by the side of it.

Some people think that the whole comfort of a bed depends on its pillows, and I am not sure that they are not right. Certainly a hard or a pappy pillow will make an otherwise comfortable bed a most unresting one. Everyone has their own way of arranging their pillows: some like them smooth and straight, while others twist and turn them till it seems as if no head could find rest. The nurse must find out which way her patient prefers before attempting to arrange the pillows. I have often seen a sick person tormented by the over zealous nurse seizing the pillow and altering what certainly seemed a most uncomfortable arrangement, but one which was in fact exactly suited to the patient's needs, and only attained after many struggles. The nurse must be always ready to turn the pillow when wanted; she can do this without fatiguing the patient by placing one hand at the back of the sick person's head, while with the other she quickly turns the pillow and slips it back into its place. I say hand advisedly. The palm hollowed inwards a little should be used. Nurses very often make use of two fingers, which, when well pressed in at the back of the head, make the turning of pillows a very torturing process. Where no second pillow is at hand, and the patient wishes to have her head higher, she can make a comfortable change for herself by doubling the corner of the pillow back or under her cheek; but no nurse can attempt such an arrangement, as it may be such an uncomfortable one, that it is only by the patient's own hand and cheek that the proper curve can be made.

From
Notes from Sick Rooms

Sources and Acknowledgements

Amis, Martin, "Mary": from *Other People* (Jonathan Cape, 1981)

Anon, "Two Love Letters": from *The Vagabond Path* edited by Iris Origo (Chatto and Windus, 1972)

Berlin, Isaiah, "An Encounter with Pasternak": from *Personal Impressions* by Isaiah Berlin, edited by Henry Hardy (The Hogarth Press, 1980)

Boland, Maureen and Bridget, "Defending the Old Wives' Garden": reprinted with permission of The Bodley Head from *Old Wives' Lore for Gardeners* by Maureen and Bridget Boland (Bodley Head, 1976)

Cavafy, C. P., "King Claudius": from *Passions and Ancient Days* (The Hogarth Press, 1972)

Clark, Kenneth, "Feminine Beauty": from *Feminine Beauty* (Weidenfeld and Nicolson, 1980)

Colegate, Isabel, "Tom Harker": from *The Shooting Party* (Hamish Hamilton, 1980)

Collins, Joan, "Lifestyle": reprinted by permission of Macmillan, London and Basingstoke, from *Joan Collins' Beauty Book* (Macmillan, 1980)

Cooper, Jilly, "The Class System": from *Class* (Eyre Methuen, 1979)

Coren, Alan, "Moby Junk": from *Tissues for Men* (Robson Books, 1980)

De Vries, Peter, "Columbine": from *Consenting Adults* (Victor Gollancz, 1981)

Farjeon, Eleanor, "A Letter from Charles Dickens": from *A Nursery in the Nineties* (Oxford University Press, 1935, n.e. 1980)

Fowles, John, "Green Chaos": from *The Tree* by John Fowles and Frank Horvat (Aurum Press, 1979). Copyright © Association for All Speech Impaired Children (AFASIC) 1979

Green, Benny, "Eccentric Cricketers": reprinted by permission of the author from *Barclays World of Cricket*, edited by E. W. Swanton (Collins, 1980)

Howard, Philip, "Standard English": from *Words Fail Me* (Hamish Hamilton, 1980)

James, Clive, "Fanny Dissected": reprinted with permission from *The New York Review of Books*. Copyright © 1980 Nyrev, Inc.

Jong, Erica, "Fanny": from *Fanny* (Granada Publishing, 1980)

Koestler, Arthur, "East and West": reprinted by permission of A. D. Peters & Co Ltd from *Bricks to Babel* (Hutchinson, 1980)

Küng, Hans, "God in China": from *Does God Exist?* (Collins, 1980)

Le Carré, John, "Karla on the Bridge": reprinted by permission of Hodder and Stoughton Ltd from *Smiley's People* (Hodder and Stoughton, 1980). Copyright © 1979 by Authors Workshop AG

Montaigne, Michel de, "Women and Men": reprinted by permission of Penguin Books Ltd from *Essays*, translated by J. M. Cohen (Penguin Classics, 1958), pages 257–64. Copyright © J. M. Cohen, 1958

Moorehead, Alan, "The Mahdi": from *The White Nile* (Hamish Hamilton, 1960)

Morris, Jan, "The Venetians in Corfu": from *The Venetian Empire* (Faber and Faber, 1980)

Motion, Andrew, "The Letter": reprinted by permission of the author

Murdoch, Iris, "In the Sea": from *Nuns and Soldiers* (Chatto and Windus, 1980)

Nasr, S. H., "Islam and the West": from *Islam and the Plight of Modern Man* (Longman, 1975)

Partridge, Eric, "What's in a Catch Phrase": from *In His Own Words* (André Deutsch, 1980)

Pasternak, Boris, "Autumn": from *Dr Zhivago* (Collins and Harvill Press, 1958)

Read, Piers Paul, "Reading": from *A Married Man* (The Alison Press/Martin Secker and Warburg, 1979)

Seymour, John "Dropping In": from *Getting It Together* (Michael Joseph, 1980)

Snowdon, Lord, "Fashion": from *Personal View* (Weidenfeld and Nicolson, 1979)

Stark, Freya, "A Letter from Persia": from *The Letters of Freya Stark* Vol. 1, edited by Lucy Moorehead (Compton Russell, 1974)

Stephen, Mrs Leslie, "Crumbs in Bed": from *Notes from Sick Rooms* (Puckerbrush Press, 1980)

Stoppard, Miriam, "The Beauty Game": from *Health Care* (Weidenfeld and Nicolson, 1980)

Tinniswood, Peter, "Our Own Dear Queen": reprinted by permission of Anthony Sheil Associates Ltd from *Tales from a Long Room* (Arrow Books, 1981)

Updike, John, "Guilt-Gems": from *Problems* (André Deutsch, 1980)

Waugh, Evelyn, "Two Letters to a Daughter": from *The Letters of Evelyn Waugh*, edited by Mark Amory (Weidenfeld and Nicolson, 1980)

Weldon, Fay, "Breakages": reprinted by permission of Anthony Sheil Associates Ltd from *Watching Me, Watching You* (Hodder and Stoughton, 1981)

York, Peter, "Style Wars": from *Style Wars* (Sidgwick and Jackson, 1980)

Illustrations by

David Davies: pages 96, 208, 238 and 249

Tim Foster: pages 46, 54, 61, 85, 89, 93, 137, 228 and 250

Julie Hazlewood: pages 27, 31, 36, 66, 77, 82, 156, 171, 189, 205, 231 and 234

Tony Kerrins: pages 5, 44, 99, 128, 148, 164, 188, 210, 213 and 253

David Sim: pages 48, 159, 162, 185, 191, 195, 217 and 222

Helen Wilson: pages 81, 113, 155, 197 and 201

The illustration on page 126 is reproduced by permission of *Graphics World*; and those on pages 150, 179, 180, 181, 182, 183 and 184 are reproduced from *1800 Woodcuts by Thomas Bewick and his School*, edited by Blanche Cirker (Dover Publications, 1962).